NO MAN'S LAND

NO MAN'S LAND

Combat & Identity in World War I

ERIC J. LEED

Professor of History
Florida International University

CAMBRIDGE UNIVERSITY PRESS

CAMBRIDGE
LONDON · NEW YORK · MELBOURNE

Published by the Syndics of the Cambridge University Press
The Pitt Building, Trumpington Street, Cambridge CB2 1RP
Bentley House, 200 Euston Road, London NW1 2DB
32 East 57th Street, New York, NY 10022, USA
296 Beaconsfield Parade, Middle Park, Melbourne 3206, Australia

© Cambridge University Press 1979

First published 1979

Printed in the United States of America
Typeset, printed and bound by Vail-Ballou Press, Inc., Binghamton, New York

Library of Congress Cataloging in Publication Data
Leed, Eric J
No man's land.
Bibliography: p.
1. European War, 1914–1918 – Psychological aspects.
2. European War, 1914–1918 – Influence and results.
3. European War, 1914–1918 – Moral aspects.   I. Title.
D523.L443   940.3'14   78–26396
ISBN 0 521 22471 3

In memory of my mother, ALICE A. LEED 1908–1972

Contents

Preface

There is much that this book is not and cannot claim to be. It is not a military history, although I have found military histories essential for assembling in my own mind the skeleton of events of World War I. Neither is it an analysis of the literature of war. Although I have used this literature extensively, I have done so to gain a purchase on experiences that lie outside the boundaries of text and narrative. And, finally, this book is not a psychohistory of the First World War. Its subject – the transformation of personality in war – would seem to fall within the concerns and competencies of psychohistory, but, as I have tried to show in the first chapter, transformations of character that appear highly subjective are often drawn from age-old conventions and traditional symbols. Thus my concern in this book is not with psychohistory per se but with the cultural repertoires of meaning drawn upon by participants to define felt alterations in themselves. The "self" appears in this investigation not as the ultimate goal of analysis but as one of those supremely important fictions used by participants to define the nature of their experience.

I have written this book as an analysis of a coherent, unified, historical experience, the aim being to isolate and define the way in which an historical event of the first magnitude contributed to the character and definition of modernity. The war contributed to the character of the age by altering the status, expectations, and character of participants. I must admit that even now – after a great deal of time spent in reading about the war, thinking about it, and occasionally dreaming about it – I still believe that the war cannot hold one's interest for very long unless one is an aficionado of military things or a member of the war generation. As a purely military event the war is of strictly limited interest. But it gains an overwhelming fascination when one looks at it in order to see how it mobilized, articulated, and modified the resources of signification available to the individuals who entered its bewildering and terrifying reality. The war experience is an ultimate confirmation of the power of men to ascribe meaning and pattern to a world, even when that world seemed to resist all patterning. The war mobilized all the cultural resources of meaning available to Europeans in the first decades of the twentieth century. It allows us to see what those resources were, not as an abstract system of thought but as something which rendered experience coherent and meaningful.

The narrowest subject of this book is the way the war changed the men who participated in it. This focus has led me to lean most heavily on the most self-conscious and introspective testimony and to prefer an intensive treatment of a few combatants to a broader analysis of the war literature. I cannot, thus, claim extensive coverage of the literature of the war. Most of my examples are drawn from German materials, although I have used British, American, and French works – as well as materials drawn from other wars – as a source of counterpoint and comparison. Because, in the last analysis, it is difficult for any history of the war to "prove" that the events of battle changed the character of participants, I have attempted to surround the transformations of war with models and insights drawn from a wide variety of fields other than history, particularly social anthropology, sociology, and psychology. At times I have preferred the strategy of "boxing in" the phenomenon of the transformation of character by events, rather than attacking this phenomenon directly. It is this strategy of circumvention which, more than anything else, has evolved into the structure and purpose of this study: to provide a cultural history of the First World War *through* men who participated in it, by retracing their discoveries and reversals that – in the more distant past – would be the subject of tragic drama rather than historical analysis.

The discussion follows the very simple but well-tested form of beginning, middle, and end. In my analysis of the beginning of the war, I have been primarily concerned with defining the ways in which the war was envisioned as a solution to basic cultural contradictions. In examining the middle, the war experience itself, I have been particularly attentive to the forms in which these contradictions reappeared in altered guise, through unexpected realities, and to the fantasies, myths, and psychological pathologies necessitated by the realities of war. But with the ending of the war the pattern of discussion breaks down, for the cessation of hostilities did not mean the end of the war experience but rather the beginning of a process in which that experience was framed, institutionalized, given ideological content, and relived in political action as well as fiction. The final chapter cannot be a conclusion. It is rather an attempt to explain why the war experience was something which could *not* be resolved, reintegrated, and covered over with the exigencies of civilian existence.

This study began some time ago in a somewhat inchoate desire to anchor the stuff of intellectual history in the ineluctable reality of historical events. I am grateful to the many people who furthered the process of coming to earth, people who taught me the difference between writing history and studying it, between the sayable and the thinkable. First and above all I am thankful to Lavina Leed who has edited, criticized, and struggled with this manuscript, often at the expense of her own work. The manuscript has gained life and clarity where it was most needed from her critical intelligence and powers of organization. Sidney Monas, of the University of Texas, from the very beginning has contributed enormously of his time, his sensitivity, and his eye for the complexity of human motives. I am also relieved to finally have the chance to thank Hayden White, of Wesleyan University, for his support and intellectual generosity. My colleagues in the History Department at Florida International University have been unfailingly supportive of this project. I have benefitted greatly from Brian Peterson's extensive knowledge of German history and from Howard Kaminsky's criticism of this book when it was in a critical phase. Much of what is most valuable in this book emerged originally from conversations with Roger Abrahams, of the University of Texas, and with Phin Capron, who have both acquainted me with a world of material I did not know existed. I am very grateful to them.

E. J. L.

1. The Structure of the War Experience

THE DISCONTINUITIES OF WAR

It would be difficult to find any war in which participants did not claim that the actualities of combat had in some way altered their character. What is astonishing about the First World War is the persistence and consistency of this claim, even in the depths of personal and generational disillusionment. In August 1914 the expectation of a profound and precipitate maturation drove many young men to the recruiting offices. Such a transformation of character was cited as fact in many letters sent home from the front, as when one German volunteer writes, "No one will come out of this war who has not become a different person";[1] or, in another instance, "I am convinced that, coming back in one piece, one will have become different in every respect."[2] With the conclusion of the war, there were many debates over whether the veteran had been brutalized or ennobled, infantilized or matured by his war experience; but there was no debate over whether a deep and profound alteration of identity had taken place.

This change of identity in war – a consistent feature of the experience of the First World War in its several phases – is the subject of this study. In the chapters that follow I will define the ways in which the experience of combat altered the status, self-conceptions, attitudes, and fantasy lives of participants. In this chapter, however, I would like to suggest some of the problems involved in approaching the subject from an historical perspective and to discuss the reasons for organizing the analysis in the way that I have. The discussion follows not a discrete series of themes or topics but what I feel is the structure of the war experience itself – a structure which underlay many differences of rank, nationality, and temperament, which guaranteed a unified war experience, and which fixed the relationship of the combatant to the society of his origin.

In approaching the question – what *was* the change which combatants felt took place within them? – it seemed immediately evident that this was a change of identity or personality that must perforce be examined with the tools of psychological analysis. But in initially attempting to do a psychohistory of the war, I encountered very real problems that were rooted both in the character of the war experience and the limitations of certain, commonly used models of subjective "change." Few, if any, veterans considered their war experience even comparable to their lives before or after the war. Many spoke of having inhabited two distinct worlds, of having seemed two distinct persons. Stuart Cloete, a British veteran, described how the combatant viewed his civilian existence during the war.

> Hard to believe. Impossible to believe. That other life, so near in time and distance, was something led by different men.
> Two lives that bore no relation to each other. That was what they felt, the bloody lot of them.[3]

The personality adapted to the vicissitudes of war seemed to be wholly incommensurate with that individual who had grown up in civilian society and was, with the conclusion of the war, expected to resume his civilian occupation and status. The psychic problems caused by the experience of war often lay in a profound sense of personal discontinuity.

On every level one finds that the war experience and the identity formed by it was placed "within brackets." David Jones felt so intensely the utter distinctness of his experience of war and peace that he entitled his fictionalized memoir of combat *In Pa-*

renthesis. Those who continued to be troubled psychically by their war experience were troubled by the sense of having lived two lives and of being unable to resolve the contradictions between them. Particularly those who had entered the war before they were twenty, and who regarded their experience as a special form of higher education, realized that they had learned skills which were unmarketable in civilian society. They were sensitized to dangers which did not exist in peacetime, as Robert Graves sheepishly reminded himself in 1919 after he picked himself up out of a roadside ditch where he had automatically taken cover from a car backfire. One of the most significant responses to the feeling of psychic and social estrangement from civilian life was the ritualization and memorialization of the war experience in veterans' groups that celebrated in songs and toasts to dead comrades the distinctiveness of their common identity.

The war experience was nothing if not an experience of radical discontinuity on every level of consciousness. This is what posed the most severe psychic contradictions for combatants, and what poses severe intellectual difficulties to anyone who wishes to understand the psychic effects of war using a model of mind that assumes the essential continuity of self and identity. Continuity often seems to be the *sine qua non* of identity. An experience which severs the thick "tissues of connectivity"[4] that weld separate events into a self is most often viewed as a *loss* of identity. Concepts of identity modeled on the process of maturation and cognitive development often presume something which war effaces: the notion that there is only one self and one sphere of existence.

Erik Erikson's theory of ego development is one that historians have found particularly useful in the construction of depth biographies. It is significant that one of Erikson's key concepts, that of ego–identity, was formed in war and in observation of men afflicted by war. Erikson developed this concept while working with cases of "combat fatigue" in the Pacific theatre during World War II. Essentially, ego–identity was a description of what men who had broken down in combat *lacked*.

It was as if, subjectively, their lives no longer hung together and never would again. There was a central disturbance of

what I then started to call ego-identity . . . This sense of identity produces the ability to experience oneself as something
that has continuity and sameness.[5]

Here the effects of war upon personality can only be seen in a
negative light as a disintegration of the identity that had been
formed in a series of critical encounters with significant others –
parents, lovers, and children. What Erikson has done is to con-
struct a model of the self that is specifically a corrective to war,
one that is designed to define therapeutically what men psychically wounded in combat can no longer believe of themselves – that they are "the same."
   Any analysis of the war experience must ultimately seek to
define the sources of discontinuity that shattered the sense of
sameness normally thought to characterize the substrata of psychic life. In war men were "estranged" from their societies, and
one must take this estrangement literally; they were "made"
strange to the men and things of their past, and made strange to
themselves. In the words of Gorch Jachs, who died in the offensives of March 1918,

   I, with my steel-hard nerves, can look the dead calmly in their
   crushed eyes, can hear badly wounded comrades groaning
   without collapsing and can do much more that I cannot say. In
   many ways I have become a riddle to myself, and often shudder at myself, am terrified at myself. And then again I feel that
   I still have the weakest, most pitying heart in the world.[6]

An analysis of war experience must confront directly this experience of being "made" strange. An examination of the identities
formed in war must come to terms with the fact that these identities were formed beyond the margins of normal social experience. This was precisely what made them so lasting, so immune
to erosion by the routines of postwar social and economic life,
and so difficult to grasp with the traditional tools of sociological
and psychological analysis.
   Increasingly it became evident that the change in themselves
cited by combatants was rooted not in specific, terrifying or hor-
rifying war experiences, but in the sense of having lived through
incommensurable social worlds – that of peace and that of war.

The sense of difference and strangeness which marked the relations of the veteran with his social origins derived from a species of structural disjunction, an imprecise fit between distinct forms of social life, which imposed upon the combatant a contradictory sense of his own status and value. Thus the question of a "change" of character necessarily became a question of how the distinctiveness of war experience and civilian experience was defined, comprehended, and portrayed.

One of the difficulties inherent in attempting to define what happens to men in war is that most of the constructs that are used in the articulation of group experiences have been generated in the attempt to understand normal social development and acculturated identities. The evanescent bonds and self-images formed in wars, revolutions, riots, carnivals, and New Year's parties are often historically invisible. They slip through the web of methods fashioned to describe the development of stable social and psychic entities. The analysis of war as a social experience and a human phenomenon has been skewed by the historian's interest in the "significant," and what is significant is almost by definition the events, persons, and transactions which contribute to the stabilization or destabilization of discrete social structures. It has generally been assumed that war has taken on its meaning once one has described the contribution of a particular war to the stability or instability of the societies and men who make it. It would be silly to argue this is not a significant issue, and I am not arguing that. I am only suggesting that the focus on the problems of social stability, class structure, and the values which ensure social cohesion inevitably colors our view of experiences which take place outside of stable institutions and class structures. They become recognizable only in so far as they function in terms of social structure.

Thus the two models that have commonly been used to define the relationship between war experience and normal social life – the "drive–discharge" model and the "cultural-patterning" model[7] – are both rooted in the assumption of the primacy of the social order, though they define the relationship of war to normal social life in quite different ways. It is worthwhile to review, in some detail, both of these models of explanation. They pervade much of our thinking about the relationship of war and peace and about the identities formed in war. They articulate a set of assumptions, deeply rooted in European culture, that operated in both the expectations and disillusionment of those who fought in the First World War. Finally, it is against both of these views that I am arguing throughout this study.

The drive–discharge model is most commonly encountered in psychoanalytic theories of war.[8] But one can also see that it is implicit in Arno Mayer's view that both war and revolution release tensions that accumulate in modernizing societies.[9] Essentially, this model holds that organized spheres of conflict – war, revolution, and warlike sports – function to discharge drives which are blocked from expression in normal social life. War, in an image which seems native to the Age of Steam, provides a "safety valve" for aggressions, drives, and needs that cannot be used in working the social mechanism. Implicitly, the distinction between peace and war is a distinction between necessity and freedom, repression and release, the blockage of a vital force inherent in men and groups, and the "expression" of that force in acts which are normally taboo. It is a short step to a "functional" relationship between peace and war: If war provides an outlet for bottled aggressions that cannot be released without the destruction of social stability, *then* war is a regrettable but necessary feature of stable societies.

War, here, becomes a world of instinctual liberty that contrasts starkly with the social world of instinctual renunciation and the deferment of gratification. It follows that the personalities formed within this arena of discharge must necessarily suffer on the scales that measure civilized behavior, that is, the tolerance of frustration. They have either been "primitivized" or infantilized, or have never had an adequate opportunity to become civilized and matured. The combatant is, apparently, not trained for that instinctual renunciation that is the lot of every civilized adult.

The drive–discharge model is more than an explanation of war and what war does (or doesn't do) to men. It was a deeply rooted cultural assumption intrinsic to the sense of liberation that many experienced in August of 1914. One of the problems in any discussion of the experience of the First World War lies in understanding the unquestionably heartfelt, intense enthusiasm for war. It is clear that war mobilized a traditional, noneconomic, and romantic vision of what war was and what it would mean. In Chapter 2, I have examined the roots of this traditional image to see how it was specified in the expectations of particular individuals. In 1914 those who went to war drew upon a fund of imagery that fixed the meaning and significance of a not-yet-experienced event and justified their celebration of war as a "liberation" from the constraints of social life. Both the fulfilment and the violations of this script were crucial in the "illumination" and disillusionment of combatants.

The drive–discharge model also describes the assumptions of those who, at the end of the war, feared that the returning veteran had been criminalized, revolutionized, or barbarized by his experience. Having been shaped in a climate of instinctual freedom, the frontsoldier might be incapable of resuming the habits of social discipline. This fear was expressed by many combatants themselves. Ludwig Lewinsohn, the Chairman of the Soldiers' Council of the 4th Army during the retreat of November 1918, felt that he might only be adding to the problems of reconstruction by leading a tribe of primitives back into the homeland. He feared that, at worst, the war had created a type that could never again adapt to the necessities of productive work. At best the soldier had been "depoliticized."

> After four and a half years of separation from the homeland many soldiers lacked any kind of political understanding. They had only one wish: peace and work. Opposite them stood the great mass of those brutalized in the field, men who were dishabituated to any kind of work; especially the youthful soldier who came into the army from the school bench, or from his apprenticeship, and who had not correctly grasped the concept of work, was drawn into sloth by long periods of idleness. Fantastic thoughts of distorted communism haunted their brains.[10]

Clearly it is impossible to dismiss the drive–discharge model out of hand. Its assumptions are inextricable from the expectations with which many millions of men went to war. Thus the notion that war was a field of instinctual liberation might itself be seen as a "cause" of war or at least of the enthusiasm for war. Many welcomed the conflict because it was commonly understood to be the occasion for the expression, in action, of drives which had no normal social outlets. But the real questions are *why* did Europeans see the war in this light, and *how* did they specify this assumption in terms of concrete expectations. Equally, with the conclusion of conflict, the notion that war had been the playing field of insubordinate libido was a crucial feature in the anxieties which surrounded the figure of the returning veteran.

The salient inadequacies of this model lie in its unrealistic portrayal of war. It sees war wholly as an expression of aggressive drives, and this was not the war experienced by

> . . . man, infinitely small, running – affrighted rabbits from the upheaval of the shells, nerve-wracked, deafened; clinging to earth, hiding eyes, whispering, "oh God!"[11]

At best the war meant a new and more total pattern of repression to which millions of men, over a period of years, became habituated. Over the rules and inhibitions native to military institutions were layered the stark, unconquerable restrictions on movement imposed by technological realities, realities which made the war primarily a defensive war. The drive–discharge model defines war as an offensive, aggressive activity. It can explain the numerous breakdowns of men in modern war only by reference to the "guilt" incurred by men who kill, violating in war rules that govern their civilian conceptions of themselves.[12] But this ignores the fact that at least one-half of tactical thinking, and more than one-half of military activity, is occupied in frustrating the aggression of the enemy. In the First World War the defense ruled. The realities of war forced a curtailment of aggression, a ritualization of violence, and the holding back of hostile impulses.

> The present day trench warfare is, as I once heard it expressed "so damn impersonal" that the individual seldom has the privilege of giving physical vent to anger. . . . One cannot be enraged at the unseen line of men or the effectual bombardment from guns miles away – at least not with any amount of satisfaction.[13]

It was the frustration of aggression in war, due to the disappearance of the enemy and the necessities of entrenchment, which, according to William Maxwell,[14] forced the combatant to turn his hostilities against "improper" targets: officers, the staff, or the "home." This act, and not the too-rare release of aggressions upon the enemy, often engendered a profound sense of guilt in combatants. In war men encountered repressions for which neither their social experience in civilian society nor their image of war had prepared them. It is in descriptions of the new psychic defenses necessitated by war and in evocations of the immobilizing, frustrating realities of fighting that one can see the emergence of a new "character" as well as a new social world.

An alternative to the notion of war as the discharge of aggressive drives is the cultural-patterning model. This, too, focuses upon the emotional experience of war as an experience of aggression, a focus that is much too narrow to encompass the cultural diversity and the varieties of experience undergone in war. But the cultural-patterning model points out something that should be self-evident: that restraints upon aggression learned in the process of socialization are not purely external rules and inhibitions that can be left behind with civilian clothes. If restraints upon aggression are truly learned, they become constituent elements in the personality of the citizen–soldier. The cultural-patterning model holds that individual aggression in war is a function of the rules and values which have governed aggression in social life. The individual who goes to war – if he is a "normal" member of his society – fears his own aggression as much as the aggression of the enemy, even though he may be less conscious of the cultural inhibitions that restrain him.

This understanding of the moral and psychic makeup of the citizen–soldier became doctrine in the American army after World War II, thanks largely to the work of S. L. A. Marshall, who interviewed thousands of men newly returned from the Pacific and European theatres. He discovered that even battle-hardened veterans of elite units – even in the most desperate straits – rarely shot directly at the enemy. Only a quarter of the men in combat units would employ their fire weapons effectively in combat.

The Army cannot unmake [Western man] . . . It must reckon with the fact that he comes from a civilization in which aggression, connected with the taking of life, is prohibited and unacceptable. The teaching and ideals of that civilization are against killing, against taking advantage. The fear of aggression has been expressed to him so strongly and absorbed by him so deeply and pervadingly – practically with his mother's milk – that it is a part of the normal man's emotional make-up. This is his greatest handicap when he enters combat. It stays his trigger-finger even though he is hardly conscious that it is a restraint upon him.[15]

Marshall's insights into the motives and behavior of combatants in World War II are also valid for those who fought in the First World War. It was well known that attacks were broken not by companies or even squads of men, but by the few members of a group who survived the barrage and could bring themselves to fire on attackers. There are many examples in the war literature of officers who were reluctant to fire upon an enemy who had inadvertently exposed himself. This job was most often handed over to a man of the ranks.[16]

It is simply incontestable that those who fought on both sides of No Man's Land were, initially at least, the products of their respective cultures. In the trenches the cultural values that normally inhibit aggression were tested with a severity they rarely encountered in time of peace. The cultural-patterning model is a corrective to the excessively stark opposition of war and peace asserted by those who see war as the discharge of repressed aggressions. However, the cultural-patterning model is, par excellence, one that focuses upon the cultural and moral continuities that underlie the experience of peace and war. It is unable to account for something which was self-evident to veterans of the First World War, namely, that the war experience was dramatically "different" from normal social life and that they, as a consequence, were "different" too.

The view which regards the patterning of aggression in society as the source for the restraints upon aggression in war preserves the social character of war experience, but it does so by effacing the discontinuities which were self-evident to combatants. The cultural inhibitions on violence explain, perhaps, the actions of the seventy-five percent of combatants who were passive in combat, but not the behavior of the twenty-five percent upon whom the fate of a battle rested. These latter could only be

regarded as defective sensibilities, insensitive to civilized restraints. It is precisely these men, however, who pose the difficulties for those who attempt to see the lives of individuals and
groups as enactments of ordering and restraining social norms.
Many veterans of the First World War acknowledged that they
had come to enjoy the risk, the spectacle of destruction, and the
sheer disorder native to the environment of war. For a few German veterans the war was the source of a blatant, wholly unphil-
osophical nihilism.

> We are soldiers and the weapon is the tool with which we
> proceed to shape ourselves. Our work is killing, and it is our
> duty to do this work well and completely . . . For every age
> expresses itself not only in practical life, in love, in science and
> art, but also in the frightful. And it is the meaning of the
> soldier to be frightful.[17]

It is too tempting to take this statement of Ernst Jünger – one of
the most significant contributors to the German war literature – as evidence for something else: as an affirmation of liberated aggression, a sign of defective sensibility. But there were
many men like Jünger who emerged from the war in 1919 affirming disorder, celebrating the "terrible." Their identification
with violence and disorder must be regarded as a cultural modal-
ity in its own right; as something rooted in a particular tradition
articulated through definite conventions, codes, and rules. As
Roger Abrahams perceptively points out in his study of rituals in
culture, not all rituals are enactments of ordering norms. Such
enactments are

> . . . paralleled in every kind of society with expressions of
> disorder – which must be understood as fully as the enact-
> ments of order in getting at the ethos of the group. Ritual,
> from this point of view, may involve an embodiment and cele-
> bration of the potentials of order and the powers of disorder
> residing at the center of the life of a group. To give primacy to
> one of these motives is misleading, and ultimately futile if
> one's aim is a full ethnographic rendering of real life.[18]

Both the drive–discharge model and the cultural-patterning
model suffer from the illusion that in order to operate effectively

in a world of disorder, men must leave their culture behind, or that their culture – in the form of inhibitions and re-straints – loses its grip upon behavior and ceases to define the identity of the actor. But men do not cease to impose meaning, pattern, and significance on the fields of their endeavor when they leave behind the precincts of civil life. Upon the field of war are projected images of what lies outside, above, or below the norm. In the literature of war one can see clearly those patterns used to shape the disorder of the environment, patterns which allow the participant to determine exactly what is anomalous, unfamiliar, uncanny, or ironical about the juxtapositions of men and things that he finds. The experience of a particular historical war, like that of the First World War, augments, modernizes, and lends emotional substance to the scenes, figures, and actions that a society marks as unacceptable alternatives to a status quo, as "things that cannot be" or "must not happen again," even though they must be prepared for.

An understanding of why men went to war in 1914, and of how they were shaped by the events of war, can only restore some balance to our view of the alternatives available to men growing up in modern industrialized society. If we wish to see war as symptomatic of something else – class tensions, sociopo-litical imbalances, or repressed drives – we must first ask the question: Why and how is war seen as an alternative to normal social life in the first place?

THE LIMINALITY OF WAR

In spite of the apparent endlessness of the First World War, its purposelessness, and the monstrous numbers of casualties, some veterans persisted in seeing their experience as an initiation. Charles Edmund Carrington writes of himself and of his genera-tion: "We are still an initiate generation, possessing a secret which can never be communicated."[19] As an initiatory experi-ence the war had produced men who shared a new, common identity. Fifty years after the conclusion of the war Carrington could write:

Middle-aged men, strenuously as they attempt to deny it, are united by a secret bond and separated from their fellows who were too old or too young to fight in the Great War. Particularly the generation of young men who were soldiers before their characters were formed, who were under twenty-five in 1914, is conscious of the distinction, for the war made them what they are. Generally speaking, this secret army presents to the world a front of silence and bitterness which it has been fashionable to describe as disenchantment.[20]

Carrington sees the cohesion and distinction of the generation as emerging from an experience that can only be compared to an initiation, to rites of passage. At first sight "rituals of passage" might seem an inappropriate description of what happens to men in modern war. Indeed, certain qualifications are in order before one can see ritual as a useful category of description for modern war. But a comparison of war experience to rituals of passage allows us to do two things: It allows us to set aside for a moment the notion that war is solely aggression and violence, and it also permits us to see the conventional nature of those discontinuities between life in times of peace and war.

Most veterans of the First World War wished to see their experience as a unique concatenation of peculiarly modern realities. But in focusing upon the transformation of men by war we are dealing with a supremely conventional theme that is at least as old as written literature. When men have left behind the boundaries of their own societies to take up arms against other men, they have traditionally called upon a world of symbols to represent their altered condition. They are seen to have either transcended purely social categories or to have fallen below them. They are merged with sacred figures or animal categories, becoming like gods or beasts, often taking on the raiment and habits of animals – feathers, wolf skins, bear shirts, and so forth. In combat their change of state has been conventionally represented as a drastic alteration of temperature, intoxication, or lust.[21] Upon his return to society, the man who has killed is often considered to be dangerous, polluted or stained until he has undergone a ritual cooling and cleansing.[22]

In Indo-European literature the character of the warrior is anomalous, and this anomalousness is rooted in the nature of his project.[23] In order to defend the security and stability of the group, or to augment its wealth, the warrior must violate the rules and norms that underpin the stability of his group. The greatest danger to any society lies in the possibility that the warrior may begin to practice against "friends" and kin the activities which are proper only against enemies and strangers. This danger, and the anomalous project of battle, is ameliorated by the ritual definition of the warrior as a man who has been temporarily separated from his social roots, set apart and placed together with strangers in a moral betwixt-and-between. If he wants to return to the life of settled domesticity, he must be re-adopted precisely as a stranger is adopted into a family or clan.

The man who goes to war undergoes rituals of passage, the rites described originally by Arnold Van Gennep. Van Gennep divided rites of passage into three phases: rites of separation, which remove an individual or group of individuals from his or their accustomed place; liminal rites, which symbolically fix the character of the "passenger" as one who is between states, places, or conditions; and finally rites of incorporation (postliminal rites), which welcome the individual back into the group. The rites of separation lend a peculiar individuality to a group.

> Among rites of separation for groups may be included a declaration of war, either tribal or familial . . . The group charged with implementing revenge is first separated from society and acquires its own individuality: its members do not re-enter society until after the performance of rites which remove that temporary individuality and re-integrate them into society . . . The ceremonies performed at the end of a vendetta or a war (peace ceremonies) are identical with rites of friendship and of adopting . . . strangers.[24]

The individuality which defines Carrington and his generation can be seen as a function of passage from the security of social life to war, and as a summary of a life on the margins. The most lasting memory of war, for Carrington and many others, is of the very image of the marginal, the liminal, the "betwixt-and-between" – No Man's Land.

> In fifty years I have never been able to rid myself of this obsession with no-man's-land and the unknown world beyond it. On this side of our wire everything is familiar and every man

is a friend, over there, beyond the wire, is the unknown, the uncanny.[25]

Astonishing numbers of those who wrote about their experience of war designate No Man's Land as their most lasting and disturbing image. This was a term that captured the essence of an experience of having been sent beyond the outer boundaries of social life, placed between the known and the unknown, the familiar and the uncanny. The experience of war was an experience of marginality, and the "change of character" undergone by the combatant could adequately be summarized as marginalization.

The rites of passage, and particularly the first two phases of passage – separation and transition (or "liminality," from *limen,* Latin for "threshold") – provide a framework for war experience and offer a way of analyzing changes that are at once subjective as well as changes in social status. But it remains to be seen exactly what "separation" and "liminality" mean and how they might illuminate the discontinuities that are central to the experience of war.

Rites of separation function, according to Van Gennep, both to mark those who have left their normal, or former, state and condition, and to make the break with the known or familiar gradual rather than abrupt. Victor Turner, who brilliantly extends the implications of Van Gennep's earlier work, notes that rites of separation and their characteristic symbols may be called upon to represent the movement of an entire society from its previous state and condition. Seasonal rituals mark moments of transition that define departure from an accustomed state into a "new" condition.

> In the case of members of a society, it involves collectively moving from all that is socially and culturally involved in an agricultural season, or from a period of peace as against one of war, from plague to community health, from a previous sociocultural state or condition to a new state or condition.[26]

The moments of collective transition, such as mobilization of a nation for war, open a gap in historical time that is filled with images of "something new." One can see in the mobilization for war in 1914 two distinct but clearly interwoven processes of separation occurring. The first removes society as a whole from familiar conditions of social life; the second removes the citizen–soldier from his civilian status. In Chapter 2, on the expectations of war, I have attempted to define the ways in which contemporaries defined this break. In general, and particularly in Germany, many insisted that the declaration of war had actualized values that, if not sacred, were at least revered – values of "community" as opposed to "society," of national unity as opposed to class conflict, of altruistic as opposed to economic and self-interested behavior. Many insisted that the war meant a structural transformation of society, the abandonment of an old order and the actualization of a new one. Gertrude Bäumer, a woman who was active in the feminist movement in Germany in 1914, wrote that the first year of the war had put the nation

> . . . under the jurisdiction of an order other than the materialistic-technical one of the Nineteenth Century. An order which did not involve production, pay, profit and loss, cost and gain, but life and death, blood and power.[27]

A second, more familiar, and ceremonial process separates those who go to war from those who remain at home. It begins with the customary "two steps forward" and proceeds through uniforming, drill, subjection to discipline, brow-beating from sergeants, and, finally, to the actual departure for the theatre of war. The sense of having lived through an earth-shattering, "moral revolution" changed the attitude of many young men toward the army. What once seemed to be the essence of subordination and loss of self became, with the collective reordering of social life, a liberation and a vehicle for self-actualization. Carl Zuckmayer, a German playwright and novelist who has written one of the most perceptive and honest memoirs of war experience, was struck by the way the "revolution of August, 1914" had changed his own attitude toward military service.

> To become a soldier, to have to serve one's year, had always been a painful and threatening idea for me during my time in the Gymnasium. It meant about face, shut-up, obedience and subordination – the loss of freedom. Now it meant the opposite: liberation. Liberation from bourgeois narrowness and

pettiness, from compulsory education and cramming, from the doubts of choosing a profession, and above all from that which we – consciously or unconsciously – felt as the saturation, the stuffy air, the petrifaction of our world.[28]

Many, like Zuckmayer, felt that the war had liberated them from the constraints of bourgeois life. It had opened up a realm of activity which was often regarded as the antithesis of economic life, of social status. The pole of war had accumulated many of the values that capitalist society had placed in the museum. In entering war Zuckmayer felt that he was proceeding toward a "new" realm of endeavor, and yet, upon closer examination, it appears that this "new" order was a synthesis of traditional values.

Too often the experience of war itself is understood merely as the collapse of expectations, as an experience that transformed initial hopes into illusions. But certain expectations were not abandoned. Particularly the expectation that the war would force a profound personal and collective transformation continued to define the relationship of the combatant to the realities of war. This transformation was specified in terms of phenomena – the barrage, the trench system, the necessities of defensive war – that were not foreseen by most of those who volunteered in 1914.

The second stage of passage, that of liminality, defines a formal situation that is closely analogous to the position of men in war. The symbols that have traditionally defined the ambiguous condition of the individual in passage as a person who is between cultural classifications and categories appear with astonishing frequency throughout the war literature. A youth undergoing initiation is no longer who he was, but neither is he what he is to become. He is "structurally, if not physically, 'invisible'."[29] He is spoken of as "dead" to the things of his past, and may be treated as his society customarily treats a corpse – buried, forced to lie immobile in a pit or ditch. The initiand is identified with the earth, with pollution and corruption.

The metaphor of dissolution is often applied to neophytes – they are allowed to go filthy and [are] identified with the earth, the generalized matter into which every specific individual is rendered down. Particular form here becomes general matter – often their very names are taken from them.[30]

The symbols of invisibility, death, burial, and pollution are particularly apt descriptions of individuals who are for a moment passing between social categories – from childhood to adulthood – or between areas of settlement. In war these are not symbols but experiences that were often much more problematic than any spectacular "horror" or deprivation.

Mary Douglas, in her study of pollution concepts in traditional societies, notes that dirt is matter out of place, and pollution is the result of any contact between substances, places, or ranks that are normally kept separate and distinct by rules and taboos.

> In short, our pollution behavior is the reaction which condemns any object or idea likely to confuse or contradict our cherished classifications.[31]

Shoes are not in themselves filthy, but on the dinner table they are. Soil in the garden is not "filth," but on the bed sheets it is often considered such. The most unsettling feature of the landscape of war, for many combatants, lay in the constant transgression of those distinctions that preserve both order and cleanliness. The men in the trenches lived with the rats that grew fat from eating the corpses of men and animals. The smell of the dead pervaded the front lines, penetrating even the deepest living quarters. The war literature is full of surprising encounters with corpses, complaints of being unable to prevent dirt, mud, and vermin from invading the most personal spaces. Pollution and the sense of having no control over the access of substances, animals, and other men to one's own body was a continuing cause of the "look" native to those who had become accustomed to trench routine. "It is said that soldiers who have been subjected to this routine for . . . prolonged periods . . . acquire an unmistakable expression of gloom, irony and disgust."[32]

One of the most outstanding examples of the polluting capacity of war through its disordering of basic categories is offered by W. H. R. Rivers, a psychologist and neurologist who was Director of the Craiglockhart Hospital for shell-shock victims during the war. One of his patients had been flung down by a shell so that his face struck the distended abdomen of a German several days dead. The young officer knew, before he lost consciousness, "that the substance which filled his mouth and produced the most horrible sensations of taste and smell was derived from the decomposed entrails of an enemy."[33] It would be difficult to find a more complete violation of the distinctions which separate the dead from the living, friend from enemy, rotten from edible, than this experience which left a lasting mark of pollution upon the young officer – Rivers considered him almost incurable. But the transgression of those boundaries between life and death, man and animal, or man and machine was so common in war that it was as much a source of irony and black humor as of horror.

Like pollution, invisibility was not a symbol in war but a reality which many found intolerable. With the onset of trench warfare, the combatant took refuge in and under the ground, and this entrenchment signaled to many the end of traditional war. Robert Michaels, a captain in the Austrian cavalry, wrote to his son that neither war nor the warrior were anything like they have been portrayed.

> Modern combat is played out almost entirely invisibly; the new way of fighting demands of the soldier that he . . . withdraw from the sight of his opponent. He cannot fight upright on the earth but must crawl into and under it; at sea he fights most securely when he is concealed under the surface of the water, and in the air when he flies so high that he no longer offers a target.[34]

The invisibility of the enemy, and the retirement of troops underground, destroyed any notion that war was a spectacle of contending humanity. The combatant could feel the "danger, but there is nothing out there, nothing to contend against."[35] The invisibility of the enemy put a premium upon auditory signals and seemed to make the war experience peculiarly subjective and intangible. "Everything about it is done within, in the ground, in man."[36] The combination of factors which produced what the Germans called the *Menschenleere* ("abandoned by men") of the battlefield utterly changed the terms of the war experience: "The war seems to us to be first a dreadful resignation, a renunciation, a humiliation."[37]

The retirement of the combatant into the soil produced a landscape suffused with ambivalence. The earth was at once one's home and the habitat of a hidden, ever-present threat. The battlefield was "empty of men" and yet it was saturated with men.

> Trenches rise up, grey clay, three or four feet above the ground. Save for one or two men – snipers at the sap-head – the country was deserted. No sign of humanity – a dead land. And yet thousands of men were there, like rabbits concealed.[38]

It was precisely the memory of having inhabited for an unimaginable length of time a landscape saturated with invisible men and controlled by an unapproachable technology that remained the longest with many combatants. The sudden appearance of the human enemy from behind the mask of technological violence produced a feeling of the *unheimlich* (uncanny). Emilio Lussu, who was a lieutenant in the Italian army on the Asiago plateau during the war, remembers the enormous impression made upon him when he finally saw the enemy he had been fighting for months.

> An unknown existence had suddenly revealed itself to us. Those strongly defended trenches, which we had attacked so many times without success, had ended by seeming to us inanimate, like desolate buildings uninhabited by men, the refuge of mysterious and terrible beings of whom we knew nothing. Now they were showing themselves to us as they really were, men and soldiers like us, in uniform like us.[39]

The invisibility of the enemy stripped him of any coherent shape and diffused his characteristic menace through the dead and cratered landscape of the front. To encounter, face to face, that which had been made strange by propaganda and countless frustrated attacks, and to realize they were "like us" was an uncanny experience. It revealed to many what they had forgotten – the intrinsic similarity of men. The penetration of the wall that separated the known from the unknown provoked a shudder of recognition in the few who accomplished it. Freud, in his analysis of the uncanny, insisted that this experience was essentially a return to something old and familiar (*heimlich*) that had become alien (*unheimlich*) through a process of repression.[40] In a sense he added only the concept of repression, as a category-making activity, to Jentsch's notion that the experience of strangeness was usually provoked by an encounter with an object that spans what are usually considered to be exclusive categories. A man who returns to life from the dead, a man who becomes a machine, a man who is part animal – this man is an impossibility as long as the exclusivity of life and death, man and machine, and human and animal is upheld. When such an impossibility is encountered, the feeling of uncanniness is the result.

But war experience is nothing if not a transgression of categories. In providing bridges across the boundaries between the visible and the invisible, the known and the unknown, the human and the inhuman, war offered numerous occasions for the shattering of distinctions that were central to orderly thought, communicable experience, and normal human relations. Much of the bewilderment, stupefaction, or sense of growing strangeness to which combatants testified can be attributed to those realities of war that broke down what Mary Douglas calls "our cherished classifications."

Nowhere is this more evident than in the theme that pervades the war literature: that of death, dying, living in the midst of death. The front is a place that dissolved the clear distinction between life and death. Death, customarily the "slash" between life/not-life, became for many in the war a "dash," a continuum of experience the end of which was the cessation of any possibility of experience. Many used death as a metaphor describing their distance from the "men and things of the past." Those who volunteered for war in 1914 often felt their "civil death" as a liberation, a release from the constraints of civilian life. But the long stay at the front transformed what Franz Schauwecker termed a "vacation from life" into a more permanent estrangement. Gotthold von Rhoden, a former student, and a volunteer and junior officer who died at the front, felt after a time that he had committed himself to a process of withdrawal from the world, a sequential elimination of ties to the familiar that could only end with his physical extinction. His separation from everything familiar was a fateful freedom.

> It seems to me as if we stand before the enemy released from everything that has formerly bound us; we stand entirely free there, death can no longer sever our ties too painfully. Our entire thoughts and feelings are completely rearranged; if I was not afraid of being misunderstood, I could almost say that we are somehow "estranged" from the men and things of our former life.[41]

Von Rhoden speaks here of what Turner calls a "structural death." The men and things of the past are dead to him as he is to them. Many acknowledged that their ties to the home became fewer and more fragile as the war continued. Siegfried Sassoon locates his own disillusionment in the perception that his home had been so radically transformed by war that there no longer seemed anything secure to which he might return. "As for me, I had more or less made up my mind to die; the idea made things seem easier. In the circumstances there didn't seem anything else to do."[42] F. C. Bartlett, in his analysis of the psychological effects of trench war, observed that any extensive stay at the front caused combatants to link thoughts of home and death. Once the desire for death was fixed in the soldier's mind, a nervous breakdown was imminent.

Death became a symbol of the discontinuity and distance that defined relationships between the front and home. But equally, death was an experience of foreclosure, of sensory deprivation, a sense of being fixed and immobilized in a minimal space. The most common soldier's dream was that of being buried in a bunker by a heavy shell. Zuckmayer admits that this dream disturbed his sleep for ten years after the conclusion of the war. The dream of living burial, of being held motionless by the weight of the earth while "a heavy shell, howling and gurgling, with ineluctable slowness then with a mad shriek came down upon me . . . ,"[43] never varied.

The peculiarly Victorian nightmare of living burial came true too often during the war. Ernst Simmel pointed out that "being buried as a result of an explosion with its total obliteration of conscious ego . . . [was] . . . the most frequent originator of war neurosis."[44] It was so common that for a period during the war hysterical paralysis as a result of premature burial earned its own pathological category as the "burial alive neurosis." What is significant about this experience is that it was often felt to be an experience of death from which the victim slowly returned to life. One Dr. P. Grasset described the common sequence of events:

> He loses consciousness, and on recovery . . . finds he can neither see, hear, nor speak. He is completely isolated from the external world for he is unable to either convey or receive impressions. My colleague, M. Foucault . . . tells me that these men probably think they have died.[45]

In war death lost the perfect, abstract clarity that it normally enjoyed as the brief moment between life and not-life. It ceased to be an abstraction and became a term defining the growing distance from which the combatant viewed his home. It described the sense of total isolation from "the external world," a sense that is most intensified in the experience of living burial. In general, death began to define the range of events that removed the frontsoldier further and further from the values, sensory certainties, and hierarchies of status that had once rendered his experience unambiguous and his "self" identifiable. In war the experience of death was given not just to those who appeared in the mortality statistics but also to those who were forced to remain in the expanding moment between the extinction of all choice and the extinction of life. The exclusive attention upon the events that threatened death expanded time. In Zuckmayer's dream the shells came with "ineluctable slowness," for others "softly" or lazily, like balloons or footballs.

> The idea of death got anchored in my head. In this state of mind, on the afternoon of the 27th two bombs came. I saw the first one coming and cried out a warning. Coming back I saw the second one. The bombs were coming rather softly. From this moment on and up to the time when it had burst, I thought I had gone, that I had been carried off and crushed.[46]

There is an astonishing congruence between the symbols of liminality and the realities of the war experience, and this congruence is not accidental. Perhaps no war before or since challenged more thoroughly the value and status of the combatant. The war effaced former dignities and precipitated the combatant into a world with no exit but wounds, death, or neurosis. To become accustomed to war was to grow familiar with a world definable only in terms of paradox. Victor Turner asserts that the symbols which characterize the liminal initiand are most often those of effacement or ambiguity: They "are often considered to be dark, invisible like a planet in eclipse. . . ; they are stripped of names and clothing, smeared with the common earth and rendered indistinguishable from animals."[47]

But the ambiguities of war and the effacement of self were only one part, the most negative part, of the war experience. Many veterans felt that there were strongly positive and intrinsically rewarding elements in their experience. They cite the comradeship that erased "artificial" social barriers, the sharing of a common destiny, and the equality of condition that transcended rank and even enmity – for it extended across No Man's Land in particular sectors of the front. These positive experiences have as much to do with the longevity of the war experience as any trauma of pollution and self-effacement. The sense of comradeship and functional equality was something to be preserved and institutionalized. Simone de Beauvoir describes how central the communal experience of war had been to one of her teachers.

> He explained to us that at the age of twenty he had discovered
> the joys of a comradeship which overcame all social barriers;
> when, after armistice, he became a student again, he was
> determined not to be deprived of that comradeship: the
> segregation which in civil life separates young middle-class
> men from working chaps was something he felt like a personal
> mutilation.[48]

The social experience of war carried over, John Keegan insists, into postwar Britain. In the trenches young, "temporary gentlemen" from the West Country and South Coast watering places encountered Durham miners, Yorkshire furnacemen, and Clydeside shipyard workers.

> In this process of discovery many of the amateur officers were
> to conceive an affection for the disadvantaged which would

eventually fuel that transformation of middle-class attitudes to the poor which has been the most important social trend in Twentieth-Century Britain.[49]

After the war the glowing memories of comradeship and common endeavor were commonly separated from the horrors of war. Emphasis of one at the expense of the other often split veterans' groups into contending factions. The controversy that erupted in Germany after the publication of Remarque's *Im Westen Nichts Neues,* in 1928, over the nature of the war experience eventually produced a liberal experience of war that emphasized the loss of youth, the death, horror, and pollution of war, and also produced a conservative experience which centered upon the experience of comradeship and community. But an adequate rendering of the war experience is not a matter of judiciously balancing its undeniably positive and negative features, but of showing how both the positive and negative sides of war are emanations of the same phenomenon. The *Gemeinschaft* experience of war, like the horrors of war, is a product of the essential liminality of war.

Veterans' groups attempted to ritualize and preserve the position of the soldier as a man who had lived beyond social categories and status distinctions. The experience of living outside of class as a declassified, or not-yet-classified, individual was productive of a sense of comradeship among those who shared this situation. The lack of status of the frontsoldiery, like the statuslessness of a liminal group, can seem to be both a painful loss of identity and a positive liberation from those social distinctions which customarily prevent the formation of close personal bonds across class lines. In going to war the soldier was stripped of the visible marks of status – clothes, address, property, insignia of social rank – that defined his place in society. The formal equality of the army was not, however, comradeship, as many young, middle-class volunteers found out. Comradeship came only after the *invisible* marks of status – attitudes, education, ways of speaking and other manners – were erased, often in painful attacks by the "society of dockworkers." Many volunteers tell of the painful ordeals that their excessive enthusiasm for war, their higher education, and their refinement cost them.

Leaving the precincts of normal social life did not mean that the soldier had entered an arena of licentiousness. On the contrary, war requires and engenders a peculiar kind of social structure very much like that which Turner sees operating in groups of initiands.

> Between neophytes and their instructors . . . and connecting neophytes with one another, exists a set of relations which compose a "social structure" of a highly specific type. It is a structure of a very simple kind: Between instructors and neophytes there is often complete authority and submission; among neophytes there is often complete equality.[50]

The comradeship that was the sacred memory of postwar veterans' groups was the product of a uniformity of condition enforced by authority and the realities of war. John Masters, who served with a regiment of Indian troops during the war, tells how he continually forbade the wearing of caste marks, only to see them reappear if he relaxed his vigilance.[51] The best description of the wedding of equality and authority is that of T. E. Lawrence, who joined the British air corps as a common recruit in 1922. He had tired of the notoriety that his exploits in the Middle East had earned him, and found the anonymity he was seeking among the rows of sleeping bodies in a barracks.

> There enwrapped us, never to be lost, the sudden comradeship of the ranks – a sympathy born half of our common defenselessness against authority . . . and half of our true equality; for except under compulsion there is no equality in the world.[52]

Like Lawrence, F. H. Keeling – a socialist and journalist before the war – joined the army in 1914 with monastic expectations. Soldiering was a ritual that he celebrated as a kind of civil religion to be prized precisely because it was the antithesis of the privacy, individuality, and family-centeredness of civilian life. The Kitchener unit he joined was "communistic in just the aspects in which communism is convenient and stimulating,"[53] and he wondered if he "could ever find a family an adequate substitute for a regiment."[54]

Socialists looking for revolutionary potential in the returning frontsoldiery in 1919 were well aware that the experience of liv-

ing on the margins of social life had given the frontsoldier a contradictory set of political motives. The equality of the ranks, the
uniformity of condition, and the propertilessness of the soldier
were born not of class consciousness but of his marginality and
his defenselessness against both authority and technology. The
comradeship of the front was inextricable from certain attitudes
toward authority: "except under compulsion there is no equality
in the world." Although he was estranged from bourgeois society and out of sympathy with a system of status distinctions
based upon inequities in the distribution of wealth, the frontsoldier was wedded to concepts of authority that were essentially
traditional – and nothing if not "reactionary" in a liberal-
democratic context. The aristocratic officer was the model for
young middle-class junior officers in Britain and Germany. Don-
ald Hankney, who was killed on the Somme in October 1916,
presents the ideal of the Christian officer, the epitome of *caritas*.

> If a blister had to be lanced, he would very likely lance it him-
> self. . . . There was something almost religious about this care
> for our feet. It seemed to have a touch of the Christ about it.[55]

In attempting to realize his role, many a young officer drew on
ancient concepts of paternalism and almost forgotten habits of
deference. These concepts acquired, in war, a new and fateful relevance for postwar society. Many descriptions of the growing
together of the ranks and the new officers could stand as descriptions of a meeting of a young squire and his dependents, or of a
new master with his pupils. "It was only the ardent desire on the
one hand to teach, to encourage, to be accepted, on the other to
learn and to be led which made intercourse between them possible."[56] The equality of life that shaped the identity of the group
at the front had nothing to do with freedom or choice. On the
contrary, this equality was a function, on the one hand, of military subordination that – in the best of circumstances – acquired
a moral and ethical force, and, on the other, a product of the
common subjection of both men and officers to the overwhelming power of fire.

Any liminal experience is a learning experience, and this is implicit in Carrington's assertion that in the war his generation
learned a "secret, which could never be communicated." But

also implicit in the notion of war as an initiation is the sense that the education acquired is qualitatively distinct from any gained indirectly through traditional "schools." Indeed, in order to deal with the war experience, one must understand the myth of experience itself, and the notion that the knowledge gained in experience is inseparable from the person who learns, and uncommunicable to those who have not shared the experience. Carl Zuckmayer termed his war experience "a piece of himself," like a part of his own body, a scar, an organic mark. But this experience is not communicable:

> I can say that . . . the experience of the war and its great, life transforming chaos has taken shape in myself, although I could never make that clear in a representation or generalization.[57]

Always the disorder, chaos, fragmentation of "cherished categories" and the juxtaposition of normally separate things and moods is designated as the source both of the knowledge that characterizes men experienced in war and the incommunicability of this knowledge. Men issuing from the dark door of war are normally characterized as "silent," and this silence might be a mask for bitterness or for "secrets." David Jones pinpoints the peculiar juxtapositions of contraries as the experience that most profoundly effects men in war.

> For I think the day by day in the wasteland, the sudden violences and long stillnesses, the sharp contours and unformed voids of that mysterious existence profoundly affected the imaginations of those who suffered it. It was a place of enchantment.[58]

In war men are *shown,* not just told, and they are shown not by an orderly presentation of reality but through radical juxtapositions of violence and stillness, utter fear and utter boredom. But the real question is: *What* did the generation learn in war? Here, Turner's description of the educational process in liminal rites is helpful. In these rites,

> The bizarre becomes the normal, and through the loosening of connections between elements customarily bound together in

certain combinations, their scrambling and recombining in monstrous, fantastic and unnatural shapes, the novices are induced to think (and think hard) about cultural experiences they had hitherto taken for granted. The novices are taught that they did not know what they thought they knew. Beneath the surface of custom was a deep structure, whose rules they had to learn through paradox and shock.[59]

The prevalence of monsters, of the bizarre and startling in ceremonies of initiation, Turner ascribes not to any desire to frighten initiates but to a desire to teach initiates to distinguish clearly the forces that shape reality as it is conceived in their culture. In liminal zones the neophyte is forced to think about those beings that buttress custom and give law its necessity. The techniques that force a conscious confrontation with cultural factors that are so familiar to have become almost unconscious are, first, the dissociation of cultural elements from their normal relationships, and then their recombination "in fantastic or monstrous shapes." The process of dissociation and recombination reveals the underpinnings of culture and "teaches the neophytes how to think with some degree of abstraction about their cultural milieu." At the same time the revelation of the forces behind reality "is believed to change their nature, transform them from one kind of human being to another."[60]

But here is a clear and obvious distinction between rites of initiation in traditional, agrarian, premodern cultures and this experience of modern war, however much war might be seen as initiatory. What is most often revealed in traditional rites is the sacred underpinnings of the group; what was revealed in war was not "sacred," even though it seemed to acquire a demonic force. In war the combatant learned to recognize realities that were most often termed "material," "technological," or "mechanical." "In general that is the most terrible thing about this war – everything becomes machine-like; one might almost term the war an industry of professionalized human slaughter."[61]

But the surprise of combatants that they were engaged in an event revelatory not of the power of men but of the power of men's means, is itself surprising. The power of modern technology could not be utterly unexpected by men who had grown up in one of the technologically most fruitful eras the world had yet seen – an era that produced, among other things, the telephone, the automobile, the airplane, notable advances in electrical and chemical engineering, and the discovery of radiation. The surprise with which many combatants realized they were fixed in the first wholly industrialized war must be attributed to two factors: the expectations shaped by a traditional image of war as a noneconomic, even anti-economic activity; and, most importantly, what might be called the "desituationing" and "resituationing" of technology.

Many welcomed the war as an escape from industrial society. But in war they learned that technology shaped the organization of men, machines, and tools just as it had in peacetime. Ernst Toller, a veteran of the war who escaped through the exit of neurosis, expresses this realization best.

> Instead of escaping the soul-killing mechanism of modern technological society, they learned that the tyranny of technology ruled even more omnipotently in war than in peace-time. The men who through daring chivalry had hoped to rescue their spiritual selves from the domination of material and technical forces discovered that in the modern war of material the triumph of the machine over the individual is carried to its most extreme form.[62]

The sheer scale of events, the inconceivable power expended in shellfire, asserted an incontestable truth, a truth many thought they "already knew": The war could not be viewed and valued as personal experience, but through the barrage one could apprehend the shape of suprapersonal and technological powers that dictated the actions and feelings of individuals. Jean Galtier-Boissier described his first contact with trench war and his surprise at the pliant, almost worshipful posture of his comrades.

> They have the air of supplicants who offer the napes of their necks to the executioner . . . The peals of thunder in all those moments had revealed the terrible disproportion between the engines of death and the tiny soldier, in whom the nervous system was not up to the magnitude of those shocks.[63]

But it was the dissociation of technology from its traditional associations that made it strange, frightening, and demonic. Technology was removed from a context in which it was comprehensible as the instrument of production and distribution – functions which made life possible and European culture dominant. It was "resituationed" into a context of destruction, work, and terror, where it made human dignity inconceivable and survival problematical. In this process of "resituationing," the neutrality of technology seemed to fade, and certain features – heretofore unsuspected – of the means that industrial civilization had developed to control nature and transcend human limitations became obvious. The dissociation of technology from its normal setting and its repositioning in a context of pure destruction made strange and monstrous that which was formerly familiar, a matter of pride and an engine of progress. David Jones was impressed precisely with the sinister, albeit "fascinating and compelling," character that technology took on in the war.

> It is not easy in considering a trench mortar barrage to give praise for the action of chemicals – full though it may be of beauty . . . [We must] . . . do gas-drill, be attuned to many new-fangled technicalities, respond to increasingly exacting mechanical demands; some fascinating and compelling, others sinister in the extreme; all requiring a new and strange direction of the mind, a new sensitivity certainly, but at a considerable cost. [64]

In the war technology was recognized as an autonomous, legislative reality. It meant not just an array of weapons and tools, but the organization of material and men. This organization – freed from the nexus of use and wont that had made it ideologically comprehensible before 1914 as a means of progress and a system for the improvement of the human condition – took on the qualities of an abstraction, a unified system of force. After the war, men talked about technology in a way that was quite different than the discussions of mechanization before 1914. Friedrich Dessauer tried to pinpoint the difference, and he insisted that before the First World War,

> Technology was not yet a theme of international discussion. The awareness that here we were dealing with something

enormous, unitary, a world-transfiguring power, appeared
only in individuals . . . They saw particular objects but not
the entirety. It needed an event which directed many eyes
toward technology, and it came in 1914 – the First World
War.[65]

The experience of war forced the combatant to face, as "unaccommodated man," the material realities that underlay social
life. Only in war did they assume a startling form. Stripped of its
productive purpose, technology could only be seen as something
"enormous and "unitary," something that shaped a world and
the men who inhabited it, independent of their wills or needs.

The symbols of the "social structure" and the kind of knowledge that characterizes liminal rites are astonishingly congruent
with the experience of modern war, and this raises certain essential questions. How is the congruence to be taken? And what
does it mean? Clearly the war was *not* a ritual event but an historical event. Rituals of initiation do not kill initiands, however
much the symbols of death might be used to characterize his
anomalous situation, and however much they might be marked
and mutilated in ritual operations. But, even if one ignored these
obvious differences, it would still be impossible to see the war as
an initiation. The purpose of initiation is the induction of the initiand into a new social position. Without rites of reaggregation, in which the initiand assumes his new place in the social
structure, the liminal phase lacks all purpose, meaning, or justification. It is in the final phase of initiation that the purpose of
the rite becomes abundantly clear.

> In the third phase, the passage is consummated. The ritual sub-
> ject, individual or corporate, is in a stable state once more and
> by virtue of this has rights and obligations of a clearly defined
> and "structural" type, and is expected to behave in accordance
> with certain norms and ethical standards.[66]

The initiand is stripped of his previous status and reduced to
"generalized" matter in order to be elevated to a new status. He
does not, like the veteran of the First World War, confront his
society with a "front of silence and bitterness." If the experience
of the war was an initiation, it remained forever problematical

what state, condition, or station the soldier was being initiated into. His relations to the society of his origins remained intrinsically problematic. The rites and symbols of veterans' groups continued to celebrate liminality, and the war experience was nothing if not a reduction of self that forced the veteran into a defensive posture vis-à-vis his society. Perhaps the nature of the war and the character of industrial society prevented any consummation of passage, any reaggregation of the former soldier with his home. If the frontsoldier changed, so too had his society, and the veteran often felt that there was no "place" to which he might return.

The veteran was a man fixed in passage who had acquired a peculiar "homelessness." The postwar career of the veteran is the subject of Chapter 6, but here it is essential to point out that in the negotiations between the changed frontsoldier and his changed home, the liminality of war was not resolved but reenacted. If anything it was the failure of any reaggregation that continued to make the war experience problematic to the veteran, and the veteran himself an ambiguous and potentially dangerous figure to his society.

But still the initial question remains: How can one account for the astonishing congruence of liminal symbols and war experience when the very reality, purpose, and status of war and ritual are so very different? This congruence is more than accidental and can be explained, I feel, by focusing our attention more closely upon the ways in which participants thought about themselves and their relationship to the events of which they became a part.

THE EVENT AS TEXT

In dealing with a "war literature," one is dealing with the testimony of men who, as a rule, had little or no control over the events which threatened their lives. The perspective of the frontsoldier who was not privy to the motives and plans of staffs dissolved into bewilderment and confusion. But this raises the question of how participants seek to make their own actions comprehensible to themselves, and how they define their relationship to realities over which they have no control.

More than anything else, the common soldier in the First World War felt that the war increasingly was separate and distinct from his own purpose and motives. Even a brief encounter with combat made the "war" seem a sequence of events that was so much larger than the human beings who prosecuted it that it defeated any personalized perspective. Many who fought felt the detachment of the meaning and significance of their actions from themselves as a personal bereavement. It is this autonomy of events of war that most often lies behind the description of the war as a machine, an automaton. Henry de Man, for example, described the war as a mechanism that moved through its "own inertia and the capacities of the once aroused masses to persevere."[67] He believed that the war "had long since become the secret dread of those who had created it."[68] As an event the war seemed to have become detached even from the wills of those putatively in charge of its conduct. This sense of inhabiting an automaton, an event that is not willed by its human participants, is also implicit in Rudolf Binding's description of the war as a glacier.

> Is mankind in this war only a moraine under the weight of a monstrous glacier? This glacier is slowly rolling down the valley; and it never seems to get lighter. When it no longer weighs on the moraine, when it is melted, only worn-out stones will be lying strewn over a wide field, and they will know nothing of the glacier . . . such is this war. It is not to be compared with a campaign. For there one leader pits his will against that of another. But in this war both adversaries lie on the ground and only the war has its will.[69]

Most combatants realized that the scale of war – its enormous violence and unimaginable number of casualties – was a function of the scale of production in industrialized nations. Marx, in viewing the phenomenon of an industrialized England, realized that now the comprehension of social life and economic relations had to be qualitatively different from that appropriate to premodern production where hand, tool, and artifact were integrated in a way obvious to the most common sense. With industrialization, a productive system emerged that – like the

Nature of the eighteenth century – required scientific laws for its description. The substructure of production that underlay modern social life was a system with no center and no periphery, which defeated from the outset any individualized perspective. "In modern industry man succeeded for the first time in making the product of his labor (the machine) work on a large scale, gratuitously like the forces of nature."[70] In modern production technology, labor and capital created a system that seemed to have a peculiar autonomy from individuals. In its fruitfulness, scale, and power, it could only be compared to nature.

Industrialized war was seen in exactly this light. It was easy to see in the blindly crushing mechanism of war the dark side of modern production described by Marx.

> Here we have, in place of the isolated machine, a mechanical monster whose body fills whole factories and whose demon power, at first veiled under the slow measured motions of his giant limbs, at length breaks out into the fast and furious whirl of his countless working organs.[71]

This sense of being a part of an event that has no single author, except perhaps a divine will, might be said to characterize the consciousness of participants in any historical event of the first magnitude. But this notion that the event is autonomous, that it has no author, is the initial assumption upon which the combatant in war erects a vision of himself and his relationship to the realities that enclose him.

The feeling that the event had gained a fearful autonomy from any set of human authorities marks the point at which the event becomes the only relevant object of study for participants. To use Paul Ricoeur's phrase, for those enmeshed in it, the event had become a "text," the correct reading of which was a matter of life and death.

> My claim is that action itself, action as meaningful, may become the object of science . . . by virtue of a kind of objectification similar to the fixation which occurs in writing. By this objectification, action is no longer a transaction . . . It constitutes a delineated pattern which has to be interpreted according to its inner connections.[72]

It is worth pursuing this analogy between a text that, when written down, gains a certain autonomy from the motives, intentions, and purposes of an author, and an historical event which, for participants, gains an autonomy and a dynamic distinct from the intentions of those who make it. Even if one has fully divined the motives of the author of a book, this does not mean that one has fully understood the meaning of a text. In the process of becoming fixed in writing, the text creates a world of connotation, association, and cross-references that might be wholly unintended by its author. Equally, the experience of war is composed of internal coherencies, routines, and the startling propinquity of normally disparate phenomena that are wholly unrelated to the intentions of any staff, high command, or statesmen. One has not "read" the war once one has divined the motives of those in command, any more than one has "read" a text after one has fully answered the question: What were the purposes of an author, and has he achieved those purposes?

In capitalizing the "War" and in confronting it as an objective structure distinct from themselves, combatants were saying that the war had become a world that enfolded them with its own logic, connections, and incongruencies. Their very immersion in this world, and their habituation to it, distinguished them, their knowledge, and their identity from those who remained outside of it. Just as the meaning of the text may not lie in the purposes of an author but in its impact upon those who imaginatively enter it, the meaning of the war was commonly felt to lie in the self-awareness, consciousness, fears, and fantasies that it engendered in those who were forced to inhabit a world of violence they had not created.

This understanding of their relationship to the war oftentimes dictated the form of expression appropriate to the knowledge gained in experience. Combatants could understand their own actions less and less as attempts to carry out certain plans that would produce given ends. The scale of war lifted their own contribution out of the rational nexus of cause and effect. To see the war as an autonomous machine having the power of spontaneous motion within it and dictating the proper motions (or motionlessness) to its human members meant that the event was fixed, not in type, but in the character of participants. The autonomy of the event forced those within it to read its marks in themselves. In war the self becomes a recording instrument, and the knowledge gained in experience was codified in the "types" of character that the war produced.

Thus one finds in the war literature a sequence of types that fix the realities of war throughout its various phases: the volunteer of 1914, the essence of idealistic expectations; the closed, unapproachable, "defensive" soldier, passively shaped by the tyranny of material; the stormtrooper (in Italy, the *arditi*), the master of the technological offensive. Each of these types embodies a different set, a different imprint of the events of war. The volunteer is the embodiment of war as a national and communal project. The exhausted, waiting, forever-enduring survivor of *Materialkrieg* is immediately recognizable as the product of industrialized warfare in its enormous scale and power. The stormtrooper is both a reality and a fantasy of aggression rooted in the massive frustration of aggressive impulses by the actualities of trench warfare.

At this point, one can clearly see at least three levels of significance operating in the transformation of character cited by combatants and attested to by those who observed men returning from war. On one level the difference that marks the identity of the frontsoldier can be seen as a psychic alteration most obvious in victims of war neurosis but observed also in many who were not admitted to the shell-shock wards. Sandor Ferenczi termed this a kind of narcissism encouraged by the constantly threatening environment of war. "The libido withdraws from the object into the ego, enhancing self-love and reducing object-love to the point of indifference."[73]

On a second level the alterations in the identity of the frontsoldier can be seen as a function of the liminality of war experience, as a record of the alteration in the relationship of the frontsoldier to his society and to the categories that define the structure of normal social experience and status. In a war that lasted too long, the frontsoldier became a "riddle to himself" and a stranger to the "men and things" of his former life. The adaptation to a life in a No Man's Land between the familiar and valued categories of social life familiarized him with the excitement and the powers that lie in the gaps of respectable existence. The fears that were focused upon the returning soldier were little different from those directed at any figure who comes in from the peripheries of social life, only in this instance the soldier was a citizen made strange by his experience.

Finally, the change of identity in the frontsoldier is a formulaic interpretation of the war appropriate to those who lived in an environment that reversed the normal relationship between actor and action. The war had become an autonomous event comprehensible only in the ways it imprinted those who could no longer see themselves, even in combination, as authors of their acts. Like ritual events, the war took on a spectacular objectivity, a programmatic status, that dictated the necessary behavior to participants. The frontsoldier is a type – in fact, many types. The existence of this type verifies the impression that the war endured through its social and psychological effects on those who lived within it. Figuratively, but also literally, the war becomes a text: "The daily monotony of *Stellungskrieg* governs everything with its thousand rules which originated out of experience but now fill thick books of service regulations."[74]

The event was fixed in character, and in this sense the war was like an initiation and representable with the symbols of liminality. The effects of the war upon participants could no more be reversed than the character given by the rites of passage could be resolved back into its constituent elements. One cannot overlook the possibility that the liberation of the event from the actions and feelings of participants was more than a switch in perspective. It fundamentally altered the repertoire of roles available to those suffering a process outside of their own control. The participant was capable of experiencing himself in a double way. He could be a functionary of those forces and energies that dominated him, gaining an enhanced, if callous, potency; or he could remain the "weakest, most pitying heart in the world," lodged within an expanded and continually threatened self-love.

2. The Community of August and the Escape from Modernity

THE LOGIC OF COMMUNITY IN 1914

For many participants, August 1914 was the last great national incarnation of the "people" as a unified moral entity. The August days were universally remembered as the "most deeply lived" days in the lives of the war generation, days that would never be forgotten and never be repeated. The sense of community that activated the crowds in the streets of European cities and bound strangers together with a kind of magical cohesion was rarely intellectualized. For many, like Carl Zuckmayer, this community was a physical and moral presence within which every individual found himself confronted with his membership in a human multitude. "I have experienced such a physical and moral condition of luminosity and euphoria two or three times since . . . but never with that sharpness and intensity."[1] With deafening unanimity almost all descriptions of August 1914 begin with "I shall never forget . . ." and end with "it will never recur . . ."

> Never will we, the generation living in 1914, forget these last days of July . . . Many may jumble what came after with those weeks . . . but the last days and nights, the emotional content of those hours which ripped through the torrent of events are unforgettable.[2]

It was difficult for contemporaries to see the logic, the assumptions, and the cultural configurations that underlay their
enthusiasm for war. The very intensity and universality of feeling seemed to dissolve any critical comprehension. August was a
celebration of community, a festival, and not something to be ra-
tionally understood. Indeed, many insisted that August 1914 was
essentially an outbreak of unreason, a madness, or a mass delusion. Magnus Hirschfeld wrote:

> It was an outbreak of madness which raged through the streets
> at that time, an explosion such as had already been experienced
> and described, but which had never been fanned into such a
> world-burning flame.[3]

The only logic which Hirschfeld could see in the outburst of enthusiasm for war was the logic of repression and release. "It was
a discharge of tensions that had built up for years. Everyone suffered from under an intolerable burden . . . which the outbreak
of war had wiped away."[4] Although he had a much more benev-
olent opinion of the enthusiasm for war, W. M. Maxwell agreed
that it was futile to try and understand the English enthusiasm of
August: "Even when we try to rationalize the matter we are left
with the feeling that reason had very little to do with it."[5] Gertrude Bäumer felt that both she and the nation were transfigured
by the declaration of war, and that this transfiguration defeated
language. It was something that could only be felt and lived
through but never understood or described.

> The plunge from out of the existing world into a completely
> different one cannot be described. For that feeling of having
> broken out of a channel buttressed by decades, of having been
> catapulted into an incalculable destiny, there are simply no ad-
> equate words or representations. There are no expressions
> suitable to the reality of this pause between two world orders –
> the fading of everything that was important yesterday and the
> summoning up of novel historical forces. In those clear sleep-
> less nights of high summer we became a "battleground of two
> epochs."[6]

But it is significant that, even while denying the rationality and
describability of the experience of August, both Hirschfeld and

Bäumer sound the theme that gave August its coherence: War was seen as the binary opposite of social life and the counterpole to normal existence in modern industrialized society. The assumption of the polarity of war and peace allowed contemporaries to experience the declaration of war as a movement from normal, familiar life to an alternative existence which differed markedly from bourgeois society. It was commonly felt that, with the declaration of war, the populations of European nations had left behind an industrial civilization with its problems and conflicts and were entering a sphere of action ruled by authority, discipline, comradeship, and common purpose. This polarity of war and social life structured the experience of August, giving the movement from peace to war its characteristic significance. It is a polarity that can be seen to function in the most intensely felt experience of community, and through it was generated a picture of what war was to be and to mean for participants.

It is not too much to say that this polarity was a deeply rooted cultural assumption native to modern European society. It came as a surprise, for example, to many European anthropologists when they found that the antithesis of war and social life was not universal in human culture. The integration of warfare, trade, and normal social life in "primitive" society was often a source of comment for Europeans and stood in contrast to their assumptions. Roger Caillois is only recapitulating what had become a standard contrast when he notes that

> Wars in primitive society . . . lack impressiveness and magnitude and cut a poor figure. They are merely interludes, expeditions for hunting, raiding or vengeance. They constitute a permanent state that forms the fabric of existence. No doubt they are a dangerous occupation, but their continuity deprives them of any exceptional character.[7]

Endemic, primitive war, with its low level of violence, could not be seen as an activity outside of the normal. The conventions of trade and warfare governing relations between social groups were often found to be interchangeable, sometimes identical.[8] The yearly siege laid by the ancient Russ on Constantinople, perhaps the best fortified city in the world in the ninth and tenth centuries, ended invariably in the peaceful trade of Russian furs, honey, and slaves for Byzantine wares and finery. Here the conventions of war and tribute concealed the actuality of economic exchange.[9] This integration of war and economic exchange, of war and normal social life, in preindustrialized society became a part of the contrasting picture that European social anthropologists held up to their own culture, a culture in which the antithesis of war and social life most often went without saying.

This antithesis shapes the dominant themes in the experience of August: the experience of community and the escape from everything implicit in the notion of modern industrial society. The experience of community was dominated by the sense that the war had altered the relationships between men and social classes. And, logically, in leaving behind the social world structured by wealth, status, professions, age, and sex, it was felt that individuals themselves had been transformed. As Walter Scheller, a theologian and humanist who participated wholeheartedly in the enthusiasm for war, wrote: "My first impression was that war changed men, and it also changed the relationship between men."[10] The crowds that Stefan Zweig observed in the streets of Vienna were no longer a threatening antisemitic "mob" or undifferentiated "mass" and the channel for the release of irrational, violent, and instinctual impulses targeted for "outsiders." With the war, the multitude had become a moral presence embodying the solidarity of the nation. Zweig's oft-quoted and moving description of the crowds mobilized by war brings together many of the particulars of the community of August.

> As never before, thousands and hundreds of thousands felt what they should have felt in peacetime, that they belong together; a city of two million, a country of nearly fifty million, felt in that hour that they were participating in a moment which would never recur; and that each one was called upon to cast his infinitesimal self into the glowing mass, and there to be purified of all selfishness. All differences of class, rank and language were flooded over at that moment by the rushing feeling of fraternity. Strangers spoke to each other in the streets, people who had avoided each other for years shook hands . . .
> Each individual experienced an exaltation of his ego; he was no

longer the isolated person of former times, he had been incor-
porated into the mass, he was a part of the people, and his person, his hitherto unnoticed person had been given meaning.[11]

There are two features of Zweig's description that need to be
emphasized. First, all the "differences of class, rank and language" were not effaced or abolished but set aside by the feeling
of fraternity and the sentiment of nationality. No one, much less
Stefan Zweig, thought that the class structure was in any way in-
ternally reshaped by the onrush of feeling that allowed the inhabitants of Vienna to forgive each other's faults and shake hands
after years of silence. The poor were made no richer, the rich no
poorer, by the declaration of war, and yet the feeling of community was nonetheless real. That structure of social positions that
would, normally, have led any observer to interpret the movement of crowds as a threat to the established order or to a designated minority, now seemed to be set aside. Secondly, the setting aside of class differences allows Zweig to abandon his
defenses, his ego, and his sense of social isolation. In Berlin,
Marianne Weber took up this same theme: "No more are we
what we had been so long: alone."[12] It is obvious that the sense
of community which Zweig joined in Vienna and Marianne
Weber celebrated in Berlin was not a matter of a new source of
solidarity, the overturn of the established order, or a realignment
of status, but rather a product of the felt removal of distinctions
of class and conscience that had prevented something "natural"
and original from expressing itself. The fixation upon status and
social selfhood, and not status itself, seemed to have been replaced by wholly other concerns. It would be a mistake to assert
that in some sense the social equality of August was a "sham"
and that nothing real changed. The declaration of war changed
the perspective from which individuals regarded each other, and
this produced feelings of equality that are impossible to discount.
Binding insisted that in August men

> . . . *were* equal. No one wished to count for more than anyone
> else. On the streets and avenues men looked each other in the
> eye and rejoiced in their togetherness. The doctor, the judge
> . . . the worker, the manufacturer . . . carried the same obliga-

tions. . . . No one grumbled. The most distasteful men were willing and amicable. There were no longer any superfluous men. It was like a rebirth.[13]

The community of August was experienced as a community in Martin Buber's sense of a new, spontaneous relationship between the "I" and the "thou." It is a matter of feeling rather than a reorganization and reorientation of public institutions, a feeling of living

> . . . no longer side by side . . . but *with* one another of a multitude of persons. And this multitude, though it moves towards one goal, yet experiences everywhere a turning to, a dynamic facing of . . . a flowing from I to thou. Community is where community happens.[14]

The community of August can be identified with that type of community that Victor Turner has called "existential" or "spontaneous" *communitas*,[15] a type that is peculiar to states of transition and passage.

The descriptions of the equality that characterized social relations during the community of August reinforce the sense that this community was the product of a structural change, a raising of the horizon of expectation, and not a change of social or psychic realities. The community of August of 1914 was a byproduct of a shift of institutional gears. But within this shift certain aspirations and longings usually drowned out by the monotonous hum of the everyday became audible. Most audible was an intense and fundamental discontent – particularly prominent in Germany – with the institutions that organized, classified, and segmented individuals into classes and degrees.

It was generally felt, in all belligerent countries, that August had terminated social hostilities and removed the moral opprobrium from social promiscuity. Edith Wharton's account of the mingling of the "dangerous classes" and middle classes in Paris in the last days of July 1914 breathes a profound relief.

> Only two days ago . . . [Parisians] . . . had been leading a thousand different lives in indifference or antagonism to each other, as alien as enemies across a frontier . . . Now . . . [they

were] . . . bumping up against each other in an instinctive
community of the nation.[16]

The declaration of war established a unanimity of fate and a kind
of anonymity of obligation in which the conventions of social
class no longer seemed to identify individuals. It was commonly
felt that the war effaced the boundaries of individuality and privacy and thus made possible a more intense and immediate
sociability. An article that appeared in the Hungarian press
warned the women of Budapest against the dangers inherent in
this promiscuous sociability.

> During the weeks of the great excitement and in the following
> months the women have fallen into a feverish passion of en-
> thusiasm . . . as if the relevance of those burdening ties of
> social and economic responsibility had suddenly been
> overthrown . . . At no time have women committed so many
> mistakes and sins as in the Autumn of this mass fever.[17]

The threats that war posed to the chastity of respectable
women and the sexual attractiveness of the uniform were themes
exploited constantly by the wartime press. The uniform made
men anonymous and public, and it was feared that women might
feel that in bestowing themselves upon the uniform they were
fulfilling a patriotic duty and, in any case, not committing the sin
involved in acquiescing sexually to a "private individual."[18]
Nursing service, jobs newly available to women, semimilitary
relief organizations, and other wartime activities created by the
war for women allowed an enormously expanded range of escape routes from the constraints of the private family. Women,
as well as men, experienced with the onset of war the collapse of
those established, traditional distinctions between an "economic" world of business and a private world of sentiment. This
felt collapse permitted a range of personal contacts that had been
impossible in their former social lives where hierarchies of status
ruled.

The best analogy to August is not the revolutionary over-
throw of an established social order but the temporary disordering or reversal of social status that takes place in festivals. Roger

Caillois's equation of modern war and premodern festivals is perhaps even a memory of the experience of August 1914. The festival uproots the individual "from his privacy and his personal or familial world." Both modern war and ancient festivals

> . . . inaugurate a period of vigorous socialization and share instruments, resources and powers in common. They interrupt the time during which individuals separately occupy themselves in very many different domains . . . In modern society, for this reason, war represents a unique moment of concentration and intense absorption in the group of everything that ordinarily tends to maintain a certain area of independence . . .[19]

There are obvious differences between the unpredictable occurrence of war and the set, periodic festival, and yet Caillois's equation is based upon the observation that both war and festivals are paradigms of collective experience that take place outside or between the separate domains of social status in which individuals ordinarily live their lives. Both war and festivals organize resources for expenditure on an "uneconomic" scale, both are "orgies of consumption" that supersede the customary legal channels by which goods and affection are distributed. Both are welcomed as an escape from privacy into a sphere of unmediated human contact. It is easy to see the similarities between the enthusiasm of August 1914 and the Indian Holi festival, the "feast of love" in which Professor McKim Marriott participated.

> Here indeed were the many village kinds of love confounded . . . all broken suddenly out of their usual narrow channels by a simultaneous increase of intensity. Boundless, unilateral love of every kind flooded over the usual compartmentalization and indifference among separated castes and families. Insubordinate libido inundated all established hierarchies of age, sex, caste, wealth and power.[20]

Many describe the beginning of war in these terms, and many were capable of assuming a double perspective upon the "incomprehensible human love" that bound strangers together. It could be enjoyed, and yet at the same time the expansion of intimacy beyond the private, familial, and convivial institutions could be – to a second, "respectable" mind – a breach of good taste, a disordering promiscuity. Zuckmayer acknowledged that even in this epiphany of communal feeling he found something "pathological, such as characterizes every crisis of the soul or experience, even the productive ones of lovers and artists."[21]

Though he regards them as evidence of individual pathologies rather than the revival of traditional conventions, Magnus Hirschfeld cites many examples of the use of the uniform as a disguise, a sexual object, a means of reversing roles.[22] Women who had a uniform made for them, went to the front, and acquitted themselves bravely were a standard theme of the wartime press. Hirschfeld cites the case of an older woman of aristocratic background who had a field-grey uniform tailored for her and who appeared publicly as an officer throughout the war. Women in particular "reacted to the war experience with a powerful increase in libido,"[23] even though this libido attached itself to the very symbols signifying uniformization of roles: stripes on officers' trousers, sailors' uniforms, the sound of marching boots, batons, pistols, and so on. Hirschfeld states that some of his women patients reported that their passion for their husbands was utterly quenched when they appeared in civilian clothes, garbed again in the costume that signaled the resumption of domestic roles.

William Maxwell, drawing upon a traditional image, recognizes that the celebration of August tapped the sources of misrule: "There was a great deal of folly about it all."[24] But it would be a mistake to regard the celebration of misrule as an outburst of "insubordinate libido" for it attached itself to the very images of *Gleichgestaltung*: the uniform and other symbols of purely formal rank. One cannot avoid the conclusion that a large portion of the enthusiasm for war was fueled by a search for some avenue of escape from privacy. This appears in Zweig's account of his own feelings, in his sense that he was "no longer the isolated person of former times," and in his intense enjoyment of being only an "infinitesimal part" of a glowing mass. The motive that thrust many out into the streets, into the recruiting offices, and onto the parade grounds and barrack yards was precisely a longing to throw off a too narrow and confining identity.

However impermanent the transfiguration of society and individuals, however quickly the emotions of August disappeared in the crushing normality of industrialized war, one cannot doubt that August required participants to experience each other and themselves in a unique way. In attempting to describe this novel experience, contemporaries drew upon a fund of oppositions: historical time and ahistorical time; society and community; mediated, differentiated experience and direct, total experience; "mechanized" life and pastoral life. These oppositions must be seen as deeply traditional and conventional. Thus it was often felt to be unfair to measure the experience of August upon the scale of significance drawn from historical duration. Like revolution, war was an event that projected participants outside of chronologically structured time. In Rilke's words, by entering war the populations of European nations had stepped outside time and into a moment in which "the past remains behind, the future hesitates, the present is without foundation."[25]

The sense of being in a process rather than a place, in an interregnum with no definable structure, was common in the experience of August. The very amorphous character of this moment intensified expectations and curiosity, just as it permitted unheard-of contacts between formerly separate classes and stations in society. In December of 1914 Thomas Mann wrote to his friend Richard Dehmel, who was fighting on the eastern front: "One wonders how it will all turn out. The anxiety and curiosity are tremendous, but it is a joyful curiosity, isn't it? It is a feeling that everything will have to be new after this profound, mighty visitation . . ."[26] Mann shared the almost universal sense that the war would bring some enormous change, that it would generate something "new." Rarely was this change specified, and one can see that it is essentially the product of an experience of consciously occupying a transitional moment, a "liminal" period between a concrete past and a future that has not yet revealed itself in any detail. Friedrich Meinecke, in an oft-quoted passage, links the very ephemerality of the moment with hopes for a generalized "change."

> The exaltation of spirit experienced during the August days of 1914, in spite of its ephemeral character, is one of the most precious, unforgettable memories of the highest sort . . . One perceived in all camps that it was not a matter merely of the

unity of a gain-seeking partnership – but that an inner renovation of our whole state and culture was needed. We generally believed, indeed, that this had already commenced and that it would progress further in the common experience of war.[27]

The feeling of being in a transition period is very prevalent in the sense of community that sprang up in August. It is incorrect to speak of the war as signaling a sudden shift from one state or condition of life to another. As Rilke, Mann, and others insist, what was so liberating and ultimately paralyzing about the war was a sense of "statelessness," the sense of living in an unspecifiable moment. With the onset of war it appeared that the secure structures of social life were dissolved into a fluid state. This allowed a mingling of separate lives, careers, and roles that would, before the war, have been regarded as intolerably promiscuous.

A common, and significant, metaphor in descriptions of August is that of fluidity and flow. Bäumer and others speak of "torrents" of events, "streams" of feeling, the "breaking out" of established channels and of "dissolving" into a process of transition. "When the pressure of practical, organizational work diminished, we became conscious of that great current in which we – mere drops – drew together."[28] This flow metaphor is used with great power in Carl Zuckmayer's description of his arrival in Germany after the crisis of July had interrupted his vacation on the Dutch coast. Here the flow that leaps through the isolated fragments of humanity – travelers in the Cologne station – is an electric current that dispels Zuckmayer's fear of war.

Then, in the enormous Cologne station droning with song, marching steps, the cries of travelers rushing through the cold, expanding, white-lead morning light, it went through me – not like an infection – but like the radiation of a current of cosmic electricity which dispelled the vague feeling of nausea from throat and stomach, built up in the skull and sent sparks flashing and glowing from head to heart. It transposed the body as well as the soul into a trance-like, enormously enhanced love of life and existence, a joy of participation, of living-along-with, a feeling, even, of grace.[29]

Trains and train stations are the setting of many conversions to the enthusiasm of August, conversions invariably spoken of as a "surrendering" to the flow of feeling that is almost palpable. This setting, along with streets, epitomized an open system through which travelers had formerly hurried to their separate destinations. But now they provide the channels for the movement of separate individuals in one unified direction, toward the project of war. Ernst Gläser's conversion to the universal enthusiasm was remarkably like that of Zuckmayer. His initial response to the threat of war was totally negative for it had interrupted a vacation in Switzerland and a budding friendship with a French boy. But Gläser, who was twelve years old in 1914, was forced by the general enthusiasm to abandon any resistance and join in what Rilke called the sudden opening of a "universal heart": "I was giddy with this incomprehensible human love . . . The world lay transfigured. The war had made everything beautiful."[30] His train crossed the German border, and its passengers felt that sudden cohesion which made "everything seem new."

This sequence of initial resistance followed by a surrender to the overwhelming flow of emotion can be found in many experiences of August. An especially telling description of resistance and surrender is that of Conrad Haenisch – a Social Democrat who had shaped an identity out of opposition to capitalist society – for his surrender was accomplished at considerable emotional cost. Haenisch acknowledged the tension between the "burning desire to throw oneself into the powerful current of the national tide"[31] and the horror of betraying his moral stance against the rule of the "political" classes. The threat of war raised this conflict with agonizing intensity. But significantly, the declaration of war resolved the contradiction between head and heart and placed the moral dilemmas of participation irrevocably in the "state" that had been left behind.

> Suddenly – I shall never forget the day and the hour – the terrible tension was resolved; until one dared to be what one was; until – despite all principles and wooden theories – one could, for the first time in almost a quarter-century, join with a full heart, a clean conscience, and without a sense of treason in the sweeping, stormy song: "Deutschland, Deutschland, über alles."[32]

In Haenisch's surrender to the flow of national emotion there is little sense that he is accommodating himself to a fait accompli – the declaration of war. The political and moral dilemma was itself set aside, not by throwing over principles but by surrender to a situation in which those principles were felt to have become irrelevant, "wooden" theories. Something more than innocence or culpability allowed Haenisch to feel, with other Social Democrats who voted war credits, that war had set aside the class structure that was identical with social inequality, injustice, and exploitation. For now material interest – the very motor of behavior in capitalist society – no longer seemed to motivate individuals, and the major obstacles to the surrender of self were gone, swept away by the declaration of community. One gets the sense from Haenisch's conversion to the enthusiasm for war that, in spite of his conscious antagonism to bourgeois society, he shared one of the essential assumptions of that world: the antithesis of war and social life. Perhaps the very fact that this assumption was shared by antagonistic social and political groups made it possible to mobilize the nation, and to speak of Europe in 1914 as *a* culture.

With thoroughgoing irony, but in very similar terms, Jules Romains describes the enthusiasm for war in France. One of the characters of Romains's novel, *Men of Good Will,* recognized that the declaration of war meant that it was no longer a matter of taking a stance toward war in general but of surrendering to the torrents of emotion filling the streets of Paris, a surrender that would resolve all doubts.

> He felt himself yielding to the general intoxication, the feverish delight of the public manifestation, the extraordinary emotional facility of it all. It was so simple: It was enough just not to resist; enough just to say yes; enough to replace the arduous thinking on events . . . by a blind acceptance of the immediate future . . . What peace in having no longer to kick against the Pricks![33]

A surrender to the "general intoxication" promised a release not only from the anxiety of having to take moral positions but also from boredom. War would be "life at last! No threat, even for a moment, of boredom . . . Get thee behind me, age of boredom, the long emptiness of inglorious peace. History begins today."[34]

Not surprisingly, many felt the sudden coalescence of energies that had been split, fragmented, and often set against each other in normal existence as a euphoric burst of vitality. It was quite common for them to term this a "release," and to see this release as a cause rather than a function of the movement from peace to war. Thus, from the perspective of 1941, Stefan Zweig sees the "release of energies" the was an effect of transition as a cause of war.

> Calmly reflecting on the past, if one asks why Europe went to war in 1914, neither reasonable ground nor provocation can be found. It had nothing to do with ideas, hardly even with petty frontiers. I cannot explain it otherwise than by this surplus of force, a tragic consequence of the internal dynamism that had accumulated in those forty years of peace and now sought violent release.[35]

But the enthusiasm was a product of the feeling that a highly segmented, functionally structured society devoted to the satisfaction of multifarious material needs had been set aside. It was replaced not with a new set of positions, statuses, and roles, but by a common project or, as contemporaries preferred, a common "destiny." "It was a great faith that came over men, and even the Fatherland was less the object of enthusiasm than the belief in a common destiny which transfigured men and made them all equal."[36] The project of war permitted, in Rilke's words, a "whole people . . . [to] . . . set their affections in tune" and effected a sudden harmony in the "web of a hundred contradictory voices."[37]

I have dwelt upon the language used by contemporaries in describing their experience of August because the metaphors most commonly used – of flow, motion, surrender to a common direction, release from emotional, social, and political contradictions – suggest that this experience, however "mystical," inchoate, and emotional, was a function of a set of cultural assumptions that fixed the relationship of peace to war and prefigures the meaning of the war. Too much is often made of the undeniable intensity and subjectivity of those feelings released in August and not enough of the cultural mechanisms, patterns, and structures that affected this release.

Thus the "surrender of self" that was such a common act in August can be seen as predicated upon the assumption that the war meant the removal of individuals from a state definable in terms of social, sexual, and political conflict, a state in which the ego was an essential mechanism of self-defense and the agent that mediated between contradictory demands and roles. "Mobilization" precipitated them into a condition of motion and flow in which normally disparate classes, sexes, and ages were brought together, not by a "new condition" but by a common direction. War was prefigured as a sphere of action in which organized collective behavior was not contradictory and conflictual. It presented a set of demands that obviated individual attentiveness to self and self-interest. The declaration of war declared the arrival of a field of endeavor that rendered collective life coherent and unidirectional.

There are many experiences that, though not historically situated, are strictly analogous to the experience of August and that can illuminate many of the features central to that experience. In his analysis of "intrinsically rewarding experiences" in play, performance, and sports, Milhalyi Csikszentmihalyi noted that many of his respondents used the metaphor of flow in trying to explain what was most pleasurable in mountain-climbing, chess-playing, or dancing. He began to call these experiences "flow states" and suggested that they are created by situations in which

> . . . action follows action according to an internal logic that seems to need no conscious intervention by the actor. He experiences it as a unified flowing from one moment to the next, in which he is in control of his actions, and in which there is little distinction between himself and his environment, between stimulus and response, or between past, present, and future.[38]

The flow state is precipitated by entry into an arena which lays down the "logic" of action, without any necessity for reflection. It is experienced when individual skills mesh harmoniously with specific conditions of action. Most significantly a "flow state" is not a release from rules, procedures, or order. It presumes the existence of structure, a "script" that both challenges the potential actor and restricts the range of possibilities facing him, rendering his objectives coherent, noncontradictory, and obtainable.

> The flow experience differs from awareness in everyday reality because it contains ordered rules that make action and the evaluation of action automatic and hence unproblematic. When contradictory actions are made possible . . . the self reappears to negotiate between the conflicting definitions of what needs to be done and the flow is interrupted.[39]

"Flow states" in games, however diffusely, emotionally, or mystically described, are the product of systems of rules, codes of behavior or sets of tasks that render action unproblematic, even automatic, rather than contradictory. Johan Huizinga's well-known definition of play says the same thing in a different way. The rules of the game and insistence upon amateurism exclude the range of materialistic, self-interested motives that constantly intervene in everyday life to force the ego to calculate the gains and losses of status normally implicit in every significant action. For Huizinga, play is "an activity connected with no material interest and no profit can be gained by it. It proceeds within its own proper boundaries of time and space according to fixed rules and in an orderly manner."[40]

It was common for those celebrating the coming of war to describe their experiences in the most mystical, religious, and elevated terms. For Thomas Mann, the war was a "visitation"; for Binding, the "touch of a god"; for Zuckmayer, war initiated a trance-like state, a state of "grace," a collective and personal transfiguration. In other situations, entry into such trance-like states is often dependent upon highly conventionalized patterns and cues. Morton Marks, for example, in his analysis of the structures that underlie passage into trance states in Afro-American music, argues that these passages occur only in highly patterned musical and rhythmic settings. The movement from normalcy to transport is cued by readily perceptible changes in cultural codes, changes in pitch, volume, rhythm, and musical instruments.[41] Similarly, the enthusiasm for war must not be viewed as the appearance of preexisting energies, bottled up in normal life and released with the declaration of emergency, but as a product of a "switch" between well-defined and quite traditional cultural modalities. The feelings of transfiguration are the spectacular product of the sense of moving away from a familiar array of institutions that are often characterized as materialistic, technological, and highly differentiated in terms of age, class, sex, and profession, toward an image of action that is specific only in offering "rules which make action . . . automatic and hence unproblematic."

The escape from privacy is a pervasive motive for many who entered military institutions. Military life was often celebrated precisely in the same terms as the community of August. It was welcomed as a rigidly structured, conventionalized existence which systematically simplified the myriad and contradictory choices that faced individuals in civilian life. Schauwecker was one of many who celebrated the loss of his paralyzing civilian "liberty."

> The petty, aimless, lounging life of peacetime is done with.
> Life has suddenly been brought back to its simplest terms.
> Every movement is scrupulously precise, every touch is deter-
> mined, every action is consciously directed toward its goal.
> Everything makes straight ahead, and everything has its clear,
> palpable meaning. . . . The building up of this life of ours is
> transparent and comprehensible to the simplest of us. We see a
> limb working quickly and smoothly, a body with all the ad-
> vantages of a machine: the Army.[42]

The army provided the antidote to the diseases that were felt to be inherent in civil society: indecision, aimlessness, and loneliness. The army was celebrated as the rigidification and institutionalization of a community articulated in such a way that it provided a set of specific conditions of action. The "petty, lounging" life of peacetime was replaced by a life replete with palpable meanings, clear precise goals, and nonconflicting demands.

The values that German volunteers like Schauwecker found in army life were also celebrated in England. F. H. Keeling had compared the rituals of soldiering to a civil religion and found his regiment a much more emotionally satisfying community than any private family. In this community the sense of the self as something that mediated between the multitude of contradictory purposes and demands is replaced by the sense of what T. E. Lawrence called "equality under compulsion." Robert Graves, whom nobody would take as a militarist, defended drill on these grounds. It expressed in palpable, active form the values of community inherent in the army, even though he realized that drill was tactically irrelevant in modern war.

> Arms drill as it should be done . . . is beautiful, especially when the company feels itself as a single being, and each movement is not a movement of every man together, but a single movement of one large creature.[43]

Clearly it was not the unstructured, chaotic expenditure of wealth and blood or the chaos and danger of war that was so prized by Graves, Lawrence, Keeling, and Schauwecker. The contrary is the case. In celebrating army life they celebrated structure and enjoyed the cohesion and purposefulness that civilian life lacked. One gets the feeling that these men – to use a term of Victor Turner's – are "playing the game of structure." Here structure performs the task of expressing and embodying certain values and longings, rather than providing a means to effect a given end. The army, pre-eminently a tool, an instrument for the attainment of specific goals, is not valued for that character but for its ability to give shape to the values of community and provide an escape from privacy. One might say of many who celebrated their escape from the petty, lounging life of peacetime what Victor Turner says of adolescent gangs and motorcycle clubs:

> These groups are playing the game of structure rather than engaging in the socioeconomic structure in real earnest. Their structure is "expressive" in the main, though it has instrumental aspects.[44]

The euphoria of August carried over into the enjoyment of training and drill and even into the early war of movement in the late summer and early fall of 1914. War was welcomed and celebrated precisely for its militaristic features.

At this point Alfred Vagts's distinction between "militarism" and the "military way" is useful. The "military way" describes the techniques of organization, mobilization, and direction – all the things that armies customarily *do*. The military way is simply the technological, efficient, rational spirit translated into military terms. It defines the problem of war as the attainment of specific geographical, tactical, and strategic goals with a minimum expenditure of energy, blood, and material. In contrast, "militarism" is a system of images, symbols, and rituals designed to express the character of the "warrior" and the character of the community in which he is at home.

> Militarism . . . presents a vast array of customs, interests, prestige, actions . . . associated with armies and wars and yet transcending true military purposes. Indeed, militarism is so constituted that it may hamper and defeat the purpose of the military way . . . Rejecting the scientific character of the military way, militarism displays the qualities of caste, cult, authority and belief.[45]

The qualities of "caste, cult, authority and belief," rather than the "military way," elicited the affirmation and enthusiasm of many former civilians. If the vicissitudes of life within the segmented, highly differentiated economic order provided the push that propelled many toward war, the symbols and values that had long been associated with military life provided the pull. These symbols and values are by no means as archaic and feudal as Vagts implies. However much the symbols of militarism and the trappings that define the aristocratic officer might derive from feudalism, it is impossible to ignore the intrinsically modern and bourgeois nature of those values embodied in militarism and expressed through the structure of the military machine. War was popularly welcomed in 1914 as an arena of action and a process rather than a place or position. It was an authoritatively structured community rather than a society in which status was a matter of property, family, sex, and education. It was a place where the individual could find anonymity in the uniform and common duties and escape the constant pressures of the family; a place of simplicity and formal poverty in stark contrast to the plenum of meaningless objects that "saturated the air" at home.

THE ESCAPE FROM MODERNITY

The enthusiasm for war in 1914 must be understood within the larger ideological and historical framework of the critique of modernization, and, in Germany, in terms of the decades-long reaction against Wilhelmian society. There is an obvious relationship between the spirit of 1914 and the German youth movements in terms of common personnel, common ideals, and common enemies. For Carl Zuckmayer, the declaration of war meant that the trend "toward liberation" from the "pettiness and littleness" of the bourgeois family, which had formerly been expressed in the youth movement, would "no longer be confined to Sunday outings and sports."[46] For now the grandiose sport of war had been entered by the society as a whole – a society suddenly transformed into a mobile community. In the project of war the romantic longings of youth had become

> . . . serious, bloodily and sacredly serious, and we did not hesitate to recognize precisely in this and not in the goals of conquest the essential significance of the war and our enthusiasm.[47]

Particularly in the war novels of Walter Flex, most prominently in *Wanderer zwischen beiden Welten,* the war provided a setting for the deployment of themes that had defined the *Wandervogel* movement. Flex's work is a celebration of a community of men, freed from economic necessity, bathing together in clear streams, wandering together through the bright world of forest-and-clearing and the dark world of war. The erotic bonds that cement the male community – the worship of the golden, doomed leader, the celebration of agrarian, antiurban life – all dominate his vision of war, just as they dominate the poetry of Wilfred Owen.[48] For many German intellectuals the war signaled an absolute break with the bourgeois world of comfort, profit, and security. In their support of the German war effort, Max Weber, Thomas Mann, and Georg Simmel mobilized the weapons originally forged by the youth movements in their rejection of Wilhelmian society. Only in the war, the defense of Germany was a defense against the *Bürgerlichkeit* – the social atomization, tradesman morality, analytical reason, and exploitative and contractual social relationships that now characterized England. The enemy – bourgeois society – was externalized and impressed upon perfidiously commercialized Albion.

The common belief that war had liberated an entire society from bourgeois normalcy allowed intensely personal identifications with the nation. In the youth movements, holiday excursions, sports, and mass meetings liberated middle-class youth from the constraints of domestic existence. In 1914 war was conceived as a more total release from modern society. As every commentator upon the enthusiasm of August notes, the feeling of liberation and release was the dominant mood. Hannah Hafkesbrink asserts that "what was remarkable in the beginning of the war was the feeling of liberation contained within it."[49] Gertrude Bäumer defines this as the key to her own feelings in August: "But even in the beginning there was the unprecedented feeling of liberation."[50] Rudolf Binding generalizes his own sense of personal release from the constraints of everyday life to the entire nation. "The hour came for Germany. There was a cry. A cry of release and liberation."[51] Zuckmayer, Schauwecker, Ernst Jünger, and others, just released from school and facing the constraints of insuring their place in middle-class society, saw this future suddenly dissolved in the drama of war. Zuckmayer felt that the bourgeois world was stood on its head and that the army – earlier felt to be the surrogate parent with its compulsion, subordination, and obedience – "now meant the opposite: liberation."[52] With only a minimum of projection, this personal liberation provided the entire significance of the war. In the war a youthful, ebullient Germany was testing and contesting the conventional international restrictions thrown around it by a doddering, bourgeois Britain. Zuckmayer, who was by no means a chauvinist, was able to identify wholly with the Germany that refused to bow to the "pressure of a world opposition that would deny it the free unfolding of its energies."[53] This national liberation from the "conspiracy of commerce" organized by Britain was rooted in that sense of personal release from the "pressing necessities of time, life, and youth."[54]

It would be difficult to exaggerate the intensity and reality of those feelings that bourgeois society now belonged to those things "left behind," to those dilemmas and identities from which individuals had been released by war. These emotions were most intense in those who felt most isolated and alienated – be they Jews, youth, Marxists, or intellectuals – from Wilhelmian society. The emotions of release were the foundation of extremely durable identifications with the nation. And the nation, in August, was seen as something that had accomplished the decisive first step in liberating itself from wholly artificial and external restraints. It is clear that the enthusiasm for war, and the identification with the nation of war, often derived from highly personal dilemmas. Thomas Mann, apologizing after the Second World War for his patriotism in the First World War, admits that in 1914 he "saw in Germany a country that lived in severe internal and external circumstances, a country that suffered hardships as an artist suffers hardships. I identified myself with that country – that was the form and content of my wartime patriotism."[55] On August 7, 1914, in a letter to his brother, Heinrich Mann, the nation was again the embodiment of the enigmatic artist, an identity that would become known to itself in the project of war. "My chief feeling is of a tremendous curiosity and, I admit it, the deepest sympathy for this execrated, indecipherable, fateful Germany."[56]

The kinship of the liberation of August and the drive for liberation from modern, urban society in the youth movements of the prewar years has been commonly acknowledged. It is explained by Christian Graf von Krockow in psychological terms. The youth movement, which first appeared in the large urban conglomerations of Berlin and Hamburg, within secure middle classes and insecure lower middle classes, was essentially a feature in the historical "flight from itself" of the German bourgeoisie. The enthusiasm for war, and the wartime propaganda against England, is "basically an expression of the bourgeois flight from itself, the projection of self-hatred, from within to without."[57] The war simply externalizes an internal dilemma, an ideological schizophrenia that prevented the German bourgeoisie from assuming the roles, values, and political character that ostensibly had been assumed by the middle class in industrialized society. War seemed to resolve the same ambivalence of the bourgeoisie toward itself and its role that sought resolution in the youth movements.

But this explanation assumes as a given what was most consciously problematic for many middle-class youth and humanists who saw modernity and bourgeois society as more confining than self-defining. The enthusiasm of August raises the whole question of stance taken by individuals who might, presumably, be categorized as bourgeois toward their role and toward the political and social values that had traditionally defined the moral stature of the bourgeoisie. The "liberation" of August allows us to see clearly those things from which many individuals believed they were "released" by war. In the negative image of what was gratefully left behind, one can also see the positive power that war held for millions who volunteered for combat.

Hannah Hafkesbrink suggests that many of the war generation felt that they had been released from an economic, materialistic, and technological order of existence. Implicitly they marched into a war that was conceived as a distinctively noneconomic field of endeavor. It was this which made the war a "moral" project, in contrast to the amorality of the marketplace.

> Grown up in an economic society providing little opportunity for the creative investment of their moral energies, they greeted with spontaneous satisfaction the prospect that war, by its demands for unconditional sacrifice, would replace the laws of selfish advantage. This relief over the destruction of an economic order to life was not limited to the younger generation.[58]

War was greeted as a liberation because it was felt to signify the destruction of an economic order. The assumption that war was essentially a pre-economic and anti-economic conflict enters into the most precisely defined expectations. Many hurried to the recruiting offices fearing that the war would be over before they could engage the enemy. This fear was prompted by the assumption that the war could not last longer than six months because the belligerent nations could not sustain the enormous waste of men and material required in modern war for any longer period. Joseph Conrad, in Poland during the outbreak of the war, clarifies the general proposition behind this fear: "War seems a material impossibility, precisely because it would be the ruin of all material interest."[59] In 1914 this was a statement of the obvious.

The destructiveness of war contrasted with the productiveness of industrialized economic life. But much more was meant and concluded from the assumption that war was intrinsically anti-economic. Because war meant a cessation of normal economic relationships, it could also be welcomed as the solution to conflicts endemic to those relationships. The declaration of war could be greeted as the elevation of conflict from the sphere of economic life, where it was disruptive of community, to the level of a contest that at once demonstrated national solidarity and provided the opportunity for individuals to grow into a moral, virtuous manhood unbound by the marketplace. Because war signalled the destruction of an economic order, it became the collecting point for ideals of a purely moral order and explicitly nonutilitarian virtues. The oft-noted idealism of the war generation is a function of this assumption. Because war is a realm of deeds distinct from material realities, it can embody everything most threatened by the massive modernization and industrialization experienced by German society in the forty years before the war. It was welcomed because it was the solution to realities that had formerly been inescapable. War meant the possibility of actualizing those values that modern life made increasingly unreal, but that were commonly felt to still be worthy of affirmation.

In contemporary accounts of August one can find a great many variations on the theme that the onset of war had set aside the most painful realities of industrial life. The war was seen as the resolution of the complexities of the "machine age."

> Because their consciousness was so much at the service of profiting from the unprecedented possibilities of power and well-being, the people of the machine age sensed the growth of their armor and the growth of those constrictions which bound them ever more narrowly until their direct experience of life was smothered. In a few men, a few circles – particularly in the youth movement – an unconscious longing broke through, a longing to move away from everything indirect and organized back into the natural and organic, from the social into the fraternal, from the political into blood kinship, from the collegial into comradeship. All of these longings

flowed together in that direct and overpowering feeling of having been dissolved in a new national and communal existence.[60]

For Bäumer the machine age produced enormous "possibilities of power," comfort, and security, but technology also armored modern men against "direct" experience. It separated them from each other and confined them to ever narrower precincts of sensibility. The longing for direct experience, unmediated by things or the technology of communication, was a dominant prewar theme in discussions of the impact of machines upon men. In E. M. Forster's "The Machine Stops," one finds precisely the same sense of the loss of authentic experience in a mechanized world that pervades Bäumer's description of the machine age. Technology "has robbed us of the sense of space and the sense of touch, it has blurred every human relation . . . it has paralyzed our bodies and our wills."[61] Technology, the source of power, is also a source of insensibility and insensitivity in H. G. Wells's novels, where the Martians, for example, who in *The War of the Worlds* are the cautionary future of the race, wear machines like carapaces and are "inhumanly" integrated with their mechanical means of motion.

In almost every contemporary presentation of the "machine age," one can find the thoroughgoing repudiation of the "economic and technological order" expressed in Bäumer's enthusiasm for war. While the technology of transportation and communication made it possible to enjoy an enormously increased variety of experiences and contacts, it also erected ever more complex facades that further removed individuals from the possibility of "direct experience." Direct experience is a code for "authentic experience." The insatiable desire for authenticity, for a direct confrontation of human wills, dominated the enthusiasm for war and shaped the expectations of those who went into combat just as it was present in the enormous appetite of the age for any relic of authentic (preindustrial) life or for anything that imitated organic forms or materials.

Thus many in August thought they had been liberated from "material" or "materialism." It is easy to consider materialism in the abstract sense as the spirit of the age; but if one wishes to understand specific expectations drawn from the polarities of war and social life, it is better to view this term concretely and literally. The materialism from which Zuckmayer, Bäumer, Binding, and a host of others thought they had escaped was not a generalized spirit but a world of things that had become intensely problematic. They escaped *to* a war conceived in wholly pastoral imagery, a war that embodied simplicity as well as discomfort, insecurity, and adventure. The war was entered by many as a return to a disciplined ordering of want and use, a return to health. In the words of the violinist, Fritz Kreisler, who spent three months in the Austrian army before he was invalided out,

> In the field all neurotic symptoms seem to disappear as if by magic, and one's whole system is charged with energy and vitality. Perhaps this is due to the open air life with its simplified standards, freed from all the complex exigencies of society's laws and unhampered by conventionalities.[62]

The power and richness of the pastoral imagery contained in the letters sent home from the front and in the war literature is astonishing.[63] And yet what underpins this image is the widespread assumption that the "release" of war was a release from houses crowded with things that had no function or place. August liberated many a bourgeois youth from shelves lined with carved cocoanuts, arcadian porcelains, gilded lilies of plaster, rooms stuffed with upholstery and damask draperies and sprinkled with handicrafts enjoying the patina of time.

Industrialization was nothing if not a revolution of "things." Antimodernists in England, France, Spain, and Germany charged that the awesome power of the infinite duplication of objects inherent in mass production devalued the symbolic significance of objects, the significance they had had in a pre-industrial economy. One need only glance at pictures of Biedermeir or Edwardian interiors, or leaf through the pages of novels fattened by long lists of precious objects – invariably goblets, inlaid tables, intricately worked book-bindings, flagons, fountains encrusted with gilded bezants – to appreciate the ironies that attended the construction of a "private," domestic world out of the products of pre-industrial crafts. The machine-age outpourings of things could only be balanced by the massing of unique, pre-industrial, and ostentatiously individualized objects, but this amassing devalued the individuality of objects as much as any uniformity of industrial production.[64]

If the "thing" was made problematic by industrial production, it was even more so when industrialization itself was conceived as an alien importation. Thorstein Veblen insisted that the importation of technology contributed unique features to the "crisis of values" attendant upon industrialization in Germany. The technology that increased the productive capacity of the German economy to formerly inconceivable levels

> . . . was not made in Germany, but was borrowed, directly or at second remove, from the English-speaking peoples . . . But British use and wont in other than the technological respect was not taken over by the German community at the same time. The result being that Germany offers what is by contrast with England an anomaly, in that it shows the working of a modern state of the industrial arts as worked out by the English but without the characteristic range of institutions and convictions that have grown up among English-speaking peoples.[65]

According to Veblen the crisis of values in Germany was both more intense, more protracted, and more self-conscious by virtue of the fact that industrialization brought together modern technology and "pre-industrial habits of mind." The Germans could not forget what it was necessary to forget in the process of modernization. But the machinery of production itself was conceived as less problematic than what industrialization produced: Class conflict, infinitely duplicated things, and new levels of consumption and security.

> The case of Germany is unexampled among western nations both as regards the abruptness, the thoroughness and amplitude of its appropriation of this technology and as regards the archaism of its cultural furniture.[66]

It is well known that industrialization produced new social classes and conflicts between them. But it also produced pressures upon the possessing classes themselves, which must be taken seriously as the source of "moral" discomfort. It is out of such conflicts that the anti-economic image of war assumed an overarching relevance. For those groups that had made work, thrift, saving, and the underconsumption of income the moral way of life, industrialization caused a crisis in what Veblen calls the "moral standard of living." They were now faced not with wrenching a surplus value from a minimal world of goods, but with consuming the surplus generated by the enormously expanded powers of production. If the traditional structure of society was to be maintained, propertied families had to replace an ethic of saving with an aesthetic of consumption. Here it was the material thing, the product of technology, and not technology itself, that became the source of moral discomfort. In Germany, it was the shopkeeper and not the industrialist, the *Spiessbürger* and not the *Stadtsbürger,* who served the immoral morality of consumption. Ernst Jünger enjoyed the ironies inherent in the popular enthusiasm for war. For war, the very embodiment of anticommercial virtues – the virtues of honor, courage, acceptance of risk and self-sacrifice; the presumptively pre-industrial virtues – was affirmed by those very purveyors of the products and consumptibles that saturated everyday life – the shopkeepers.

> It was no longer a dream, one stood in it with both feet. And it was not an adventure at which the shopkeeper could sneer. It was at once the highest honor and a necessary duty. The heroic feeling that a commercial age had slammed into the museums burst out, bright and living.[67]

It was with such an image – an image of war as the antithesis of the boredom, materiality, and mechanization of everyday life – affirmed even by the shopkeeping embodiments of the "commercialized" age, that countless sons of the middle class, apprenticed in the youth movements, entered the first wholly industrialized war.

But the anti-economic image of war, though it gained renewed force during the period of industrialization, was not prepared for the occasion of 1914. The antithesis of war and society, the polarity basic to the expectations of August, was an intrinsic element in the work that had become doctrine for nineteenth-century civilians and military men – Clausewitz's *On War*. Here the romantic image of war rests upon the polarity between war and real economic and political life that is at the heart of Clausewitz's famous dictum: "War is the prosecution of politics by other means." The very "otherness" of war allows it to stand as the alternative means to politics and diplomacy. War, from Clausewitz's time, became by definition a realm of violence that was properly free of qualifying realities. Political policy, industrial capacity, natural resources, population, military morale, and national cohesion – all were variables that defined the actuality of particular campaigns but never the essence of war itself. War was a "second world," an "alternative existence" a distinct medium of action that was shaped, distended, and sculpted by the realities of economic, political, and social life but never penetrated by those realities.

The "otherness" of war that is so essential to Clausewitz's vision of war and to the enthusiasm of August provided flesh to an image of personality that presumably grows and flourishes in war. For Clausewitz, war was a "free activity of the human soul"; of all branches of human activity war was "most like a gambling game."[68] The very liberty, incertitude, and chanciness that made war like a serious game also made it a sphere of activity creative of a unique kind of "genius." The genius of war was the man who could maintain his equilibrium and grow within the medium of violence, incertitude, and misinformation. Within this continually shifting, chaotic medium, he was the man capable of "imagining" the outlines of the coming combat, formulating a plan, and actualizing this plan in his disposition of troops. The medium of war tested and defined the moral character of those who could operate within it. The medium guaranteed that the man of war was the embodiment not of destructive, but of creative powers. He was the figure who was flexible enough to alter his plan in the face of events and courageous enough to withstand the invasion of doubts until he had transformed his vision into history.

Unquestionably, Clausewitz's "genius of war" was an officer, a general cut to the Napoleonic mold. But through countless editions, abridgements, and popularizations, the romantic image of the personality native to war had become democratized and generalized to the nation by 1914.

> In this inner liberation of the entire nation from its dead con-
> ventions, in this bursting into the uncertain, into the enormous
> risk, completely indifferent as to whether it swallowed us up,
> we saw the meaning of war and the source of our enthusi-
> asm.[69]

But it is clear that what liberated the youth of 1914 from the "dead conventions" of bourgeois existence was another quite traditional and conventional image of war – which itself died on the western front.

It is easy to see that the idealism of the generation, the peculiar innocence with which the volunteers of 1914 marched into war, was a function not of inexperience but of an assumption that smacks of the archaic: that there are at least *two* worlds of feeling, and *two* levels upon which life might be lived. Even to contemporaries, their initial expectations later seemed to be characteristic of a "lost" world that continued to maintain in mind the possibility of an alternative to "normal" social and economic life. The enthusiasm and liberation of August rests upon a thoroughgoing bifurcation of values, which in turn is rooted in the polarization of peace and war. It was this polarity that required the entry into war to be seen as an entry into a field of freedom, uncertainty, and risk, a field upon which a character and an identity would be realized – a character who was the antithesis of "economic man."

To see the assumptions that underlay the enthusiasm for war in August is to immediately recognize their roots in European culture and in the historical experience of the nineteenth century – particularly that experience of industrialization that revolutionized the conditions of social and economic life. The image of war was the counterweight of industrialization and modernization. The validity of this image of war lay, of course, not in its realism or verisimilitude but in the way it articulated and preserved alternatives to modern life and values. But if, as Ernst Gombrich maintains, "the test of an image is not its life-likeness but its efficacy within a context of action,"[70] this image of war was anything but efficacious within the context of *Materialkrieg*. It was an image which guaranteed that the experience of war would be a "disillusionment" in which those who had hoped to escape the "soul-killing mechanism of modern technological society" would recognize, and resign themselves to, the inescapability of modern realities. Many of those at home also suffered a disillusionment. Those who were most vociferous in welcoming war as the arrival of the alternative to the "machine age" admitted with Gertrude Bäumer that

> . . . facts forced us to confront the central contradiction of our situation – the contradiction of the survival and continuation of an individualistic, capitalistic, profit-directed economy within the very midst of the unconditional solidarity of the people.[71]

The actualities of war were found to express with deadly accuracy those dilemmas of modernity that many felt had been resolved in August.

CONCLUSION: THE PERSISTENCE OF EXPECTATIONS

In this chapter I have been arguing implicitly and explicitly against a view of war that has pervaded scholarship on the causes of war in general and on the enthusiasm for war in August 1914 in particular. This view, which has been developed with particular sophistication in psychoanalytic studies of the causes of war but which is also recognizable in works of social and economic history, finds the cause of war in the tensions endemic within modernizing societies. This, I believe, is correct. But the view that enthusiasm for war is powered by drives generated by closed, highly differentiated, conflict-producing social and psychic structures is marred by an unspoken corollary – that war constitutes, in itself, a vacuum of value, a free field for the release of energies originating in the life of societies. It is this assumption that does not bear up when the logic underlying the enthusiasm of those who went to war in 1914 is examined closely. Those who marched onto European battlefields in 1914 had a highly specific and concrete image of what war meant, an image that was deeply rooted in the past and in their culture. In most cases, war was not seen as a "free field" for the release of drives, but as a structured medium of violence that rendered action, social life, and the self unproblematic and "whole." As such, war could be welcomed as a cure, a release, or a liberation from the pathologies of experience, human interaction, and psychic disequilibrium that were seen to be increasingly endemic to life in modern technological society.

The drive–discharge model that has pervaded discussion of the "internal" causes of war is perhaps a valuable and accurate tool in the analysis of what those who welcomed the escape of war felt they were escaping *from*. But without an analysis of what, precisely, the men who volunteered for service in 1914 felt they were escaping *to* we cannot begin to see the magnet and the magnitude of the war experience. It is particularly hard for anyone who lived through the realities of war or was born after 1918 to acknowledge what was so obvious to everybody in 1914: The enthusiasm for war was not simply the negation of modern society, with its constraints and constrictions; it was also the *affirmation* of war with *its* particular constraints. This affirmation focused not on the destructiveness of war or the opportunities for "libidinal insubordination" that war created, but upon the moral and cultural values and the image of character and community that had come to be invested in war.

My purpose in analyzing expectations and the enthusiasm for war in detail has been to highlight the character of 1914 as an affirmation of basic cultural values that are sometimes regarded as "uncharacteristic" of that thing which we call the "European mind," bourgeois culture, or industrial civilization. The joyful abandonment of individuality, the search for an escape from privacy, the enjoyment of a life of obedience and equality under compulsion – all were an escape not from freedom but from *contradiction*. The attractions of the traditional image of war lay in its presentation of the possibility of noncontradictory action that did not require an "ego" and in the possibility of unmediated, *authentic* contact between human wills.

A structuralist approach to war allows one to see more clearly the cultural polarities that underlay the enthusiasm of August and continued to govern the experience of war even in the depths of disillusionment. For the essential experience of August was one of transition between two modalities of social life that were often held to be antitheses. The sense of living in the transition from "society" to community gives rise, in 1914, to the most diverse expectations of change, and this expectation lasts. It continues to define the consciousness of combatants and veterans long after the realities of war had been left behind.

One last justification for looking so closely at the expectations of war is that they were not only the summary of culturally derived images of alternatives to an economic order but continuing, lasting motifs in the war experience itself. The expectations of change, of community, of an abandonment of privacy were not discarded as "illusions" in the face of the realities of war. One might say that these expectations, literally and figuratively, went underground. The community of the front, or, as Ernst Jünger called it, the "technological" collective, existed in a world that was constructed by the frontsoldier not to preserve values, but to protect men from a threatening technological world that seemed to outstrip and transcend its human victims. One can find, in Jünger's description of men in a bunker, all of the expectations of August, concretized and materialized. This community is welded together by the sheer weight of the firepower directed against it. It is a group inseparable from the absolutely finite, minimal space of their refuge.

> How could one breathe freely in these holes where wood-sheathed walls were eaten by yellow mold, in which the small flickering lights of candles swam in the haze, and glistening great-coats hung on the damp, grossly heavy beams? That was a constricted nest of huddled-up, dirty men, full of steam, reeking with sweat and tobacco fumes. At times one man stood up, took his rifle in his fist and disappeared. Then another lumbered in – dull, exhausted in watching – and took the empty place, a change hardly noticed. Words ripped out like the curt impact of shells detonating outside, were attached to each other in monotonous conversation. They were so woven together, so twisted onto the same wheel of fate, that they understood each other almost without speaking. Everyone wandered through the same nocturnal landscape; a gesture, a curse, a wise-crack were the flares that for a moment rent the darkness veiling the precipice.[72]

In this description it is clear that the antithesis between the differentiated, structured technological world of external and material necessities and the world of community acquired quite different valences. The "human refuge" from material exigencies is constricted to microcosmic proportions by the formless materiality of the earth. The inside space is totally filled by men, by their odors and exhalations. It almost seems as if this space were opened by the injection of human beings into the body of the earth. The men themselves are interchangeably "woven together," as anonymous and silent as the "heavy beams" holding apart the walls. They exist in a constricted, minimal, and threatened space that is barely maintained by their human density against the pressure of alien firepower outside. The ties that join these men are not the ties of sentiment or feeling – those have long since disappeared. Their bonds are formed by the space they share and by the necessities of survival and work in a dark and destructive world. The formal integration of the self with the mass that was celebrated in August 1914, and on the training field, is replaced by functionally joined individuals, each disguised by the impermeability of uniforms and silence.

It is perhaps true, as Edmund Leach claims, that the polarities that a culture constructs to mediate its central contradictions are made to be abridged in experience. But it is also true that experience provides the material in which cultural polarities are resuscitated and redefined. At the front the antithesis of society and community becomes an antithesis of "home" and "front." The antithesis of a technological and human world is mapped upon the landscape of war to define the tension between the "external" world of physical, threatening forces and an "internal" world of mechanical solidarity and fantasy.

3. War in the Labyrinth: The Realities of War

EXPERIENCE, RITUAL, AND METAPHOR

How do men acquire knowledge directly from their physical reality and how do they translate their knowledge into language? This is the problem addressed in this chapter. Perhaps the best way to see the dimensions of the problem is to return to the conventional equation of war experience and rituals of passage. It is common to find this equation in most war literature. Indeed, it is so common that its absurdity is scarcely evident. As has already been pointed out, rites of initiation do not maim, gas, kill, or psychically destroy novices. War is not staged to instruct combatants or to provide the signs of their maturation. Rites of initiation are designed to induct individuals into well defined social niches. War, certainly the First World War, did not do this. On the contrary, those who returned from the front were often bewildered about where they fit in the society of their origins, or were convinced that they no longer had a social place to which they might return.

In spite of the obviously different motives explicit in wars and initiation rites, they have often been equated. This equation rests, I believe, on the similarities between the kinds of knowledge acquired in these very different sets of events as well as upon the contrast between this kind of knowledge and normal learning experiences. In war, as in ritual, individuals learn not simply through the manipulation of language but through their immersion in the dramatic structure of physical events. The experience of war, like the experience of initiation, is primarily a nonverbal, concrete, multichannel learning experience that can never adequately be reproduced in mere words. This is what Rudolf Bind ing meant when he observed that "war is a silent teacher and he who learns becomes silent too."[1] In combat the individual must become sensitive to the patterns, recurrences, and constancies behind the events that threaten him. Familiarity with the structure of events that dictate the chances of his survival is a matter of the utmost importance.

But there is another significant parallel between the kinds of knowledge acquired in the experience of war and that acquired in rituals of passage. The knowledge gained in war was rarely regarded as something alienable, something that could be taught, a tool or a method. Rather, it was most often described as something that was a part of the combatant's body, like a chemical substance in the veins, a mark, a scar, a set of reflexes, a part of the individual's very potency. The best analogy to the knowledge acquired in war is perhaps to sexual knowledge, a knowledge that transforms the character and condition of the knower from that of an innocent to that of a bearer and administrator of a potent wisdom. This raises another issue that must be examined in the light of the realities of war. How do realities become "selves," how does knowledge gained from experience become a defining element of a personality, a persona? This is the issue examined in the discussion of the "defensive personality" native to trench warfare.

Finally, and perhaps most importantly, the learning experience of war, like that of initiation, equips the individual with a kind of knowledge that could be called "disjunctive" rather than integrative. What men learned in the war set them irrevocably apart from those others who stood outside of it. The war experience established the boundaries within the larger "generation," between those who fought and those who were "too old or too young" to fight in the Great War. But the knowledge acquired in battle is disjunctive in another sense, in the sense that it segments the lives of combatants into a "before" and an "after." The knowledge and "self" acquired in war could only with difficulty be integrated into a continuous self. It is significant that in combat men learned things that were not cumulative, things that did not enhance but devalued what they formerly thought they knew, things that made initial attitudes, truths, and assumptions into lies, illusions, and falsehoods. The character of the knowledge is reflected in the image of the veteran who is conventionally "cynical," suspicious of general truths, resistant to the pressure of big words like "honor," "glory," "truth," for his experience has taught him the sheer relativity of the things he once believed to be true.

To point out the disjunctive nature of the knowledge acquired in war is to say nothing more than that this knowledge is the product of a change that is irreversible, as irreversible as the collapse of a familiar, beloved world, as irreversible as the spilling of blood. The themes that are so prominent in Erich Maria Remarque's *All Quiet on the Western Front* – the theme of the loss of youth, of premature aging, of disillusionment – suggest merely that the knowledge of war is lived knowledge, a part of the individual's body, that sets the boundaries between his present and past, between himself and others.

Anyone who examines the experience of the First World War must talk about "disillusionment." In the discussion that follows I argue that disillusionment was most often a function of the combatant's social status or, more exactly, of his sense of social contradiction imposed upon him by his social status. Invariably the disillusionment of literate, upper- or middle-class soldiers – often volunteers – came with the apprehension of the industrial character of the war. Those who crossed the boundaries between peace and war expecting release from the constraints and constrictions of bourgeois society learned that the membranes that separated peace from war were permeable. They let through those fundamental realities that underlay civil life. In war these technological realities fashioned a physical structure, a trench system, a labyrinthine world that dictated the behavior, social relations, and self-conception of the combatant. In other words, the disillusionment of many volunteers is identical with a felt sense of proletarianization on the part of those who, in civilian life, were not and would not normally have become proletarians. Disillusionment is a process in which individuals are stripped of their former dignities, dignities that they often did not know they possessed. This process, too, is irreversible and its outcome is an inward turning, an attempt on the part of combatants to derive their identities from the realities of war, from their relations to their comrades, and to their enemies who became – ultimately – more familiar and respected than those who stood outside the dramatic structure of war.

An analysis of the realities of war, how men learned them, how they came to represent them to themselves and others, can illuminate important epistemological issues. Once one takes these issues seriously, one can begin to suggest an answer to the historical question of how and why the experience of war became a paradigmatic reality for combatants, a model that was mapped upon quite unmilitary domains after the war. Paul Fussell has shown how the metaphors and language of war were, in the 1920s, projected upon political, sexual, familial, and educational realities. Whether or not men actually viewed their social and political world with different eyes, the language of contest and struggle became almost obligatory to anyone who wanted to communicate the seriousness of an issue. Here one must deal with the problem of how the realities of war were composed by combatants into a set of images that provided the roots of metaphor, an explanatory structure, which could be generalized to a variety of settings.

It is not an overstatement to say that many combatants came to understand everything in the terms of their war experience. They could do this because the war experience, through the metaphors derived from it, became something that could encompass everything. Examples of how the war experience was mapped upon political, familial, and sexual domains are easy to come by. Perhaps the best example is provided by Ernst Jünger who, while working for the political mobilization of veterans in 1925, wrote:

> For us politics is the prosecution of war by other means. But this political war is waged increasingly in the form of trench warfare, in a situation of tactical confusion in which the energies feel constrained because there is no clear, unbounded

space. And it is no wonder that the longing for the great deed, for the great national, political figure rises ever more frequently and despairingly.[2]

One can see here the peculiar reversibility of those metaphors drawn from the war experience. On the one hand politics is equated with war – not an uncommon equation. But as soon as the parallel is drawn the specific reality of the First World War, trench warfare, imposes itself as a peculiar vision of politics. The political reality is identified as a frustrating stasis, chaos, constraint, and the fragmentation of energies. The political situation is, like the reality of trench warfare, a situation of deeply interlocked contradictions irresolvable by those enmeshed by them. On the other hand, any claustrophobic situation, be it political, sexual, or psychic, can call up the image of the trench labyrinth. Through this image the former combatant returns to the reality of war, to the lived experience of utter constraint and frustration, and to memories that were often best forgotten.

Perhaps this is the appropriate place to define how I am using such terms as "metaphor" and to distance myself from a literary analysis of the war experience. I am not primarily interested in how the experience of war was integrated, through pre-existing literary or cultural structures, with tradition. Neither am I interested in where the metaphors that order the experience of war are drawn from. I am concerned much more with how these metaphors are used, verified, integrated into an historical experience to acquire meanings and associations that they did not previously have. What I regard as the primary, obligating metaphor of trench warfare – that of the labyrinth – has a long and rich history stretching back at least to the Palace of Minos. But a review of this history can explain nothing about how the image of the labyrinth was synchronized, through the lived experience of combatants, with the constancies of their physical setting. None of the images, conventions, motifs, and metaphors that prevail in the literature of the First World War are new. But this is not important, and to show exactly how they are not new would tell us very little about the war experience or what men made of it. What is important is to show how these metaphors became the vehicle for the explication of the deepest feelings and experiences of men caught in the web of an apparently irresolvable set of physical and psychic contradictions built and maintained by the force of an industrial technology.

Once there is a wedding of the symbolic world of language and the nonsymbolic world of physical experience, the realities of war become "things to think with," to fantasize with, to apply in action within political and social contexts. But this wedding is rarely a "free" choice, the metaphors chosen rarely the product of an aesthetic decision. The image of the labyrinth appears again and again in the reports of combatants not because of its inherent elegance, but because of its obviousness. It was a metaphor that suggested the fragmentary, disintegrated, and disjunctive nature of the landscape traversed by the combatants of trench warfare.

> When moving about in the trenches you turn a corner every few yards, which makes it seem like walking in a maze. It is impossible to keep your sense of direction and infinitely tiring to proceed at all. When the trenches have been fought over the confusion becomes all the greater. Instead of neat, parallel trench lines, you make the best use of existing trenches which might run in any direction other than the one you would prefer, until an old battlefield, like that of the Somme, became a labyrinth of trenches without any plan.[3]

Here Charles Carrington cites all the properties of the trench labyrinth. The soldier moving toward a spcific destination is faced with an awesome profusion of choices, all subtly wrong, all a slight misdirection. Movement through the trenches creates anxiety over the correct path, anxiety that culminates in the feeling that one may be lost. Carrington stresses the effects of the "historicity" of the complex he is negotiating. It was a system that, though perhaps initially constructed according to plan, has been effaced, built up, partially erased by shell-fire and one more reconstructed. After a period of time and countless accomodations there is no direct path to one's destination, only a sequence of disorienting bypaths. The net effect of the complexity and historicity of the system is a sense of inhabiting a bewildering complex of compromises that produces confusion and psychic fatigue.

Franz Schauwecker uses the labyrinth image to make a different point: Trench war is an environment that can never be known abstractly or from the outside. Onlookers could never understand a reality that must be crawled through and lived in. This life, in turn, equips the inhabitant with a knowledge that is difficult to generalize or explain. "The position became a net-like maze, a labyrinth through which only those with the most exact familiarity could hurry swiftly and safely."[4]

Like all metaphors, that of the labyrinth is the use of the familiar to portray the ineffable. It is difficult to point to the precise place where the image of the labyrinth ceases to be a mere description of the physical properties of the trench system and becomes a symbol of the fate of men in war. But increasingly the image expressed the feeling that the war that was begun to realize the destinies of the nations involved had become a conundrum and a mystery. The war was a knot, a deeply tangled web of cross purposes that defeated the best efforts of those caught within the labyrinth. The mystery of an individual's fate is deeply involved in the "mystery" of the war. Henri Massis, with the image of the labyrinth, evokes the mystery that the war and his own future had become.

> Finally here is the trench we are to occupy: a commonplace hummock, but its intertwined pattern of communicating trenches and paths make it a secret thing, a labyrinth full of mystery and danger.[5]

On another level the image of the labyrinth represents the feeling – necessary if any set of conditions is to be truly called a reality – of the inescapability of the environment of war. As the idea of an exit becomes ever more vague and distant, the trench labyrinth becomes the summation of everything that confounds the desire for release and transcendence. Carrington had stressed those features of the trench maze that permitted a paralyzing freedom of choice. But this illusion of choice is gone in Henri Barbusse's description of the labyrinth. The totality of the environment is reinforced by the massiveness of the earth and the absence of exterior walls. The trench is a system with no externality.

A little further on the real trenches lay – one long burrow . . .
To go down into that never-ending pit is to plunge into the
sudden twilight smelling thickly of earth; to feel cut off from
the world and close to the terrible heart of things. Round bend
after bend you go, scraping twin walls, a prisoner held length-
wise, framed in by the formless antitheses of the earth, and the
breath is buffeted out of your body by the thrust of the walls.[6]

Here the trench labyrinth abolishes all hope of escape. In
stressing the totality of the environment, Barbusse touches upon
perhaps the deepest level of significance lodged in the image of
the labyrinth. He suggests that the trench maze, a totally en-
closed world, a true "underground," may be an initiatory structure that leads the combatant close to the "terrible heart of
things." To reach this center, he must undergo a series of ordeals
the survival of which will unalterably change his existential status.

The metaphor of the labyrinth works on a series of levels. It is
a picture of the reality defining the experience of combatants.
But it is a picture that can be used to define a war in which the
meanings of human activity have gone astray or turned inward.
At the same time it defines the structure within which the psychological and existential transformations that made the frontsoldiers "what they are" took place. But before the realities of
war and the personality shaped by these realities can be examined, it is essential to see how men were stripped of their former
dignities to find themselves in a war that violated their most
meaningful expectations.

SOCIAL CLASS AND DISILLUSIONMENT:
THE VOLUNTEER AND THE WORKER

Disillusionment has long been an important theme in European
literature, and it is only natural that the most literate combatants
would use this theme to present the sequence of their abandoned
attitudes and mental states. But, at least in Christian doctrine,
disillusionment had been regarded as a positive experience. It
was a painful but necessary awakening from the enchantment ex-
ercised by material and sensual realities, an awakening from the

world of mere appearances. Through their disillusionment, those following the path of Christian enlightenment acquired wisdom. They grew toward an awareness of the supreme good, their own mortality, their place within a world created and disposed according to the mysterious purposes of God. But in the First World War disillusionment describes not an ascent toward grace but a spiritual and social descent. It was commonly asserted that in the war men had lost their ideals, their sense of good, their higher purpose. They were compelled to resign themselves to the omnipotence of those material realities that were already familiar to the industrial working classes – realities that were described as "industrialized" and "technological." In the war disillusionment signifies a loss of social and existential status or, more exactly, a process of self-definition through realities that had a significantly lower moral and existential value than abandoned expectations. In Stefan Zweig's description of the disillusionment of his generation, learned realities acquire a rather odious quality when placed against the grandeur and delicacy of initial ideals: "The war of 1914 . . . knew nothing of realities; it still presumed a delusion, the dream of a better, a righteous and peaceful world."[7]

Those who entered the war as educated volunteers, spent a year or less in the ranks, and then went to officers' training school to rejoin the ranks of their own class, often learned two things in their encounter with the uniformed lower orders. They learned, first of all, that their attitude toward the social significance of war, toward the nation, toward the meaning of combat was rarely shared by the dockworkers, farmers, laborers, miners, and factory workers who made up their companies. More importantly, they often concluded that their conception of the war as a community of fate in which all class differences would be submerged was an "illusion," a function of their initial innocence and idealism. They understood that the First World War was a peculiar sort of war in that the realities of fighting rendered their own expectations absurd, and the attitudes and behavior of the "men" realistic, canonical, even exemplary.

It is important to understand that this is not a necessary effect of war in general, but of the particular kind of war fought between 1914–1918. It was a war in which Don Quixote assumed the features of a Sancho Panza, not, as the traditional tale would have it, the other way around. In a war in which the opposite was the case, in which the reigning ideologies of war worked for the integration of the common soldier into a national and communal project, it is doubtful that the common soldier would have had the power to inflict himself so bruisingly upon the attitudes and self-conceptions of upper- and middle-class volunteers. Class tensions, antisemitism, racism can be found in any national army at war. What is unusual about the First World War is that the encounter with this tension often collapsed the entire "meaning" of the war in its ideological aspect. This was particularly true in the German army, where the dichotomy between the *Kriegsfreiwilliger* (volunteer) and the "common soldier" was much more sharply drawn than in the British, French, or American armies. Here, too, the disillusionment was greater, for the war had been entered as a release from the tensions generated by extremely rapid modernization. The image of the war as a classless enterprise was much more dominant in Germany, and thus it was particularly vulnerable to the realities of a war that expressed, even amplified the class hatreds endemic to bourgeois society.

The manner in which a knowledge of social realities was acquired in the context of war is particularly clear in the experience of two men, Carl Zuckmayer and Franz Schauwecker. Both had volunteered for a war that had made actual the dream of a natural community. It was with these expectations that both were confronted, in war, with the stigma of their class identities. Zuckmayer immediately recognized the source of the "unbelievably coarse" tricks played on him by his comrades. By education and class he was an *Einjahriger,* someone who by virtue of passing the *Abitur* was to spend one year in the ranks before being elevated to the status of officer. "Well-to-do civilians who played the 'reserve officer' were hated by the men. To this class we would belong. Now they had us in their grasp and took their revenge beforehand."[8] After the war Zuckmayer became a playwright and a novelist, Schauwecker a radical nationalist and one of the leading "front-literati" in Germany. Paradoxically enough, Schauwecker's postwar nationalism centered upon the *Gemeinschaft* of the front, the community of which, in reality, he had been the designated victim. Both men became aware of the implications of their former status in a war that stripped them of their dignities.

Zuckmayer was the son of a prosperous Rhenish manufacturer of bottlecaps. In July of 1914 he had been sent by his father to the sea-coast of Holland in order to separate him from his first love – a girl of "good" family. There he wrote poetry, waged a "desperate struggle against the narrowness of compulsory education, no longer tolerable to . . . [his] . . . suddenly awakened moral and intellectual energies,"[9] and had an affair with a servant girl. When the threat of war became acute, he entrained for Germany and immediately volunteered for war. He goes out of his way to stress the significance of his voluntary decision to "go." It was the disinterestedness of this act that fixed the character of the volunteer and created dimensions of moral significance to the war that went far beyond the mere state of emergency.

> It was self-evident, there was no question, no doubt any longer: We would go along, everyone, and there was no covert compulsion to this – I can testify to that. It was not as if one would be embarrassed before the others to remain behind. One can say that it was perhaps a kind of hypnosis, a mass decision, but with no pressure, no coercion of consciousness.[10]

This free act of thousands of men, ambiguously committed with no compulsion but under "mass hypnosis," made the war as a whole something more than an act in defense of the nation. It transformed the war into a popular movement, the spontaneous expression of a self-sacrificing sense of community. The act of volunteering made the entry into war a chosen liberation rather than an acquiescence to an overriding necessity. Zuckmayer insists that this original act of himself and his contemporaries forever conditioned his war experience, and separated him from those who joined even a year later. For those of the class of Erich Maria Remarque, who joined the war late in 1915 after having been subjected to the jingoism of their teachers, and who entered directly into a mysteriously immobilized war, combat was meaningful only as a demonstration of the superiority of material over men.[11]

But the volitional entry into the war, so crucial to the meaning of August 1914, was also an act that brought the volunteer into the sharpest possible opposition to the common soldier. To the common soldier, called up with his unit, the volunteer was a "gambler, a player, a doubtful character," intent upon throwing away the comfort and security that were the greatest goods in life. The difference in attitude between the volunteer and the soldier was often a reflection of class, and this difference often resulted in the victimization and humiliation of the volunteer.

> For these "people of the *Volk*" whom, on our part, we first got to know and understand here, life was the highest good. Whoever thoughtlessly risked it in the sense that he "voluntarily" set out into danger without being called up was to them – at the very least – a gambler, a player, a doubtful character . . . Our mentality was as foreign to them and as incomprehensible as, at that time, that of a Ruhr mine-worker, or a Polish farm laborer, was to us. And although most of them were not organized socialists, they felt toward us a kind of class hostility, or at least a class barrier.[12]

Differences of social class now appeared as different modes of entry into the war, voluntary or compulsory. But with these different modes of entry came different attitudes toward the war. For the soldier–worker the war meant a new range of tasks that were dirty, hard, and compulsory. For the soldier–player the war offered a range of roles that contained the possibility of realizing virtues obsolescent in modern industrial society. The class line that divided the volunteer from the "volk" was as obvious to the "men" as it was to the *Einjahriger*. Karl Jannack, illegitimate son of a railroad worker and member of the SPD Bremen before the war, found the social structure of the trenches very familiar.

> Now one must understand that at that time there were two different groups of reserve people: replacements for men and officer candidates. Of the first there is little to say on the face of it; they disappeared into the trenches like ourselves. The others were almost all volunteers, mostly graduates of secondary schools and sons of wealthy tradesmen, high officials, or senators. With them came their fathers with their automobiles. Their cars were always packed full with parcels.[13]

But in war, unlike peace, the "men" could inflict themselves directly and disillusioningly upon the "volunteer." The rude welcome given the "gambler and player" in the trenches is not without its irony. Zuckmayer realized that the suspicion and resentment directed at him was targeted for a representative of a particular station in life, for young men who were the beneficiaries of wealth, advantages, and possibilities of consumption beyond the reach of the common soldier. And yet it was precisely these things that he had repudiated in the act of volunteering.

It was the feeling of being punished for what he had repudiated of his own free will and further mocked for the frivolity of his voluntary sacrifice that more than anything else gave Zuckmayer the feeling of being "delivered into a world of enemies who were much worse than the shell-spewing enemies over there," and who were, with the exception of his corporal, "all sadistic devils . . ."[14] Zuckmayer felt as if he was being humiliated for his social status and mocked for his rejection of that status. This double-bind appears clearly in the impossible position in which he was placed by the stream of packages sent him by his mother. They were material reminders of the "stuffy, petrified" world he had left behind. If he did not share them with his squad, he was a bad comrade, ostracized and isolated; when he did share, he was regarded as a privileged individual who had condescended to share his wealth and was resented for his patronization of the "people." These tensions were resolved only by his removal to officers' training school where he was with men of his own class.

Zuckmayer understood the painful irony of his brief stay amidst the people. The act of volunteering had made the declaration of war a release and a liberation, but this was received by his comrades as an act that demonstrated the freedom from necessity enjoyed by men of his class. Franz Schauwecker, too, expected to find in war a community of men bound by ties of honor and discipline, untainted by calculations of material advantage. He, too, was victimized by his comrades precisely for his free repudiation of the advantages of his station, and further made to suffer for being that which he had rejected in the act of volunteering. But Schauwecker suffered the *Gemeinschaft* of the trenches for three and a half years, an unusually long time in the ranks for one of his station.

In the 1920s and 1930s Schauwecker was one of those spokesmen of veterans' nationalism who attempted to redefine the war experience into a national experience. The almost obsessive fixation upon the *Gemeinschaft* of the front as well as the peculiar nature of that community leads one to suspect that Scahuwecker's postwar nationalism was an attempt to close and bind the wounding realities of war. Schauwecker's war books focus upon that tightly knit body of men in the trenches. They are men isolated from the home, enduring the unendurable, who contain the hope for a "future Germany." But when one looks closely at his experience of war, one finds that nothing was more problematical than that complex of cooperation, unity of will, and cessation of individual ego that was supposed to have characterized the *Frontgemeinschaft*.

He entered the war at the age of twenty-four, already an educated man (Berlin, Munich, Göttigen) and planning an academic career. As the son of a customs official in Hamburg, his youth was spent in sanitary isolation from the "people." In August 1914 he added the disadvantage of being a volunteer to the already serious inconveniences caused by his status as an educated, if morally uncomfortable, member of the upper middle class. His status, education, and idealism made him the target of hatred among the dockworkers who made up the majority of his company.

> To undergo fire and wounds and all the rack of the front was spared no one, but I passed a whole half-year under an additional backbreaking yoke of contempt, spite and humiliation. . . . Inside my company my own comrades – for the most part dockworkers from Stettin – played tricks on me with genuine rapture whenever possible, even after the first big battle, because they, the men of action, saw in me the ill-developed, physically inferior, and further, the foolish war volunteer, the puerile player with life and death, and because they, the socialist workers, suspected in me the pampered, well-to-do privileged man of education.

I was the only educated man in the company . . . That means:
I stood alone, which is to say, I was solitary, which signifies I
was forsaken. The sensation of being pushed out was always
with me.[15]

He was refused seconds in the chow line while all of his
comrades had their plates filled again. His painfully cleaned rifle
was repeatedly exchanged for a dirty one just before inspection.
After the baptism of fire that was to make all members of the
company equal, his iron rations were stolen and he was punished – tied to a tree for three, three-hour stretches in the depths
of the Polish winter – for eating them. He suffered the mocking
sympathy of his comrades, including the one who had taken and
eaten his rations.

Schauwecker's experience of the *Gemeinschaft* of the front was
that of a victim. The overt forms of victimization ended with a
fight that gained him some respect from the society of "dockworkers." And yet throughout the three and a half years that
Schauwecker spent in the ranks, he continued to feel the subtler
forms of deprivation earned him by his education.

The years-long life on an inhabited but infertile island, among
men whom one goes past, speaks to in passing, deals with in
passing, calls to without receiving an answer, who stand in the
sun without casting a shadow, that made one not only de-
pressed and confused but indifferent and listless.[16]

The picture of exclusion and isolation was increasingly qualified. Schauwecker learned to keep silent, to listen, and to defend
himself physically against his comrades. He was capable of casting off the verbal talents that made him a figure of suspicion and
of acquiring the endurance and strength required of the soldier.
The common hardships, grievances, and experiences created
some minimal comradeship in his company, from which he was
not excluded. But this comradeship was not of the magnitude of
his expectations. It is difficult to miss the diminuendo of enthusiasm in his description of the "transformation" that the war had
worked in the "soul" of the frontsoldier.

Softly and gradually began that transformation of the interior,
in the life of the soul, which for the sensitive and educated man

occurred with such agonizing hesitation and slowness, in a
school hard to the point of cruelty, educating with the bare
fists of primitive ways of life, terrible precisely for the reason
that it developed and shaped only the physical and instinctual
in man.[17]

Schauwecker found a relationship with the "socialist workers" in
his company not on the moral plane of *Gemeinschaft* as was expected but on the base level of common, physical deprivation
and hardship, to which his education merely added another range
of burdens. The organic interdependence of a male community,
the cessation of individuality, the submergence of class differences – all of his expectations – cast no shadows in the glare
of realities.

The story of the humiliating apprenticeship of the volunteer is
told by many others. Most often the humiliation was ended not
by the integration of the volunteer into the "people," but by his
promotion into the ranks of his own class and by the gradual replacement of the "old boys" in the ranks by draftees. And yet
this initial confrontation between the volunteer and the men of
the "people" is one not just of class but one of expectation. The
volunteer, according to Schauwecker, was "the most basically
despised and hated creature at the front." His disillusionment
was incomprehensible because it was based upon expectations
that were often foreign to the majority in the ranks. "They cried
crocodile tears over his disillusionment, laughed at his stupidity,
jeered at his weakness in service and on the march."[18] In their
professionalism, their willingness to dodge odious duties, work
the system to their advantage and, particularly, in their attitude
toward self-sacrifice, they differed fundamentally from many
volunteers.

To the "people" the war was something to survive; for Schauwecker it was a singular opportunity to escape from a career that
he had not chosen, an opportunity for self-realization within a
national body. But the fundamental difference between the "play
spirit" of the volunteer and the men who regarded the war as
work lay in the contradictory attitudes toward life at the front.
For the volunteer, life was something that gained validity in sacrifice; for the worker it was something to be preserved at all

costs. This attitude contributed greatly to the style of war in which Schauwecker lived for three years. The front was constructed out of unofficial agreements between "enemies" that tended to limit the level of hostilities to the minimum in which survival was possible.

> In a quiet position everything is done to maintain, if at all possible, the calm. If one knocks out the opponent's bunkers or blockhouses the other does the same, and both lay exposed under the open sky and no one has won anything . . . For this reason orders for patrols to take prisoners find little approval and few volunteers. The opportunity [for success] is too slight and life seems too precious for such pettiness. Every purposeless hostility for the sake of wanting . . . hostility in itself appears to the frontsoldier as something frivolous, as immoral playing with the highest good in life, and such play is undertaken only because of hate, ambition, or desire for decorations.[19]

The lesson of the front was simple enough: the frontsoldier preferred survival to self-sacrifice. The volunteer was hated and despised not only because he often represented a higher social status but also because his ethic of sacrifice and selflessness could produce actions that would threaten the uneasy truce in which life could be preserved. The realities of war, both social and physical, eviscerated the ideology most fully embodied in the volunteer. It was this, it seemed to Schauwecker and others, that deprived the war of all meaning and made it an endless slaughter, a "maw and a belly" fed with human lives.

By 1929, ten years after the conclusion of the war, Schauwecker was sufficiently distant from these paralyzing realities that he could again style the war experience as one of nationality and community, affirming the slogan of *Soldatisches Nationalismus:* "In 1914 the German people marched forth. In November, 1918, the German nation returned. In between lay the breakthrough of nationalism into the political reality as a being and fact."[20] The vagueness of what happened "in between" is dispelled when one sees the character of the front community that is being idealized. His later nationalism was modeled upon Schauwecker's most devastating experience, for the front community was a projection of Schauwecker's "isolation," "loneliness," and sense of having been cut off from life. His own sense of abandonment becomes a property of the frontsoldiery as a whole. "And so we marched back with no banners flying, with no band, without any of the glitter of fame, without any reward other than that which we have within us – abandoned by the whole world."[21] The front was an isolated, cut-off world of marginalized men among whom all the correlates of identity had turned inward. It was this front that laid claim to the title of "nation" that the home had abandoned. "It has been hammered into us with blood and dirt and sweat for four years; we are not for ourselves alone. We are a complete, closed body, a nation."[22]

It would seem that in Zuckmayer's and Schauwecker's encounter with "the people" in war, their early expectation of a classless national experience becomes an illusion. Both recognized that they had entered the war as "players," individuals who could not be taken seriously by those common soldiers whose boots were encrusted with realities. Their expectations were formed into a dream of an earlier time, a time in which an escape from the bourgeois world into its moral antithesis still seemed possible. They had believed that the war was the negation of material interests and found themselves in the midst of *Materialkrieg*. They felt in August that the war would shatter all artificial social distinctions and melt all shards of the national conscience into one crystalline whole. They found that this, perhaps, was true. But the unity of the front came with the abandonment of ideals and purpose. It came as the result of a felt proletarianization in a war that was not play, but work.

The realization that war was work and that the comradeship of soldiers was little different than common subjection to the necessity of labor was the essence of the disillusionment of the volunteer. The particulars of Zuckmayer's disillusionment can be found in the letters and journals of many volunteers.

And now disillusionment rattled down on me. The really hard school of war had begun, which was hell – but not because of the dangers or terrors. Everything was completely different than we had imagined it, above all: the "comradeship"! Here it was a matter of learning how to be a "common man" whom nobody released or relieved and who had to do his grey, anonymous dirty work instead of "heroic" deeds! One had to undergo the hardest things, so difficult to endure in the following years at the front: the monstrous boredom, the exhaustion, the unheroic, mechanical day-to-day of war in which terror, fear and death were inserted like the striking of a time-clock in an endless industrial process.[23]

War was not a place for heroism, not a medium of violence that favored men of exceptional courage and vision. The change of character experienced in war is synonymous with a social descent, "learning how to become a common man." The comradeship of war comes from a common sense of proletarianization, subjection to common burdens of never-ending labor. The men in this war are only anonymous fellow-sufferers of an "endless industrial process." But what is even worse: war is a "monstrous boredom," punctuated only by intense anxiety. With this realization Zuckmayer abandons an expectation that was so fundamental to his initial enthusiasm for war that it was never stated – war would allow gratifications, pleasures, and satisfactions that were either tabooed or proscribed in a life devoted to the fulfillment of social obligations. War had revealed its monstrousness to the volunteer, but this monstrousness was just a grossly distorted version of the "mechanical day-to-day" of an industrialized life. The life of the worker was the model for the soldier in an industrialized war.

The disillusionment of many volunteers centered upon the realization that war was labor. As Ernst Jünger, a man whose vision of war was that of an arena of adventure and heroism, admitted: "We had long since exchanged heroism's iridescent mantle for the dirty smock of the day-laborer."[24] This war was a matter of holes and ditches, a place where the sewer worker, the miner, and the ditch-digger were at home. The "heroic warrior" was more alienated from the reality of war than he had ever been from the realities of social life in prewar Germany.

The romantic, mobile image of battle became one of monotonous, dangerous labor which made its demands day and night.

Heroism became an unvarnished, dreary changing of the
night-watch, entrenchment, carrying parties, hunger and inac-
tive perseverence in danger.[25]

Not many volunteers had as heavy an emotional investment in
war as the antithesis of modern industrial society as Jünger and
Zuckmayer. Other volunteers were content to describe their
"work-war" ruefully, sadly, or ironically. "The workers wait
for night, the enemy waits for night; for he knows: then we will
work on the strengthening of our most advanced strong points.
Thus the whole of life lies in darkness."[26] Another volunteer
cannot help but appreciate the irony inherent in the contrast between the image of war held at home and what he is doing.
"What I want to write is that our midday break is over and we
have to go to work again. Work? Yes, if only you could see it:
we are perfect moles."[27]

The irony is implicit: Those at home would understand the
realities of war if only they would see them in terms of night
shifts, intermittent industrial disasters, lunches and coffee breaks,
the nervous and physical exhaustion of men ending their eight-
to ten-hour shifts. But many of those who suffered the disillusionment of the work-war did not wish to disabuse those at
home of an image of war that made the activity meaningful to
them. The very similitude of war and industrial production, of
combat and labor, began to stand between the front and home
and to generate the silence that was to characterize those who did
not wish to relive their humiliation in words.

Against the background of the particular disillusionments of
volunteers, one can begin to unravel the paradox of the war as a
social experience productive of a particular species of social
knowledge: It was an experience of a "classless" life in which the
differences and tensions of class were intensely felt between individuals and within individuals. But one cannot ignore the sense
that "comradeship" changed its meaning in the context of trench
warfare. It meant one thing in the enthusiasm of August and
another thing in the endless "industrial process" that was war. In
August the enthusiasm for war rested upon the assumption that
community was a matter of will, volition, sentiment, and consciousness. Once the material basis of class feeling had been

swept away by the declaration of the moral alternative of war, no barriers existed any longer to a coalescence of fellow-feeling that was natural, organic, imminent below the artificialities of social and economic life. The experience of many volunteers showed that this sense of community was illusory. Their very expectations and enthusiasm for war marked them in the eyes of the bricklayers and dockworkers who filled the ranks as "them," members of society who enjoyed a singular freedom from necessity.[28] The volunteer saw the war as the fruition of his freedom, the "common man," as the fruition of the necessities that bound him to his job and place. The role that material and physical necessities – food, drink, work, defecation, coarse language, and rough treatment – play in the disillusionment of volunteers is significant. For these are the things that constituted an ultimate good for those in the ranks and the ultimate irrelevancies of life for many volunteers.

The comradeship that Zuckmayer, Schauwecker, and many other volunteers found and accepted was not a product of sentiment but of the material conditions of life in the trenches. It was a comradeship much less exalted, luminous, and altruistic than expected. The truths revealed by war were commonplaces rather than the revelations one might expect from the uncommon place of battle. Henry de Man, a Belgian socialist before the war, joined the Belgian contingent of the allied forces and was puzzled that men continued to fight after they had lost their ideals, principles, faith in the aims of war. He understood the compulsions that kept the men in the trenches – the fire of the enemy in front and the officer's pistol in the rear – but these, he believed, were irrelevant to the "ethic" and sense of duty that he saw around him. This was an ethic that had little in common with the high honor of acting as defender of the nation; it was rooted in the commonplace "desire not to disappoint others who expected something of you. It is this instinct that makes it normal for the least educated of common laborers to do his job well."[29] The values that held the army together were identical with the "pride of a man in his work," for in this war, as de Man pointed out, fighting was not just *like* work; "most of a soldier's duty *is* work."[30] This was the basis of the comradeship found in war, a comradeship rooted in those minimal human connections permitted, even required, in a world in which everyone was a potential victim of the anonymous forces of chemicals and steel.

The awareness that was was work and the warrior a day-laborer was not disillusioning for the men in Schauwecker's company or for the Welsh miners under Robert Graves's command. They continued, as in peacetime, to dig holes and ditches. The work was similar, only the cave-ins and explosions were more frequent and the foremen wore uniforms. But this war was disillusioning for those who expected to find in war a moral sphere of action, a community joined by the organic bonds of nationality, a world that was meaningful in so far as it contrasted with the work-a-day world of peacetime. But in this war those sons of the bourgeoisie who were initially defined by their idealistic expectations became familiar with activities and human relationships that were wholly unfamiliar to them, and would have remained so if they had followed their normal civilian careers.

It is difficult to see the disillusionment of the volunteer as anything other than a militarized proletarianization, a process in which they lost a social "self" they didn't know they possessed. As Zuckmayer, Schauwecker, Robert Graves, Siegfried Sassoon, and countless others learned, it was decidedly more painful to be stripped of those positive and wholly internalized values of bourgeois culture – the values of equality within freedom from necessity, the vision of a unique individuality, of a community based upon a common will – than it was to leave behind the negative features of this culture, codified as "materialism," "egotism," the "machine age," "class conflict." In their disillusionment one can see the loss of an internalized and idealized positive status that was difficult to replace. In their reaction to the work-war, their resignation to meaningless, boring, endless, and dangerous jobs, many of the uniformed upper and middle classes took on the bitterness and resentment formerly identified with their social inferiors. This bitterness was directed at the "managers" of war, the staff, as well as at those at home who enjoyed "security and comfort" and could not understand the suffering of the men at the front. This translation of social resentment, of a sense of being a victim of injustice, into military terms continued in veteran's groups after the war.

But perhaps the most significant effect of the social experience of war was the diminution of both the guilt and the romanticism with which morally uncomfortable sons of the bourgeoisie had formerly regarded their social inferiors. The bruising disillusionment of the volunteer could be regarded as the expiation of a long accumulated social guilt. Even the war in general could be regarded in this light. Jünger came to regard his initial expectation, that the war would mean a release from materialism, with great irony in the light of what came after – a war in which the soldier suffered "orgies of materiel," the release upon himself of millions of man-hours of labor "objectified" in millions of tons of explosive shells. Jünger saw *Materialkrieg* as an atonement for sins that, like original sin, its penitents did not feel they had committed. The industrialized war punished the sons for the sins of the fathers.

> Here an entire generation expiates its long accumulated guilt, here it experiences inwardly the collapse of an entire era and its outlook. Certainly the majority experience this as animals, they suffer without knowing why . . . Indeed here an age that saw the highest ideal in material suffers a fearful chastisement through material itself.[31]

This war was not simply work but alienated work, a war which destroyed the balance of Marx's observation that capitalist society meant the destruction of men for the production of goods. Here, in the trenches, the only purpose of war came to seem the destruction of both goods and men. At the same time the actuality of war raised with new intensity and concreteness the problems that had been "solved" with its declaration: the relationship between victimizing and victimized social classes, the relationship of men to the means of production that in war became the means of destruction, the relationship between owners, "managers," and workers of war. All of these issues are crystallized in the presentiment that war was work. At the very least, the reality of war effaced any lingering hope that there was an order of existence separate and distinct from the economic order of "production, pay and profit." If the volunteer entered the war as a "player" he quickly became a "common man" bound to his often self-destructive labors. In an unexpected way the war was a modernizing experience for millions of men of all classes who had never experienced an industrial environment. It collapsed any assumption that there are two distinct spheres of value and action, a pre-industrial and an industrial world.

The world of war was not a world of freedom. The immobilized sufferer of material was denied any "free play" except that of fantasy, and even his fantasies were a product of the constrictions, pressures, and denials that shaped his life. In the narrow confines of the trench, war became work – not in the ethical sense but in the oldest sense of the term. It was not a vocation, not a process in which the individual shaped his identity and endowed the world of matter with value. It was work as a necessary suffering, a continuous travail, and, hopefully, the expiation of a "long-accumulated guilt" administered by a world of men's means that had become a rebel and an enemy, at once alien and all powerful.

THE TACTICAL REALITIES OF CHAOS

Between 1914 and 1918 many millions of men learned the realities of life in industrialized societies in military contexts. It is important to understand what the realities of war actually were and how they were perceived to be a crystallization of technological and economic development. It is also important to understand how combatants perceived the "order" that underlay their reality. This order was first conceived as a "tactical" picture. Trench warfare slowly forced a revision of tactical preconceptions and, ultimately, transformed defensive thinking.

At bottom the realities of war revealed the power that technology wielded over the possibilities of human movement. The superiority of defensive firepower over attacking troops was the one, obvious, unquestionable fact of life and war – both for the staffs and the troops in the line. This superiority convinced Ernst Toller that he was participating in an enormous irony in which combatants were compelled to learn "that the tyranny of technology ruled even more omnipotently in war than in peacetime."[32] The bewilderment of the commanders was often as great as the disillusionment of those soldiers who entered the war with an "offensive" conception of the soldierly character. In the first years of war it slowly became clear that trench warfare was a situation born out of a century of technological development.

J. F. C. Fuller points out that the Napoleonic musket had an effective range of 100 yards. The invention of the minibullet improved the range of the musket to the point where the American Civil War soldier had some hope of hitting a target 500 yards away. By 1900 European soldiers were equipped with a small-bore, magazine rifle firing smokeless powder that was sighted in at 2,000 yards. This twenty-fold increase in range over the course of a century meant that attacking troops stayed under defensive fire for a much longer period of time, incurring much heavier casualties. Fuller calculated that the prone rifleman behind earthen ramparts enjoyed only one-eighth the visibility of the semi-erect attacker. In terms of tactical bookkeeping, this meant that 1,000 defenders lying prone and firing at 2,000 attackers had an advantage of 7,500 bullets.

The tactical significance of the increased range of the modern rifle was brought home in the Boer War. Because of rapid rifle fire and smokeless powder it was possible to use "extensions unheard of in former battles and in consequence overlap every frontal attack."[33] In spite of the thinness of this enormously extended defensive line, it could be held. With the addition of machineguns and barbed wire, the security of the defensive line and the effectiveness of the defender were enormously enhanced.

But it was the development of the quick-firing artillery piece that ultimately dictated those "laws" that regulated life and death at the front. The quick-firing gun forced the enemy to entrench, and entrenchment forced artillery to take up positions behind the skyline and adopt indirect laying. Indirect fire further complicated the defensive system for it required observation points, telephone communications, signal lights, runners, and the specialization of artillery fire.

In drawing up his conclusions on the Russo-Japanese war, J. M. Homes, a major in the British army who was attached to the Japanese staff, was newly impressed by the dominance of modern artillery: "I saw that artillery is now the decisive arm and that all other arms are auxiliary to it."[34] It was in the Russo-Japanese war, too, that there was a sudden, dramatic increase in the number of psychiatric casualties. R. L. Richards attributed this increase to the conditions of modern war and, particularly, to the dominance of artillery.

> The tremendous endurance, bodily and mental, required for the days of fighting over increasingly large areas and the mysterious and widely destructive effects of modern artillery fire will test men as they have never been tested before. We can surely count, then, on a larger percentage of mental diseases . . . in a future war.[35]

I. S. Block, too, drew the necessary conclusions from prewar industrial development. In 1895 he predicted that "everybody will be entrenched in the next war. It will be a great war of entrenchment."[36] But these pre-1914 premonitions and predictions did not lessen the surprise of Allied generals when the German army entrenched after their retreat from the Marne in September of 1914. "The Allied generals were completely baffled by the decision of the Germans to dig in."[37] As the "temporary" stabilization of the front began to seem ever more permanent, those in charge of the war admitted their frustration. They seemed to be fighting a war that was the outcome of no strategic plans, or even the frustration of strategic plans. Lord Kitchener confessed: "I don't know what is to be done – this isn't war."[38] The frustration was felt even more intensely in the trenches than at the higher levels of command, for in the trenches the stalemate was not simply a tactical problem but a problem of keeping dry, fed, and alive. What was a baffling tactical problem to the staff was a daily reality for those in the line.

When the rules of trench warfare began to be recorded in tactical manuals, it was learned that artillery was both the cause and the solution of the immobilization of the war. With sufficient artillery, even the most strongly held defensive position could be battered down. It was assumed that by doubling and tripling offensive firepower, the second and third lines of resistance could be blown away and the break-in would become a break-through. Invariably the problem of resolving the immobility of war was put in quantitative terms. It was a question of massing sufficient numbers of guns, shells, attackers, and reserves at select points along the line and, by sheer chemical and human mass, offsetting the superior effectiveness of defensive firepower. This logic was most ruthlessly prosecuted at the Third Battle of Ypres (Paschendaele) where, after a preparatory barrage of four and a half million shells fired by 3,000 medium and 1,000 heavy guns (one gun to every six yards of front, four and three-quarters tons of shells thrown on every linear yard of front), and at a cost of $110,000,000, an entire British army was swallowed in the mud of Flanders. This single battle, which cost approximately 300,000 British casualties, was proof to R. C. Sherriff that the army staff had lost all contact with the realities of the war they were supposed to be directing. "I needed no souvenir to remind me of the monstrous disgrace of Paschendaele. It was proof, if proof was needed, that the Generals had lost all touch with reality."[39]

But in actuality the disgrace of Paschendaele, as well as similar bloody and futile battles on the Somme, in the Champagne, and before Arras and Mons, demonstrated not a difference of opinion between frontsoldiers and staff on the nature of the war's tactical realities, but different attitudes toward those realities. For the frontsoldier the superiority of defensive firepower dictated what was possible and impossible within his world. But for the staff this superiority was a tactical problem that had to be solved before they could "get on with the real war." It was soon obvious that the solution would cost an intolerable number of lives.

In tactical terms, it is easy to describe what happened again and again on the western front. Most often, attacks were hung up on barbed wire, stopped by a machinegun and a few riflemen who had survived the preparatory barrage. But even when an initial attack was successful, it could generate no offensive thrust. The heavier the bombardment used to create a hole in the opposing lines, the more difficult it was to move masses of troops and equipment necessary for a breakthrough across the torn and cratered front. In the removal of defenses, artillery could create difficult, if not impassable, terrain. By the time roads were built so that supplies, guns, and reserves could be brought up to capitalize on the successful attack, the enemy would have dug a new line of defense. Even if all these difficulties were overcome, if a break-in became a break-through, there were further technological limitations on the offensive. Erich von Ludendorff learned in 1915 that an offensive was usually limited to 100 miles, the distance men and animals could move the enormous quantities of supplies required by modern armies from a railhead.

This warfare was often treated as seige warfare. But in fact it differed from a normal seige because new "walls" could be created more easily than old "walls" could be knocked down. Behind each breach made in a defensive system, in this trench warfare, new lines of trenches could be dug and manned before the attacking force could get its own guns up over the desert of mud and ruin which they had themselves created.[40]

The rifle, the artillery piece, the machinegun, barbed wire, and the spade locked up the front. Until a mechanical means of mobility could be found – as it was later in the primitive tank – the tactics of advance and penetration were exercises in futility. The war seemed, in the trenches, to become an affair not between offensive and defensive forces, but between "implacable mechanisms and diggers. The machinery of war would wipe out the results of months of digging, but in "several days . . . the spades of the diggers re-establish the equilibrium and everything begins again."[41]

The central contradiction of trench warfare, a contradiction that came to define the deepest emotional responses of those living within the defensive system, arose from problems inherent in the technology of war. In this war the means of attaining specific military objectives came to seem dysfunctional, creating as many obstacles as it cleared away. It is not surprising that the barrage is often described in aesthetic terms and appreciated as a spectacle, a dawn, a sunset, a display of fireworks. For it seemed to lack any utilitarian value. Whatever the quantity of shells poured upon the front there was never an end to the immobilization of war.

But it was not as if men, in 1915, lacked any means of conceptualizing the realities of war. Perhaps there is only one adequate conceptualization of war's reality, that of Clausewitz. Following the method of Kant, Clausewitz located the physical realities of war in everything that qualified, distorted, frustrated, minimized the abstract essence of war and its movement toward an extreme of violence. He saw the reality of war as "friction," something that cannot be imagined, for it qualifies every imagination of war. "Everything is simple in war, but the simplest thing is difficult. These difficulties accumulate and produce a friction which no man can imagine exactly who has not seen war."[42] All of those frictions that frustrate the actualization of a plan – weather, accidents, fatigue, inadequate intelligence – deserve the title "realities" of war. Clausewitz portrayed real war as "movement in a resistant medium. Just as a man immersed in water is unable to perform with ease and regularity the most natural and simplest movement, that of walking, so too in war, with ordinary powers, one cannot keep even to the line of mediocrity."[43]

In the First World War the "resistant medium" was conceived not as water but as fire. In one of his most suggestive formulae, Ernst Jünger describes the frontsoldier as existing within the "gravitational pull of the realm of fire."[44] The mathematics of trench war were calculated in terms of an inverse ratio between the intensity of fire and the mobility of the attacking force. As the intensity of fire increased, the mobility of the attacker decreased. As the voltage rose in the energized force-field of the trench system, so too did the force dragging on the limbs of those attempting to cross the front, to the point where the most exhausting human efforts could produce only one or two painful steps forward.

Jünger's image suggests the degree to which human movement had become a problem of physics in which the individual soldier labored under the most severe disadvantages. It also suggests the degree to which those frustrating, retarding forces that Clausewitz suggests constitute the reality of war had become overpowering. In this war the reality was immobility enforced by the technological domination of defensive firepower. This fact had great significance for a redefinition of the soldierly character, which in this war could have little in common with the aggressive, offensive image that had traditionally defined the soldierly role.

The realities of trench warfare necessarily precipitated a transformation in defensive thinking. Early in the period of trench war it was understood that defense meant the holding of the first line of trenches. The second and third lines of the trench system functioned as a refuge upon which beaten defenders could fall back and as the collecting place for reserves who would go forward to replace casualties. This emphasis upon the first line of

defense was both irrational and murderous, as was clearly demonstrated at the Somme where battalion after battalion of German troops were poured into the front line to be consumed by
British artillery. The rigid concentration on the first line was
butchery in a war in which the balance was held by long-range,
indirectly laid guns invisible to the eyes of defenders.

The early fixation on the maintenance of a rigid, impenetrable
line was incomprehensible in purely tactical terms, and one must
search the often dysfunctional elements of military tradition for
an explanation of the hold that the concept retained over tactical
defensive thinking. The line was the clearest representation of the
uncompromising defensive posture. It was the most perfect representation of boundaries, the outer limit of one's territory. In a
sense the line perfectly embodied the agonistic element in war.
Enemy penetration of the defensive line and the occupation of
that space marked out as the defender's own, meant the loss of a
battle. The winning or losing of a contest of arms, even after the
Napoleonic revolution in the art of war, could often be a matter
of the integrity of one's line, the holding of the ground one had
sworn to defend, or at least of the continued presence of defensive forces in the territory they had taken up.

By 1916 the "plane defense" had emerged as an alternative to
the concentration on the first line of resistance, and this new
defensive system lent a new flexibility to trench warfare. The
first line would be lightly held and would be given up if the
enemy reached the trenches. Then it would be retaken by fresh
counterattacking forces issuing from the second and third lines of
trenches. Ernst Jünger compared the plane defense to a "steel
sinew" that would bend and give way to an attack, then snap
back and sweep the attackers – exhausted and handicapped by
the difficulties of supply and reinforcement over shell-torn
ground – out of the conquered trenches and back to their starting
point. The plane defense had the added advantage of dispersing
the enemy barrage that now had to concentrate upon two, three,
or even four lines of resistance rather than just one. But this advantage remained only until the quantity of enemy artillery was
trebled or quadrupled.

Jünger, who helped write German tactical manuals in 1921,
finds the plane defense tactically sound but psychologically debil-

itating. Even beyond the deleterious effect upon the morale of defenders in giving up territory, the evasion of the enemy attack was contrary to the nature of war as Jünger wished to understand it. "The evasion [*Ausweichung*] as it was so aptly named, did not recommend itself to the mind of the German soldier; and he would never have been capable of adequately adjusting himself to it."[45] It was in the nature of war to seek a "decision and not the evasion of a decision." War was perhaps the only human activity that could tolerate no compromise; "only the unconditional will endure."[46] The plane defense, by multiplying the lines of resistance and making the first line an object of contention rather than a space to be held unconditionally, served to compound the myriad compromises already inherent in the practice of trench warfare.

The most adequate conceptualization of defense, "defense in depth," began to take shape toward the end of the war. Significantly this conception of defense relinquishes any conception of the line, single, or multiple. Defense in depth meant the fragmentation of coherence, the shattering of any clear, geometrical structure, the dissolution of the company into small, independent squads and pockets of defenders. Defense, given the realities of trench warfare, could only be thought of as a net, a labyrinth that entices, confuses, entraps, and then dissolves the force of the opponent's attack.

> We must come to an irrevocable break with the idea of the line from which, for historical and disciplinary reasons, we were never truly able to detach ourselves during the entire war. For that reason the comparison with the "steel sinew" which I advanced above is false; the correct picture is that of a net, into which the enemy may be capable of penetrating here and there only to be immediately crushed to earth from all sides by fiery meshes.[47]

Jünger proposed for future wars a defense in which the line was dissolved into a system of detached strong points, machine-gun nests, blockhouses, and bunkers. In effect this kind of defense is a direct translation of the realities of trench warfare. Werner Beumelberg pointed out that the modern defense in depth first appeared accidentally in the Allied double attack on

Béthume and Arras in the Champagne in May of 1915. After a barrage of a half million shells, which was seen as a "horrible extravagance" at that time, the attack foundered on disconnected "cut-off" islands of resistance left after the decimation of the German first line of trenches. "Out of these islands of resistance originate the masters of defensive war, upon whom all depends, later, when the defensive battles take on their most grandiose, terrible form."[48]

This picture of defense can be found in the greatest battles on the western front. For those who fought it, the Battle of Verdun was an experience of complete and utter chaos. It was, according to a French participant, a "battle of very small units, each directing its own fate, to the degree that enemy fire did not totally destroy them."[49] At Verdun the combatant fought from shellhole to shellhole in a landscape dismembered by explosives where there were no trenches and it was impossible to tell French from German; all were the color of the soil. Movement by day was out of the question, by night frightening and bewildering. "Units were lost in the maze without a knowledgeable guide." In this unstructured space, time also lost its form and coherence. "Time stopped for violence to pass, and the alternating periods of violence and stillness, of savage bombardments followed by sudden silence, blended to render time dimensionless, indistinct."[50]

In description after description of the major battles of the war one perception always emerges: Modern battle is the fragmentation of spatial and temporal unities. It is the creation of a system with no center and no periphery in which men, both attackers and defenders, are lost. Jünger only imposes upon the reality of chaos the image of the net and the lines of a maze. Schauwecker only deifies the survivors of the battles of material, seeing them, in Darwinian fashion, as men who are selected by the storms of explosives and thus superior in their hardness, their impenetrability from those now disappeared. "Now the soldier was no longer considered 'cannonfodder,' or regarded as a 'steer on a slaughter bench.' "[51] The war of machines seemed to revive, through the technology of battle, the romantic vision of war embodied in those individuals who had survived the "monstrous outpourings of material."[52] It was these individuals who deserved the title "masters of defensive war."

The hero of this war was not an "offensive" but a "defensive" personality. This required a radical transvaluation of many expectations, values, and images of war. The system of defense fashioned by the superiority of defensive fire over human mobility fundamentally reshaped the idea of military virtue, the unofficial personality of the soldier, the frontsoldier's vision of his enemy. The changed role and self-conception of the soldier was a necessary response to this new landscape of war so obviously fashioned by tools forged in the factories of European nations.

THE DEFENSIVE PERSONALITY

A. E. Ashworth, in his study of the sociology of trench warfare, argues that war in general is not necessarily an "alienating" experience. If violence is officially sponsored by the state, has the unqualified support of society, and is directed at an object – the enemy – that remains strange and hateful, violence is "to some extent a meaningful expression of one's personality; its performance does not involve self-estrangement and there exists no disjunction between emotion and activity."[53] The purpose of training is to identify the soldier as an aggressor and to get the soldier to accept that identification. The purpose of propaganda is to place the act of violence within a moral universe by identifying the enemy as something that lies on the boundaries between the inhuman and the human, as something without a "soul," and thus the proper object of hostility. As long as training and propaganda are successful, the soldier operates within a moral and ethical structure and his acts can be experienced as confirmations of his identifications, his identity. As Dr. Chaim Shatan points out in his analysis of Viet Nam veterans, the purpose of training is to get the soldier to "pattern himself after his persecutors (his officers)"; if successful, this will cause the trainee to undergo a "psychological regression during which his character is restructured into a combat personality."[54] Behavior in war is patterned on the drill field. There, the training officer treats the trainee in the same way that he wants the soldier to treat the enemy in battle. To escape the low and painful status of victim and target of aggression, the mantle of the aggressor is assumed with more or less guilt. In so far as this identification with the aggressor is successfully maintained, in so far as the "offensive personality" accords with the actualities of combat, the soldier's activity in war – all the shooting, maiming, and killing – is perceived as moral, legitimate, and meaningful. But the erosion of these identifications in the explosive rhetoric of battle, the dismantling of the sense of self as offensive executor of a national will upon a quasi-human enemy, has incalculable consequences for the soldier's conception of himself, for his subjective experience of war, for his relations with the enemy, and for his stance toward the home and those administering his war.

Trench warfare, perhaps more than any kind of war before or after, eroded officially sponsored conceptions of the soldierly self as an agent of aggression. It produced a kind of personality, a defensive personality, molded by identifications with the victims of a war dominated by "impersonal" aggressors of chemicals and steel. Everyone who had been in the trenches for any length of time immediately recognized the difference between his attitude toward the enemy and that of those who remained at home. Jean Norton Cru is able to distinguish on the basis of this different attitude toward the enemy, the work of those who really experienced the war from that of people who only visited the trenches or wrote about the war from the safety of the rear areas. In describing the work of the Abbé Bessières, a medical orderly at the front throughout the entire war, he commends the Abbé's "impartiality which was always rare among those who were not in the trenches."[55] Bessieres ascribed the peculiar smell of the Germans to the impermeability of their uniforms rather than to their inherent bestiality, as civilians did. F. H. Keeling was shocked and disgusted when he encountered the ferocity of civilians, especially that of women. "I met a lady – a war nurse in the hospital where I was after Hooge – whose catlike ferocity of sentiments about Germans and Germany simply made me sick. A dose of shelling would cure a lot in that one."[56] Keeling felt that the war had demilitarized him, confronted him with realities in which it was impossible to maintain the aggressions reinforced by propaganda. He regarded both the militarism and pacifism of those "at home" as attitudes based upon a false reality deliberately maintained. Those who knew what it was to be victims in common under the weight of the barrage constituted the best hope for a "practical" pacifism. "It is the soldiers who will be good pacifists."[57]

In a war in which all combatants were victims of material, in which an industrial technology was the "true" aggressor, identification with the enemy and his dominant motive – survival – was logical, even necessary. One need only cite the many cases of fraternization, the unofficial agreements between officially declared enemies that established and maintained "quiet sectors" on the front, to show that this was a war that dramatically altered the identities and personalities of combatants. Often this alteration was brought to the attention of authorities when it assumed a pathological form. For however admirable and humane was the "identification with the enemy," it was also the source of a profound, deeply felt conflict, in which the combatant was forced to repudiate self-conceptions sponsored by his society and often shared by himself. Unquestionably the breakdown of the "offensive personality" in the realities of defensive war was one of the major causes of war neurosis. Indeed, for extreme cases of departure from official norms there was even a pathological category: "neurotic sympathy with the enemy." Dr. R. Steiner, a German neurophysician, treated a 26-year-old noncommissioned officer – a merchant in civilian life – for this ailment. The sergeant ordered his men not to shoot at the enemy because it had occurred to him in a dream that the enemy was human, that French soldiers had wives and children.[58] Perhaps the best illustration of the psychic conflicts that could be precipitated by the breakdown of identifications with the aggressor is a case of "neurotic identification" treated by Otto Binswanger. Under hypnosis the soldier cried out: " 'Do you see, do you see the enemy there? Has he a father and a mother? Has he a wife? I'll not kill him.' At the same time he cried hard and continually made trigger movements with his right forefinger."[59]

But these are individual cases, and perhaps the best indication of how general was the estrangement from the "offensive norms" proper to the soldier in battle lies in the many unofficial agreements that limited hostility at the front. The restrictions that were placed upon hostile behavior at the front, restrictions that ritualized violence, came not from any humane tradition or attitudes of professional military respect. They came from out of the realities of war themselves. The "offensive spirit" that was supposed to characterize relations between belligerents was clearly suicide in a war in which contact with the enemy was a relative constant, something measured not in hours but in days, even years.

The standardized hostility and aggressive hatred that was supposed to define the soldierly character could not be upheld in a situation in which defensive war had become a way of life. A mortar shell fired into the opposing line of trenches brought two or more in response. Mortar squads were not popular among the *Frontschwein,* the *poilus,* and the Tommies. Every burst of machinegun fire would be repaid with an extended strafing. Every volley of rifle fire would be returned in kind. These were the realities of war, realities that could periodically stimulate a spiral of revenge, but that most often operated to restrict hostility and routinize the business of trench war.

The agreements arrived at through conversations in explosives covered many of the necessities of life in sectors where no offensive was under way. It was common courtesy not to interrupt an enemy's mealtimes with indiscriminate sniping. Certain points of the trenches, known to both sides, were regularly strafed; the morning barrage was limited to an obligatory five or six rounds after which normal trench life would continue. In certain sectors there were extraordinary agreements that provided for the safe removal of the wounded, the repair of trenches and wire, sunbathing on the first days of spring, and the cutting of grass and the harvesting of fruit in No Man's Land. A case of the breach of such an agreement is reported by Weygand. He tells of a soldier who climbed out of the trenches to pick apples from the trees between the trench lines. But when he began to pelt the French lines with the fruit, rather than – as permitted – harvesting them for himself and his comrades, he was fired upon and had to be rescued under covering fire.[60] When Basil Liddell-Hart went into the line in September 1915, his battalion occupied a sector where the French had previously established a peaceful coexistence with the Germans, to such a point that they shared the shelter of undestroyed houses in No Man's Land, and it was possible to drill a battalion in full view of the enemy without being fired upon. The truce was ended by the British policy of "constant harassment."[61]

Even during major battles, the settlement of differences between legally declared belligerents was not uncommon. During the Battle of Verdun, at a place where both sides were holding their positions only tenuously, a volunteer reported: "It has been quiet in this position for several days; the French had orders to throw hand grenades frequently at us during the night; he threw them, as agreed, with a 'German comrade,' to the right and left of the trench."[62] The degree to which this ritualization and limitation of hostile activity was the product, not of a prewar ethic, but of the sheer proximity of enemies, is clearly demonstrated in Fritz Kreisler's description of the period of trench warfare that intervened in the Austrian retreat of 1914. In this brief period the unquestioned hostility that prevailed in the open campaigns suddenly broke down. "The salient feature of these three days' fighting was the extraordinary lack of hatred."[63] The cessation of hostilities began with a "red-bearded Russian" leaping up and down in the opposing line of trenches, and Kreisler witnessed the transformation of "the enemy" into "human individuals who can actually be recognized."[64] After this, fraternization proceeded literally by leaps and bounds, the Russian leaping forward, an Austrian soldier bounding toward him until they met in the center of No Man's Land to be joined by their comrades.

These and other examples of identification with the enemy, momentary cessation of hostilities, the ritualization of violence, indicate how the realities of war – the limitations placed upon the escalation of violence – emerged from the combatant's response to the physical realities of his life in the trenches. Such a response might be regarded as an admirable demonstration of man's humanity to man in a deadly situation. But it must also be regarded as the source of much of the alienation, the sense of the purposelessness and meaninglessness of war, the feelings that became general in the trenches. Even more importantly, identification with the enemy must be regarded as the most important source of the estrangement of those in the trenches from those who demanded offensive activity of the soldier and strove to maintain the aggressive role of the combatant: the staffs and the "home."

The erosion of hostility in trench warfare had the effect of intensifying the hatred of front-line troops for the staff. "Trench soldiers hate the staff and the staff know it. The principal disagreement seems to be about the extent to which trench conditions should modify discipline."[65] Here discipline refers less to military dress and courtesy than to relations with the enemy. In many units and sectors, "the spirit in the trenches was largely defensive; the idea being not to stir the Germans into more than their usual hostility."[66] All the while the staffs continued to demand offensive behavior, fire ascendancy, patrols, harassment, and other measures that were designed to disturb the delicate equilibrium in which life was barely possible. As units became more absorbed into the routines of trench warfare, their distance from the staff and from the military role enforced by the staff increased. In official terms their morale often declined and their discipline became loose.

If the realities of war and the necessities of life in the trenches distanced combat troops from those who managed the war, they placed an even greater distance between the front and the "home." Estrangement from the offensive norms of combat implies, as Ashworth points out, estrangement from those values and beliefs upheld and affirmed by a society at war. "The resentment shown by many combatants to those on the 'home front' who have disseminated such bellicosity may be interpreted as symptomatic of the former's isolation from the goals and standards of society at war."[67] Indeed, the most feeling complaint of those at the front was that the violence demanded of them was not an expression of their "selves" but of their societies, speaking through the voice of a "mindless, soul-killing machine." The return to the home was often like a return to a strange land, while return to the front could be even a relief. Robert Graves, like many others, admitted: "England looked strange to us returned soldiers. We could not understand the war madness that ran about everywhere looking for a pseudo-military outlet. The civilians talked a foreign language; and it was newspaper language."[68]

But the soldier's estrangement from the role and image of the offensive warrior had a significant effect upon the psychological state of the troops at the front; for with this estrangement he had lost most of the sources of legitimation of his own activity, of his own death. "Courage," "honor," "self-sacrifice," "heroism" now belonged to those distant, "unreal" worlds outside of the trench system. Wilhelm von Schramm insisted that the invisibility of the enemy, the *Menschenleere* of the battlefield, and the routines of trench war completed the decay of military style and virtue begun with the French Revolution and mass conscription. "In this complete formlessness and dispersion, every action of the leader, every art . . . defeat and victory, even military honor, was finally brought to absurdity."[69] The frontsoldier lacked any of those accoutrements and insignia that were the sign of the military being at war. Henri Massis, too, reflected that all those satisfactions and virtues that had traditionally been proper to armies at war had now been effaced. Everything about trench war was internal, was "done within, in the ground, in man."[70] The removal of all signs of an offensive character, with the retreat into the soil, entailed a basic tranformation of the soldierly type. The soldier of trench warfare was humble, patient, enduring, an individual whose purpose was to survive a war that was a "dreadful resignation, a renunciation, a humiliation."

Given the character of the war, the personality of the soldier was necessarily woven from his role as silent sufferer of the will of material. He was not the offensive administrator of pain, himself psychically armored against any disturbing consciousness of his target as a human being. Henri Massis sees the war as a place of random death, a place that developed the most common virtues, an ability to wait.

> Soldiers without pleasure in warring, they wait. For what? Nothing and everything, for death can bury them here during this desolate assignment without their testing their own strength against it; death is as if oblivious, mindless. It does not want their courage . . . for in this war it demands a harder virtue: it wants to be waited for, at every hour, with patience. It is not at all the adventure of a heroic moment, the exalted passage of the hero into eternity, the sublime vocation of the warrior. It is less solemn: it takes whom it will, when it will, in the most humble posture, always imposing its ceaseless presence, requiring us to be always ready.[71]

Here Massis sees, in the Christian mold, that figure which Zuckmayer had called the common man, the man who had come to a consciousness of himself as an eminently replaceable component of an endless industrial process. At the very least, the realities of war radically lowered the individual's sense of his own worth and value, while requiring the erection of massive defenses against an impersonal, indifferently hostile world of firepower.

But this raises the question of how the realities of war become conscious and unconscious selves? The conscious self of the frontsoldier might be seen as the internalization of the elements of his "job," a job that imposes upon him a certain sense of his own reduced status. In finding his way into the war the volunteer first learned, often painfully, the illusory status of the ideological conception of himself and his comrades as national personas, armed defenders of a unified community. In his initial disillusionment he lost a transcendent view of himself and his role, he lost his ideological contact with the home and all that it represented. But in the context of trench warfare, an even more radical estrangement takes place. The frontsoldier increasingly found himself distanced from all professional, military sources and concepts of selfhood. In the erosion of the "offensive character" by the realities of defensive war, the frontsoldier was stripped of all those symbols of "caste, cult and belief" that constitute "militarism" and a means of identifying the military character and community. Certainly one cannot claim that military conceptions of the soldierly role were repudiated en masse. If this was so the war would have stopped for revolution to pass. But there did come to exist an intense, destructive tension between official conceptions of the soldierly self and the frontsoldier's conception of what he was and what it was possible for him to do and be within the defensive system. It is against the background of this tension that we must understand war neurosis as an attempt, through the neurotic symptom, to repudiate a role that, objectively, was self-destructive. The therapies administered to men who broke down in war must be understood as an attempt to reimpose officially sponsored conceptions of the offensive, aggressive self, by reinforcing the moral universe in which that self was at home.

In essence, the unassailable superiority of defensive firepower equipped the frontsoldier with a set of dominant motives that could not be recognized as legitimate, proper, and manly by those responsible for winning the war. His strivings for a minimum of security in an exclusively threatening and destructive world became a bond with the "enemy," those "other" inhabitants and victims of the dramatic structure of war. These motives also provided a bond with his comrades, those who shared realities and knew what they implied for the chances of a continued survival. This collective estrangement from the military role gave the frontsoldiery a sense of having a collective, "clandestine" self, which could not be made visible to those "outside" the war. They would not recognize it or understand it. This sense of having an invisible personality unquestionably contributed to the vitality and cohesion of veterans' groups after the war. A few realized, however, with Charles Carrington, that their sense of comradeship, their sense of themselves as veterans, was rooted in a complex pathology. "The 1916 fixation had caught me and stunted my mental growth, so that even ten years later I was retarded and adolescent. I could not escape from the comradeship of the trenches which had become a mental internment camp."[72]

If character is, as Wilhelm Reich defined it, the sum total of those strategies that an individual evolves to defend himself against threatening definitions of himself by the "outside" world on the one hand, and against purely internal fears and anxieties on the other, then it must be recognized that the frontsoldier acquired in war a distinct character. In defending himself against the definition of himself as an aggressive, offensive agent of a national will, he was forced to internalize a decidedly diminished sense of his status as an anonymous worker in a bleak and threatening world. If trench warfare was nothing other than a set of compromises that assumed a physical, material form, the personality of the frontsoldier was woven of an even more impacted set of compromises between official motives proper to soldiers in battle and "unofficial" motives proper to men seeking to continue their lives.

But the realities of war supplied the frontsoldier not just with a conscious conception of himself as a proletarian in uniform. They also supplied him with an unconscious self expressed in characteristic fantasies, dreams, and neurotic symptoms. An exploration of this unconscious self occupies Chapters 4 and 5, but here it is possible to indicate the direction of analysis. The change of character that many expected upon entering the war was pred-

icated upon an initial vision of themselves as aggressive, offen-
sively motivated, and guiltless. Given the realities of trench warfare, these early expectations became a dream, a fantasy, even an
obsession of those who were psychologically most wedded to
this conception. Trench warfare is a paradigm of compromise, of
the repression of aggressive energies. As such, the image of aggression takes on a characteristic energy, which, in Ernst
Jünger's fantasy of the offensive, is frankly sexual. "We will
force open the closed door and enter by force into the forbidden
land. And for us who have for so long been forced to accumulate
in desolate fields of shell holes, the idea of this thrust into the
depths holds a compelling fascination."[73] The dream of force-
fully violating a peaceful landscape, of thrusting deep and vio-
lently into an "unbounded space," the dream of an elite of spe-
cialists in penetration, armored against suffering and pleasure:
these dreams are fueled by the reality of defense, the reality of a
war in which everyone is a "common man." In the context of the
realities of trench warfare, abandoned hopes and self-images, initial illusions, take on an added energy and a fantastic form. These
"illusions" become the dream of those "accumulating in desolate
fields," or lost in the labyrinth of trenches.

It is in this context that one must understand the popular,
postwar notion that the war had schooled millions of men in the
arts of aggression. The fear that was focused upon the returning
soldiery and the suspicion that veterans were behind the "crime
wave" that swept European nations after the war were products
of pre-existing images of the kind of personality formed outside
of the boundaries of civilization. Few suspected that the realities
of this war were realities that frustrated aggression and turned all
acts of hostility inward. The realities of war equipped the soldier
with a fund of repressed motives, images of an aggressive self
that often assumed fantastic form. These motives could not be
acted upon in the context of war. But after its conclusion they
could be acted out in the relative security of postwar social and
political life.

4. Myth and Modern War

MYTH AND REALITY

Paul Fussell, in his rich and masterful analysis of the British war literature, notes the ironic contrast between the actualities of war and the kind of consciousness that this war engendered. It was the first modern, mechanized, and industrialized war, and yet it produced myths, fantasies, and legends that are reminiscent of more archaic mentalities. "That such a myth-ridden world could take shape in the midst of a war representing a triumph of modern industrialization, materialism and mechanism is an anomaly worth considering."[1] It is this anomaly that will be considered in this chapter. The imaginative productions of combatants, the myths, fantasies, and rituals that were native to trench warfare seem to stand in stark contrast to the modernity of war. And yet upon closer analysis those fantasies and myths can be seen as characteristic features, even necessary emanations of technological warfare.

Often the fantasies and legends that were generated at the front are cited in order that they may be set aside. Jean Norton Cru,[2] for example, spends the first chapter of his review of the French war literature dispelling legends propagated in the trenches and behind the lines. Indeed, the folklore of war – British, French, and German – supplied copious materials to those who wished to further blacken the enemy or project their own anxieties or hopes on the blank field that lay across No Man's Land. The myths and legends of war are often regarded simply as falsehoods, or distorted impressions that interfere with a clear understanding of the actualities of experience. Reports of the "officer spy," of a shepherd betraying the positions of batteries by the arrangement of his sheep, of the transposition of the trench into a river of blood, of crucified Canadians, Germans, or Frenchmen, of the angel of Mons, of the "German corpse-rendering works," and of the army of deserters living beneath No Man's Land were all popular legends, figures, and descriptions. But they were not *true* and thus seem only to obscure the actualities of war.

While one must observe the distinction between significant and silly legends propagated in the war, it is arguable that, in general, the myths and fantasies of war cannot be regarded as false imprints of phenomenal realities. They were the necessary articulation of the combatant's experience of realities. In the most significant myths one can find a "reading" of the constraints that immobilized the lives of those in the trenches, a reading that, imaginatively, solved the deadlock of the front and the stasis of the individual. The technological actualities that immobilized the front also eviscerated previous conceptions of war and the warrior. The myths and fantasies of war attempt to revive these conceptions in a new landscape. They attempt to close the gap between the surprising realities of life and initial expectations.

There can be no doubt that, for example, the myth of the army of deserters inhabiting No Man's Land and living from what can be scavenged from corpses is an illusion. And yet those who propagate and participate in such illusions are seeking not a false impression but a consistent projection that restructures the chaos of impression and events that inhabit their living space. The myths and fantasies of war are firmly anchored in the realities of war, however much they might mobilize traditional themes, images, and formulas.

One must see illusion in general, and the myths and fantasies of war in particular, as an attempt to dissolve and resolve the constraints upon vision and action that define the reality of war. It is first necessary to see what these constraints were. There is abundant evidence in constant citations and complaints that the war imposed upon its inhabitants a restricted and fragmented consciousness that made it ever more difficult to distinguish what was true, what was false, and what was rightly to be feared. The impact of war upon the sensorium of combatants is the point where one must begin to understand the necessity of illusion, fantasy, and myth. Invisibility rendered combatants' hearing more valuable than their sight in locating threats. Immobility made movement a magical, fantastic possibility to be specified in dreams, legends, and myths (the spy officer, for example, is pre-eminently mobile and sharp-sighted).

The priorities of discussion flow from this view of the relationship between the realities and the fantasies of war. First one must define the ways in which the actualities of war shape a unique consciousness. Only then does it become apparent that the fantasies that appear within the war literature in general are constructions designed to resolve a problematic reality. The fantasies of war rarely appear in a consistent narrative, but only as fragments of experience. For this reason it is fruitful to see how one individual – Ernst Jünger – shaped a consistent reading of his war experience and wove the fragmented images of war into a coherent vision. But before embarking upon this analysis, one must clarify the anomaly noted by Paul Fussell and look more closely at the relationship between the realities and the fantasies of war. Fussell suggests that war forced its participants to move "towards myth, towards a revival of the cultic, the sacrificial, the prophetic, the sacramental, and the universally significant."[3] But must one assume, because combatants ransacked their memories for phrases, lines, and images from a literary and ritual tradition adequate to their experience, that the war effected a kind of regression toward a more archaic mentality? Many psychologists assumed this, although their terms of description were rarely literary: The war had "barbarized," "primitivized," or "infantilized" its psychic victims.

The assumption that underlies much discussion of the imaginative productions of war is that belief, myth, ritual, and legend are characteristic of a particular phase of cultural and psychological development. If individuals, en masse, move in this direction, this can only be a regression to an earlier cultural and psychic stage that civilized adults have abandoned. This assumption conceals an hypothesis about the relationship of reality and myth. War effects a psychic regression toward a place where the restraints of reality do not operate. The myths and fantasies of war are an escape, a flight from constraining modern realities that in war were translated into military terms. The actualities of war, in sum, necessitated a movement toward fantasy and myth, which, in turn, have their cultural and psychic place on the continuum that leads from the primitive to the civilized or from the infantile to the adult.

Much confusion is caused by this attempt to spatialize and temporalize comprehension and perception. It is a simplification to see the characteristic fantasies of combatants – even the most obvious escapist fantasies of flight – purely and simply as a movement away from the oppressive actualities of trench warfare. Perhaps, to avoid this simplification, it is better to dispense immediately with the word "fantasy," which has too many connotations of escape from the real and problematical into the unreal, and to use the word "myth" instead – however arguable that term has become. Discussions of myth, which have been stimulated primarily by the French structuralists, focus precisely upon the relationship of the myth to the realities of a social and cultural context. In these discussions the term has been modernized, and it is worthwhile reviewing this discussion in order to see some of the alternatives to the "regressive" notion of myth.

Initially, myth was seen as nothing but a sacred tale, a narrative that defined sacred realities in terms of observable phenomena.[4] It was thus difficult to speak of myth in the context of secular, desacralized societies. But with Malinowski and the functionalist school of anthropology, myth was seen as fulfilling certain needs characteristic of all societies: Myths provided "charters" of social institutions and religious customs explaining where these institutions and customs had originated and why they must be respected. Malinowski defined the terms of all future debate over the relationship of myth to social reality. It became a question of how myths functioned in a social and cultural context. Increasingly the role of myth has been defined less as charters of social reality than as a story that mediates the contradictions, tensions, and conflicts inherent in the real world of social relations. If there is a consensus upon what myths mean, it lies in the notion that myths mediate unpalatable cultural contradictions. But the question of *how* this mediation takes place is still a matter of debate.

One can see the terms of this debate in the differences between Roland Barthes and Claude Lévi-Strauss over the precise function of those mediations that myth accomplishes. According to Barthes, myths alleviate contradictions by supplying a "metalanguage" that removes signs from the context of signification. In a sense myth performs the operation of transforming a sign into a symbol, a process that removes its direct relationship to the contradictions that constitute historical reality. "We reach here the very principle of myth: It transforms history into nature."[5] Myth performs the function of alleviating social contradictions because it is a type of speech that drains forms (signifiers) of their native content (the signified) and combines these forms into new stories, images, and performances that permit an audience to find pleasure in what – in their everyday lives – is most problematical.

> In passing from history to nature myth acts economically: It abolishes the complexity of human acts, it gives them the simplicity of essence, it does away with all dialectics . . . It organizes a world which is without contradictions because it is without depth, a world wide open and wallowing in the evident. It establishes a blissful clarity: Things appear to mean something by themselves.[6]

Myth accomplishes, this time linguistically, a flight from contradiction. However, it is difficult to see, in Barthes's discussion, any real difference between myth and fantasy, legend, melodrama, or romance. They all accomplish a depoliticization of reality, and all are forms of false consciousness.

Lévi-Strauss offers an understanding of myth, certain features of which are useful in the context of the war experience. He sees myth neither as a charter of social reality nor as a flight from the contradictions inherent in this reality; rather, myth is an often unconscious "speculation" that has a complex relation to the culture that generates it. In the context of his analysis of the story of Asdiwal, a myth of the Tsimshian Indians located on the northwest seacoast of North America, he insists that the depictions of the pure matrilocal and patrilocal residence that appear in the story must be read cautiously in the context of a society that has neither of these kinds of residence in their pure form.

> Mythical speculations about types of residence which are exclusively patrilocal or matrilocal do not, therefore, have anything to do with the reality of the structure of Tsimshian society, but rather with its inherent possibilities and its latent potentialities. Such speculations do not, in the last analysis, seek to depict what is real, but to justify the shortcomings of reality . . . This step, which is fitting for mythical thought, implies an admission (but in the veiled language of myth) that the social facts when thus examined are marred by an insurmountable contradiction, a contradiction which, like the hero of the myth, Tsimshian society cannot understand and prefers to forget.[7]

Here myth performs the function of isolating, focusing upon, and framing one or more of the myriad aspects of the social context to reveal its "inherent possibilities," while also acknowledging, in a backhanded fashion, the improbability and unreality of that aspect when pushed to the extreme. Mythic thought, as it is traced by Lévi-Strauss, operates with the assumption that truth lies not in a careful description of the mutually qualifying realities of status, authority, lineage, feast, famine, age, and sex that make up the social fabric. It lies in selecting certain data from that reality and pushing them to their extremes.

Myths alleviate contradictions by reframing the elements that conflict in reality. In so doing they change nothing and "explain nothing . . . merely shift the difficulty elsewhere, but at least . . . [they] . . . appear to attenuate its crying illogicality."[8] The difference between Barthes's and Lévi-Strauss's views of myth lies in the subtle but real difference between the alleviation of contradictions by means of a shift of linguistic level, a kind of linguistic Aufhebung, and the insistence upon the speculative, creative, and illuminating power of myth. For Lévi-Strauss, myths show signs of a process of selection, categorization, and recombination that make the social, technological, and economic facts of life narratable. The elements drawn from the environment are reframed according to a variety of schemata: geographical (north/south), cosmological (heaven/earth/underworld), or gustatory (edible/inedible).

Similarly, in the context of the war, certain facts of the war experience are selected for signification, not because they are unreal but because they are central to the human experience of war. One can see in the war literature the reintegration of the phenomenal realities of war within a new and imaginative topography. The dimensions of height and depth, in particular, were exploited to reveal the possibilities that are so inextricably confounded at the surface of the trench labyrinth. Visions of the sky and its inhabitants – pilots – were assigned values that only those in the trenches can assign. The underground – a real theatre of war in the mining and countermining that went on under the trench system – drives the realities of war to an imaginable extreme where they provide the setting for a new type of hero. In short, the aerial and underground dimensions of warfare – aspects of the phenomenal realities of war – provide the details of a schema that allows participants to sort out their experience, to intensify certain features, and to recombine them in stories that accomplish those modifications of expectations required by a work-war, the industrialization of human slaughter.

Beside the vertical schema that articulates the problem of mobility, visibility, and vision, one finds the horizontal articulation of the front into zones of danger. This, too, is quite a traditional formula, and one only has to remember Clausewitz's famous description of battle to locate its origins. The rear areas, the reserve trenches, the front line, No Man's Land, the enemy front lines, reserve trenches, and rear areas: these describe facing, opposed systems that define the realities of life and movement. The rhythm of three to four days in the line, three days in reserve, and four or more days at rest behind the lines was observed in all the belligerent armies, and this produced a characteristic rhythm of retirement and advance that can be found in every infantryman's journal.

The rear areas in particular provided the setting for the development of pastoral themes, and the forward lines for those evocations of the increasingly demonic world of mechanism. The war literature is replete with scenes bedecked with flowers, moldering ivy-colored walls, aimless, contemplative wandering through summer days that stand next to descriptions of "wounded trees and wounded men," crater fields, the lunar landscape that is dominated by a mechanical, nonhuman presence. It is tempting to see the contrast of pastoral and technological themes in terms of the opposition of machine and garden that has become such a standard feature in discussions of industrialization and myths – particularly in American cultural history.[9]

But here I will examine the interaction between the natural and technological dimensions of warfare in terms of what had become the obsession of troops, staff, and all who were required to deal in any way with the realities of war: mobility. The focus on the problem of mobility and the way this problem finds a mythical solution changes the valences of meaning woven into pastoral and technological themes. *Both* the pastoral world and the technological world provide settings for passage. They fix images of different kinds of mobility. The soldier resting and recuperating behind the lines moves through a relaxed, nonresisting landscape that continually offers him only the picturesque, never the problematical. His mobility is characteristically aimless and the occasion for a ruminative chewing of his experience. The landscape is an aid to contemplation and memory. The movement forward through a technologically dominated world, however much it took the form of dreams, was directed, impulsive motion that could only be accomplished through the expenditure of enormous stores of energy. It is motion that evokes not contemplation of a visually delightful field but thoughts of penetration and violation. Technological motion is pre-eminently necessitated motion that is visualized, often, in the sadistic terms of puncture, rape, and dismemberment of a passive object.

If the pastoral and technological settings of war provide the context for the resolution of what had become most problematical, they also provide the terms for the statement and articulation of the problem. One must recognize that the relation of the pastoral to the mechanical is not purely and simply an antithesis. There is a positive and negative pastoral image to be found in the war literature, just as there are positive and negative visions of the technological world. The positive and negative poles within the pastoral have often been obscured by the tendency to see it as a state or a place coincident with all that is natural, rather than as a setting of action. The hero of the pastoral is not the gardener rooted to the scenes of his labor, but the shepherd who enjoys his wandering, semipropertiless, and aimless life. The immobilizing natural world, the earth, and the activities proper to that setting – digging and rooting – are precisely what the frontsoldier wishes to be liberated *from*. The soldier mucking about in holes and ditches sees himself and is often seen by others in terms of the negative pastoral vision, as a brute, a peasant, a stupefied consciousness, bound by the necessity of labor.

Similarly the "machine" constitutes an image that is negative in so far as it is immobilizing and alienating, and positive in so far as it is enabling, mobilizing, and an integrating system. In both incarnations, as an overawing authority that decrees the condition of immobility and as a means of mobilization, the inherent possibilities of technological reality are pushed to an extreme. The machine is a term that acquires metaphorical prominence in the war literature both as a description of the problem and a vehicle for its solution. The machine is at once an autonomous, "legislative force" and an articulation of human potencies and drives.

Both the pastoral and technological motifs in the war literature are bifurcations and redefinitions of the problems that the realities of war present to combatants: the problems of potency, mobility, and visibility. This becomes evident first when one approaches the consciousness native to the trenches.

FRAGMENTATION OF VISION AND THE DREAM OF FLYING

The actualities of combat on the surface of the trench system produced a profound disorientation in most of those who inhabited it. This disorientation in turn generated a need for a coherent vision, the kind of vision attributed to the flier, the pilot who enjoyed an aerial perspective. The feeling of being lost in the trenches – while often a literal experience – is also a metaphor for the effects of trench warfare upon the sensory perceptions of combatants. The constriction of vision, the loss of any secure orientation in space or time, were perceptual structures that provided the basis for reminiscences and for experiences of déjà vu like that reported years after the war by J. R. Ackerley. As he was wandering through the streets of a town in India, he returned to the trenches. "The streets became narrower and narrower as I turned and turned . . . until I felt I was back in the trenches. . ."[10]

The realities of trench war posed problems for those who wished to memorialize their experience. Fritz Kreisler was only one of those who, in a reminiscence written no more than six months after he left the eastern front, apologizes for the formlessness of his recollections. He was unable to organize his memories in any sequential order and suggests that he was not the only victim of this disability. The "curious indifference of the memory to the values of time and space" was "characteristic of most people I have met who were in the war . . ."[11]

> One gets into a strange psychological, almost hypnotic state while on the firing line which probably prevents the mind from observing and noticing things in a normal way.[12]

The invisibility of the enemy and the necessity of hiding in the earth, the layered intricacy of the defensive system, the ear-shattering roar of the barrage, and the fatigue caused by the day and night shifts, combined to shatter those stable structures that can customarily be used to sequentialize experience. Hearing became much more important than vision as an index of what was real and threatening. Kreisler reports that his musical training certainly contributed to his survival, for he was able, by ear alone, to single out the shells that were coming closest, gauge their trajectory, caliber, and speed. He tells with some pride that his trained ear was also used as an offensive weapon when he aided his artillery in locating the position of a particularly effective enemy battery.

Many report that the physical setting of war effected a peculiar narrowing of comprehension, a stripping away of any sense of periphery, a fixing of their gaze to a narrow strip of uninteresting ground. This radical curtailment of vision enhanced the possibilities of projection. Ernst Jünger, in visiting a familiar stretch of trench a decade after the conclusion of the war, remembers not any specific incident but a generalized set of projections that were necessitated by the impossible narrowness of the spot.

How often I have stood like this; in such places as this! A short piece of trench lies before me, a tiny part of the immense front. But still this black hole of the dugout entrance, a dead eye suffused with darkness and secrets, this sentry post, these three or four wires which, overhead, slice through the pale sky, are an entire world which enfolds me as simply and significantly as the scenery of a powerful drama.[13]

Many veterans who later returned to the sites of their combat in order to refresh their memories remark upon the overwhelming sense of spatial incongruity. The trenches as they now appeared were much smaller, narrower, more restricted than they were felt to have been during the war. Touring veterans, like those who return to the settings of their childhood, were stunned by the gap between the way things now appeared to be and the way they were felt to be before. There was a significant discontinuity between the visual field and the space as imagined and lived in. In Jünger's striking metaphor, the difference between seeing the trenches after the fact and when he actually lived in them was like the difference between seeing a cavity in one's tooth and feeling it with the tongue. In the war the restricted space of habitation had been stretched by fantasy. Now it was regarded from the outside, in its objective appearance.

The wild face of the landscape projects a series of nightmares upon the fantasy which the mind continually tried to reject as unbelievable. In the long run, this was a greater strain than one thinks.[14]

It is significant for the lasting effects of the war experience that what most often was remembered was not an impression, a stimulus that was somehow preserved, but a perspective, a construction that was placed over the realities of war. The shards of experience that appear in the memoirs and journals can be recognized by their curvature as fragments of a once whole vase, as chips of a cognitive, conscious structure that contrasted sharply with what was normal before the war and after it. As one volunteer reported to his parents, in an attempt to define the differences between their perspective and his: "You must understand how narrow one's horizons become; one can't think of the general situation and judges of it entirely on the basis of one's own."[15] The recall of the war seemed to bring forth images that had once served to define the place and position of the combatant in his experiential field, images that highlighted the discontinuity of dimension and spatial awareness between the accustomed spaces of civilian life and the radically curtailed field of the combatant. The curtailment of this field encouraged the projection of hopes upon the war as well as the expansion of other senses – pre-eminently, that of hearing.

Robert Graves recently discussed, in an interview with Leslie Smith, the difficulties that attended any description of the realities of war to civilians. The problem of incomprehension had much to do with the dominantly aural impressions received by combatants, impressions that could not be imagistically conveyed.

> GRAVES   The funny thing was you went home on leave for six weeks, or six days, but the idea of being and staying at home was awful because you were with people who didn't understand what this was all about.
>
> SMITH   Didn't you try to tell them?
>
> GRAVES   You couldn't: you can't communicate noise, noise never stopped for one moment – ever.[16]

Indeed, "minds were broken by the continual roaring." The superiority of machines over men was announced in "peals of thunder" that buckled the earth and drove those huddling underground very close to their breaking point. There was a consensus among combatants: The conditions of neurosis were created not by the sight of exploding chemicals but by the deafening sound and vibration of the barrage, which defenders were required to suffer for hours, even days.

J. C. Carothers, in his analysis of those sensory organizations that seem to distinguish modern from premodern cultures, argues that sound and magic are peculiarly compatible, as are

sight, vision, and demystification. He claims, in an argument
that Marshall McLuhan and Walter Ong have made familiar, that
the ear becomes a purely secondary organ in literate cultures.

> For living effectively in the modern western world a well-
> developed sense of spatio-temporal relations and of causal rela-
> tionship on mechanistic lines is required, and this is highly
> dependent on a habit of visual, as opposed to auditory, synthe-
> sis. The world of magic governed by animistic powers could,
> it was argued, pass away only when man's attention became
> focused more on the relatively objective . . . visual world. [17]

However one might object to this construction of culture
around the individual sensorium, there is evidence for the view
that the shutting down of any possibility of "visual synthesis"
creates a climate of fear and anxiety that is an appropriate setting
for the practice of magic. Many reported that, even counter to
their temperaments, they became superstitious under the barrage
and began to see their world and themselves as manipulated by
malevolent forces that might be propitiated by spells and rituals.
Robert Graves acknowledges that he "became superstitious too: I
found myself believing in signs of the most trivial nature." [18] The
circumstances of this war, the dominance of sound, and the impossibility of effective, active defense produced a notion of the
relationship between individuals and the forces that governed
them that seems much closer to magic than to any technological
spirit. Charles Carrington describes how his own thought processes bent under the weight of the barrage. His recourse to
spells, rituals, and fantasies was designed to give him some control, however spurious, over the forces that dominated him.

> I got into a thoroughly neurotic state during the day . . . You
> think of absurd omens and fetishes to ward off the shell you
> hear coming. A strong inward feeling compels you to sit in a
> certain position, to touch a particular object, to whistle so
> many bars of a tune silently between your teeth. If you com-
> plete the charm in time you are safe – until the next one. This
> absurdity becomes a dark overpowering fatalism. You con-
> template with horror that you have made a slip in the self-

imposed ritual, or that the sign of your invention shows
against you. You image that the shells are more deliberate
and accurate than could be possible.

So all the day you listened, calculated, hoped or despaired
making bargains with fate, laying odds with yourself on the
chances of these various horrors.[19]

Here is evidence of the anomaly that Fussell has pointed out.
The sheer scale of technologically administered violence seemed
to force the regression of combatants to forms of thought and action that were magical, irrational, and mythic. One need not go
on, as many medical officers and psychotherapists did, to assume
that this regression retraced the steps of modernization. But even
if one dispenses with the idea of regression, one is faced with
abundant evidence that the consciousness native to trench warfare was in striking contrast to the problem-solving activity that
is customarily termed rational, scientific, or technological.

Men became superstitious in war. Their use of magic, ritual,
spell, and omen seemed to be an unavoidable response to the
total loss of individual control over the conditions of life and
death. Carrington's magic is not a communal but an individual
and solitary activity, but still it is behavior within a situation that
approximates the technological impotence that Malinowski insisted underlay reliance on magic. Magic is an appropriate resort
in situations where the basis of survival could not be guaranteed
by any available technology. Magic is functional behavior in the
sense that the spell often alleviates anxieties that would otherwise
paralyze any capacity for action. The reliance upon magic defenses and fantasy invulnerabilities can be seen as the result of
that profound sense of individual impotence before technologically administered violence that suffuses all descriptions of war.
But the magical consciousness, Carothers argues, is also a result
of the foreclosure upon any possibility of visual synthesis and the
increasing reliance upon sound. Sounds indicate dangerous
movement. The rustle of grass in No Man's Land, the click of
wire, the whistle of an incoming shell, the soft crump of a mortar
firing – all announce a potential death against which the only
defense was earth and ritual.

I would like to suggest one other possible link between the

sounds of war and the change of conscious state attested to by combatants. Graves, Carrington, and many others noted that the roaring chaos of the barrage effected a kind of hypnotic condition that shattered any rational pattern of cause and effect, allowing, even demanding, magical reversals. This state was often described in terms of a loss of coherence and the disappearance of any sense of temporal sequence. It created the setting for irrational thoughts and unbidden associations. All through the history of psychology, students of cognition have insisted upon a distinction between two different and often dichotomous organizations of thought. These dichotomies – variously termed irrational/rational, primary thought processes/secondary thought processes, intuitive/analytic, and magical/technological – have defined different structures of cognitive organization. Ulric Neisser prefers to call these two organizations "parallel" and "sequential." Sequential processes "make only those tests which are appropriate in the light of previous test outcomes."[20] Each image and idea follows from a prior, necessary image or idea. In contrast to sequential processing, in which ideas are ordered one at a time, parallel thought processes carry out "many activities simultaneously, or at least independently."[21] Seen in toto, parallel processes lack any coherent sequence. Neisser suggests that "pandemonium" is an appropriate term for parallel processes, as is Freud's "primary processes." "Freud might not have objected to describing the primary process as a shouting horde of demons."[22] This distinction between parallel thought processes, which are multilevel, diffuse, and apparently chaotic, and sequential processes, which focus upon the ordered, successive solution of problems, offers a framework for the interpretation of the change of conscious state suffered by those under shellfire.

Implicit in the anomaly noted by Fussell – that is, the contrast between modern industrialized war and the magical, ritualistic behavior within it – is the concept that these are contrasts between mentalities, between a technological spirit and apparently archaic clusters of belief. Magic is more than ineffective technology; it works on the basis of correspondences, analogies, and associations that presume a multivalent world of significances. Technology, as it has been defined in the western world, focuses attention upon a verifiable relationship between means and ends, between cause and effect. Francis Bacon distinguished science from magic on the grounds that science produces works, results that can be traced back to an absolutely minimum set of necessary causes. These results were to be described in a language free of "fancy," imagination, or cultural prejudice. It is notable, also, that the earliest definitions of modern science – those offered by Bacon, Galileo, and Descartes – relied to a much greater extent than before upon the metaphor of visualization and the notion of the innocent, inductive eye. The visual field, the technological spirit and sequential thought processes, when they make only those tests that are suggested by the outcome of previous tests, mutually ratify one another. Visual synthesis cuts through the myriad of correspondences that underlie every magical act.

It could be argued that the deterioration of the visual field experienced by many in trench warfare removed those visual markers that allow an observer to direct his attention to what comes first and what later. Certain situations, like that of trench war, seem designed to disorder sequential thought processes and to disorient the participant. Particularly in African culture, noise or the rapid oscillation between sequentially ordered notes and thickly layered, staggered patterns of rhythm are used to key movement into a trance, a spirit possession, or other altered states of consciousness. Rodney Needham, for example, suggests that percussion instruments dominate ritual settings because they have a strong, physiologically disorienting effect. Like thunder or gunfire, drums "shake the environment."[23] The drummer is the central figure in the Haitian voodoo ceremony. "It is the drummers," Frances Huxley claims, "who largely provoke dissociation; they are skillful in reading the signs, and by quickening, altering or breaking the rhythm they usually force the crisis on those who are ready for it."[24] Morton Marks describes in great detail how the break between order (speaking or playing one by one) and noise (speaking all at once) is a central characteristic of African and Afro-American performances. The oscillation between order and noise conveys the information that certain kinds of behavior usually associated with trance states are now appropriate.[25]

This digression into the fields of cognitive psychology and ethnomusicology suggests, I think, some of the possible connections between the noise of bombardment and the altered state of consciousness described by combatants, as well as the mythic, magical mentality seen by Fussell as an effect of the war. The constriction of vision eliminated most of those signs that allow individuals to collectively order their experience in terms of problems to be solved in some kind of rational sequence. The sheer volume of noise that dominated the front was experienced as supremely disorienting. The background of continuous noise limited the information that could be derived from the environment of war and forced those cowering in the bunkers and burrows underground to impose some pattern on, or decipher the meaning of the tapestry of detonations outside. Naturally, this chaotic world was judged entirely on the basis of the individual's own perspective, a perspective that mobilized deeply layered anxieties, animistic images, and surprising and unbidden associations.

For the vast majority of Europeans who fought in the war, noise meant nothing but chaos; it caused nothing but fear, stupefaction, and dull resignation. Precisely because there was no cultural convention to call forth an appropriate switch of the soldier's "inner state" during the transition from order to noise during the war, the barrage most often effected a transition into neurosis, breakdown, or mental disorder. The last defense against the murderous and brutalizing realities of war lay in bleak irony, projection, fantasy, or the assumption of a neurotic symptom.

The curtailment of vision effected not simply the incidence of neurosis but also contributed to the "textualization" of the events of war discussed above. The war assumed an awesome autonomy from the motives and purposes of combatants. Increasingly it was spoken of in anthropomorphic terms, or described as an automaton – an organization that authored and authorized actions no longer attributable to individual motives. The rationality, purposes, and intentions of the war were increasingly mysterious to combatants. In turn, their own role and welfare seemed to depend increasingly upon a correct reading of the mysterious intentions of the organization that dictated their lives and deaths.

It is worth following the course by which the war became

meaningless for many participants in individual terms. For this process was not merely a change of attitude but a function of the transformation of perspective and consciousness necessitated by the realities of war. The very first impression of war was, for many, an acknowledgement of the peculiar incongruity between its meaning and its actuality. The space within which the war was fought was much too narrow for its world-historical significance. The very narrowness of the stage upon which combatants performed seemed to open a gap between meaning and action. Herbert Weisser, a German volunteer, was gently puzzled by this ambiguity in his first encounter with trench war.

> Yesterday I was in the trenches. There I could see the actual war for the very first time. Everything takes place in a very narrow (but certainly very long) strip of ground which seems much, much too narrow for its gigantic significance.[26]

The initial ideological frame of war did not accord with its spatial dimensions. Increasing familiarity with the actualities of war convinced Weisser that it was only a waste of men, a reckless, meaningless expenditure of energy, and a complete denial of the "urge to productivity." He could only hope that the greatness of the war that was so firmly fixed in his expectations would reappear after the war was over – as a memory. "I believe that I will recognize the greatness of this time after three to five years and find pleasure in it."[27]

The actual experience of war did not bring combatants, as they had hoped, closer to its meaning. Rather, familiarity with combat distanced the individual from the purpose and the significance of the project in which he was engaged. The struggle to fit expectations into the actuality of war, a struggle that ended in incomprehension and a peculiar kind of animism, is nicely illustrated in the war letters of a Lt. Edward F. Graham, of Rochester, New York. As a news writer for the Brooklyn *Times* who had accompanied Henry Ford's peace party to Europe in 1916, Graham was convinced that he knew the meaning of the war and had clearly grasped its ideological significance.

> The world is breaking up. The desperate contest between justice and empire . . . is now on. You should be proud to have

me . . . participate in the struggle as a part of the human wall against a second Dark Ages.[28]

But at the front the clarity of the confrontation between the forces of darkness and civilization was increasingly obscured by the sheer scale of the event. From the inside, the enormity of war effaced any personal perspective. Whatever the rank of the individual, whatever his authority in the chain of command, any rational comprehension of the meaning of the event in terms of plan, order, and the execution of order was impossible.

> This grim, continuous effort grips the faculties and dwarfs all frivolity. There is something to this thing . . . civilians and their dwellings and doings are mere cinema to us. This is an effort, so huge and complicated that no mind can grasp it – a man throws a hand grenade at a Boche – a general throws an army – the result is very real and useful but in neither case does the operator grasp the subtle processes involved.[29]

The war was still a human project even though it had passed beyond the powers of comprehension available to one man, whether infantryman or general. But it is only a small step from the realization that the war is subject to no individual will to the belief that the war is governed by a will that is suprapersonal and inhuman. The movement is animism is taken in Graham's last letter – in which the war becomes a gigantic, incomprehensible, and malevolent beast. Men are reduced in scale. They are recognizable only by their smallness and abjectness. On August 21, 1918 – less than three months before the armistice – Graham was killed by an artillery shell that exploded in the entrance of a dugout where he and his squad had taken refuge from a fierce German shelling. His mother later received his notebook and a two-paragraph fragment of a letter, dated August 20.

> This is a cowering war – pigmy man huddles in little holes and caves praying to escape the blows of the giant who pounds the earth with blind hammers.[30]

The war retained its magnitude for Graham, even though it evolved from a morally comprehensible historical event into a system that defeated any personalized perspective, and, finally,

into an autonomous persona characterized by indifference to the
human suffering "he" was inflicting. Graham ends by asking the
question that many asked, a question that was appropriate to the
modern paradigm of mass suffering: Why do men who are
wholly diminished by their reality, whose convictions have become illusions, and who have lost any sense of purpose continue
to suffer to no end?

Many preferred not to ask this question and attributed the lost
purpose and meaning to a future perspective or to a fantasy creature somewhere "above" the front who could locate the pattern
in the chaos inhabited by the frontsoldier. Franz Schauwecker
was one of those who ascribed the lost coherence to the being
who somehow rose above the labyrinth of the front.

> All private roads wander incoherently, on their own account,
> but behind and above stands, somewhere, a meaning which
> orders the million bends and corners and slippery places into
> an organic whole . . . Only an eye which can gain perspective
> will survey the whole.[31]

For Schauwecker, as for others, the war had become a mysterious fate and an indecipherable destiny. Incapable of relinquishing
the possibility of meaning in his own suffering, he projected that
meaning to a location above the front. The perspective that had
been stripped from the frontsoldier, bewildered by the "million
bends and corners" of his dwelling, was bestowed upon an "eye"
free from restraint and distortion.

The aerial perspective – the perspective assumed to belong to
the flier – was one of the most significant myths of war. The
necessity of this myth lay precisely in those constrictions that so
fragmented the perceptions and purpose of the frontsoldier. The
myth of the flier, of adventure in the air as the last home of
chivalric endeavor, is clearly a compensatory notion. It serves to
keep open the realm of purpose and meaning with which many
entered the war. The flier is a figure woven out of the expectations defeated by the actualities of war. By assuming the perspective of the flier, the frontsoldier could gain some psychic distance
from the crushing actualities of trench war. The aerial eye orders
the twists and turns of the trench labyrinth into an organic whole
and reinvests the actuality of war with its initial purposes. The

flier, in fact and fantasy, keeps open the possibility of an escape. Many took advantage of this possibility. Erich von Ludendorff had initially advised his sons to join the "decisive military arm, the infantry." They did so, but Ludendorff ruefully acknowledges, "as it happened to many of our young men, the freedom of the air drew them from the trenches,"[32] and his sons became pilots.

The mystique of the flier and of flying was one of the most obvious contributions of the war to the fantasies of the 1920s and 1930s. The flier was engaged in individual rather than collective combat. He was identifiable rather than anonymous. The flier, like heroes such as T. E. Lawrence, fought preindustrial war with modern technology and inherited the values – mobility, honor, vision and visibility – that had formerly surrounded the heavily armored cavalryman but that had been lost by the infantryman. The most brilliant poet of flight, St. Exupéry, was too young to fight in the war, and yet in his novels he exploited themes and images that had initially been developed in accounts of aerial warfare above the front. The metaphors of war are prominent in St. Exupéry's work precisely where he reasserts the concept of heroism that had most obviously been made nonsense of in trench warfare: The happiness of the hero lay not in security but in risk, in adventure and self-transcendence. In *Night Flight,* the form-giving, Nietzschean hero is reincarnated in Rivière, the manager of the airline carrying mail across the Andes, who justifies the firing of a mechanic in the following terms: "We can command events and they obey us; and thus we are creators. These humble men, too, are things and we create them, or cast them aside when mischief comes about through them."[33]

In the war the flier was a saving reality. His existence provided a concrete location for those expectations of adventure, liberation, and self-distinction with which many had entered the war. Ernst Jünger visited an airdrome behind the front in March of 1918, and his description of the pilot is the occasion for the revival of almost abandoned expectations. The aviators were mostly former cavalrymen who, through their relationship to their machines, had revived their elite status and their superiority over the humble masses in the trenches. The fliers were at once embodiments of an old spirit of chivalry and initiates in the secrets of steel and explosives. Their machines enabled them to rise to a height where, once again, war was a unified, human project. The aviator had the eyes that had been removed from the frontsoldier.

> When they soar into the heights from which the front appears as a thin net, visible to the eyes of the frontsoldier as a row of dots, there occurs in their risky enterprise a fiery wedding of the spirit of old chivalry and the cold austerity of our forms of labor.[34]

Paul Fussell notes the prominence of the sky in British war literature. This is a recurrent motif in nineteenth-century literature in general and one that often appears in depictions of war, most memorably perhaps in Tolstoy's *War and Peace* when Andrei, wounded on the field of Austerlitz and contemplating his own mortality, faces the "eternal sky." Trench warfare intensified an already considerable interest in the sky-scapes, sunrises, sunsets, and atmospheric phenomena that had long since been singled out by Ruskin as essential themes of pictorial representation. A few combatants were quite conscious of the appropriateness of the sky as an over-arching motif of industrial war. Max Plowman asked:

> Was it Ruskin who said that the upper and more glorious half of Nature's pageant goes unseen by the majority of people? . . . Well, the trenches have altered that. Shutting off the landscape, they compel us to observe the sky; and when it is a canopy of blue flecked with white clouds . . . and when the earth below is a shell-stricken waste, one looks with delight, recalling perhaps the days when, as a small boy, one lay on the garden lawn at home counting the clouds as they passed.[35]

The sky was often used to great effect in drawing out the ironies implicit in the human project of war. "When a participant in the war wants an ironic effect, a conventional way to achieve one is simply to juxtapose a sunrise or sunset with the unlovely physical details of the war that man has made."[36] Sky and earth have always offered an almost inexhaustible fund of pathetic or ironic contrasts between impassivity and turmoil, eternality and mortality, and the ineffable and material. The focus upon the sky and its inhabitants can only be intensified by a world in which death is the most immediate fate of its inhabitants. Indeed, F. C. Bartlett, in his analysis of the psychological effects of trench warfare, felt that death and the desire for death as an "honorable escape" from war was a preoccupation particularly of those men who had "high ideals of duty." He agreed with MacCurdy's view that the desire for death was a recurrent fixation in those who ultimately broke down under the strains of war.

Given the circumstances of war, one can see how something that had served the purposes of literary juxtapositions assumes a psychological potency. Freud, in his analysis of dreams in which the dreamer envisions his own death, claimed that such dreams always dramatized a split of consciousness. The observer always witnessed his own death as a spectacle, while surviving as an observer. The very ability to presume an aerial perspective over the scene of one's demise acted as a guarantee of survival and ensured that one's personal demise was only a dream.

The realities of war forced combatants to assume an observing relationship to themselves. This ability became a habit of perspective that Jünger called "stereoscopic" vision, a vision that allowed the individual, as victimizer, to observe himself as victim. The sky is charged with intense significance: It *must* be the residence of the observer watching himself struggle through the nightmare of war, for only then will the eye survive the dismemberment of the body. The fantasy creature that observes the front and orders the million bends and turns into a coherent pattern of purpose and meaning is a reconstituted self, a projected identity, a mythic persona called "the War."

> If there were a creature that could with a glance effortlessly span the Alps and the sea, this activity would seem to him a dainty battle of ants, a delicate hammering in an integrated factory. But to us who see nothing but a minute section, our small fate overwhelms us and death appears to us in a terrible form. We can only surmise that what happens here forms a part of a larger order, and that the threads upon which we wriggle so strenuously and so apparently without purpose are somewhere woven together into a fabric of meaning, the unity of which escapes us.[37]

The mythic, religious, and ritual dimensions of warfare grow directly out of the "mechanized slaughter" that was World War I. Many surmised into existence a godlike eye out of their own constricted vision, a leviathan who does not suffer out of their own suffering, and a creature of will and purpose out of their impotence and purposelessness. While recognizing the irrationality inherent in the act of projecting upon a fantasy creature everything that they had lost, the very possibility of its existence guaranteed what had become most problematical in the war – a continued existence and a continuity of meaning.

WAR IN THE UNDERGROUND

If the aerial dimension of warfare provided a setting for self-estrangement, self-transcendence, and self-observation, the war fought in the underground mines and galleries beneath the trench system served as the locale that totalized the most oppressive realities of trench warfare. Trench warfare in general was a war of engineers, but the theatre of war that was dominated exclusively by engineers was the war of mining and counter-mining under No Man's Land. The silence, darkness, disorientation, and almost unbelievable psychic tension suffered by mining soldiers was an intensification of the experience of trench warfare. In mining, entrenchment – a defensive tactic that immobilized the war – became an offensive act. The underground soldier drove silently through the soil, chalk, and clay that had barely been scratched by the trench system on the surface. The earth was the prison of the *Frontschwein,* but it was also the medium of combat and movement for the pioneer and engineer.

It is much easier to articulate the schema of height and surface and to see the way in which it provides a distancing dimension of experience than it is to define the distinctions between surface and underground. The frontsoldier and the sapper share a common medium – the earth. They are interchangeable figures, for the sapper is a miner who has been armed and the frontsoldier is an infantryman who has been transformed into a digger. One distinction lay, clearly, in the different terms used by front-soldiers and by sappers in defining their relationship to the earth and in developing the implications contained in the medium of the soil for their own sense of themselves and their status.

Frontsoldiers described themselves as modern cave men. The experience that had initially been welcomed as a release from confining social convention and the beginning of a simpler, more natural, and healthier life had become, with trench warfare, an existence within "a new dimension of foulness, a tunnel life lived in a troll kingdom in which immobility never brought peace and activity scarcely ever brought mobility."[38] The barbarization that many felt they had undergone in war is always related to the trench environment, an environment described by Barbusse as a "troglodyte world." The caves, the cave men, the filth and dirt of war, and the sense of being lost in an endless morass gave combatants the feeling that they were living a precivilized life that had little in common with any industrialized, technological environment. Henri Barbusse deployed the "troglodyte" formula throughout his war novels. It seems odd only to a civilian when one of the *poilus* in *Under Fire* finds a stone-age axe while digging a communications trench and adopts it as a supplementary sidearm. The club was a much more popular weapon in the trenches than the bayonet, and one only has to tour the exhibit of fearsome, nail-studded knobkerries in the Imperial War Museum to make the equation between modern war and primeval combat that became automatic for those who wrote of their war experience.

At the surface of the trench system the images of barbarization implicit in the image of the soldier as troglodyte codify the sense that trench warfare reduces men, pollutes them, and pushes them outside of the temporal and spatial fringes of civilization. This becomes explicit in the sometimes ironic, sometimes pathetic references that countless soldier made to themselves as vermin, moles, gophers, rats, and rabbits. "Pigmy man" huddling in little holes and caves is certainly not the man who walks on the face of the earth, under the sky, but the creature who lives in it and digs through it.

In what way have we sinned, that we should be treated worse than animals? Hunted from place to place, cold, filthy and in rags . . . in the end we are destroyed like vermin. Will they *never* make peace?[39]

The cave and its inhabitants – supply the formulas of self-regard appropriate to the surface of trench warfare. But beneath the surface, in the true underground, different formulas are often employed. The medium of the soil enhances rather than diminishes human stature and military virtues. H. D. Trounce, a lieutenant of Royal Engineers, insisted that in "no species of land warfare is a cool head and a clear brain combined with decisive energetic action and determined courage, more required than in the conduct of these military operations."[40] The extreme tension involved in mining beneath an enemy sap, and listening to conversations of the enemy through a few yards of earth, must be totally suppressed. The aim of mining warfare is to get beneath the enemy and blow up the tunnels he is driving toward one's own trenches, as well as to undermine his trenches. The underground war is a war of small groups – safe from the pervasive threat of shellfire that dominates trench war – racing through the earth toward the enemy lines. Just as the flier can fly above the realm of fire, the digger can tunnel below it. This fact makes the sapper, like the flier, a figure of imaginative resolution for those who inhabit the surface.

Underground warfare draws upon a complex of conventional symbols, both ancient and modern, that have been keyed to the notion of change and human transformation as a recombination of elements rather than transcendence. The function of the mine, both as symbol and reality, is to eradicate any hope of escape, liberation, or transcendence, thereby focusing attention upon interior, chemical, and organic reactions. The mine, like the smithy and ultimately the factory, is the scene of mechanical operations that confer a socially ambiguous status upon their practitioners. Their occupation at once makes them masters of the material world and stunts, cripples, or otherwise marks them as creatures who are foreign to the surface and its social graces, manners, and hierarchies.

It is worth reviewing, briefly, the complex of symbols that have defined the activities and status of the worker in the underground before going on to examine narratives of underground warfare themselves. Mircea Eliade, in one of the very few studies of the myths, taboos, and mysteries that have surrounded technological processes, points out that miners, smiths, and alchemists have always been regarded as practitioners of transformations. These activities have been regarded as ambiguous, potentially dangerous, and occasionally bordering upon the heretical. One cannot read the materials assembled by Eliade without coming to the conclusion that even the earliest ideologies of work, and particularly those of the alchemist, serve as a defense against the ambiguities of their position with regard to structures of authority and belief, as well as justifications for the process they practiced. Thus miners saw themselves not as violators of a maternal earth but as midwives of natural transformations. The miner merely collaborates in the birth of metals, retiring periodically to allow the embryo ores to renew themselves. Similarly, the songs, spells, and rites of smelters and smiths identify the furnace as an artificial womb that hastens with fire the gestation of pure metals from out of the native ores. The alchemist takes the further step, seeing his operations as both the perfection of matter and of himself.

> Alchemy prolongs and consummates a very old dream of Homo Faber: collaboration in the perfecting of matter while at the same time securing perfection for himself. . . In taking upon himself the responsibility for changing matter, man puts himself in the place of time.[41]

Eliade finds that the symbols accompanying the work of miners and smiths are the same as those that accompany rites of passage in general – symbols of death, sexuality, and rebirth. Indeed, it would be surprising if technological procedures were *not* understood and justified in terms of those symbols that define changes of state, location, or status. But the point that emerges most clearly from Eliade's study is the anomalous position of the smith, miner, and alchemist within his society. He most often was classed with the magician. A Yakut proverb identifies the first smith, the first potter, and the first shaman as blood brothers. In Africa, itinerant smiths were regarded as pariahs by the Boris of the White Nile, while the Bololo of the Congo regard them as culture heroes. In East and North Africa, in Hamitic pastoral cultures, the smiths are of low caste. In the true iron civilization of Africa, they enjoy the prestige of an aristocracy. In both instances, those who practice the transformation of metals are a race apart. Their skills endow them with enormous power that is respected and feared.

The technician traditionally belonged to that category of individuals classed as magicians precisely because they were identified with the transmutations they practiced. They were grouped as magicians with other professions – barbers, actors, gravediggers, shepherds – who enjoyed a similarly ambiguous status.[42] As Marcel Mauss points out, the category of magicians, or those to whom were ascribed magical powers, was often very large. Members of superceded religions or conquered races commonly were feared as witches. Jews in western Europe were considered more likely to exercise their malevolence in occult practices, just as Scandinavians saw the Finns and the Lapps as sorcerers. In Mauss's review of the social position of those felt to have magical powers, he concludes that a magician was anyone who had a social status above, below, or outside the norm.

This ambiguity of status, and the ascription of extraordinary power to the men engaged in material transformations, was not set aside by industrialization. The mystique that surrounded the successful inventor in the United States during the nineteenth century exploits his status as a culture hero. The ambiguous status or low status of the engineer in Europe was very much a source of complaint and a stimulus for the self-promotion of engineers. Friedrich Dessauer, himself an engineer, became an explicator of technology in 1906 because he felt that his profession was looked down upon and abominated by men of culture and intellect. His defensive tone and his assertion of the power of the technologist hearken back to the most ancient ambiguities that surrounded men who were at home with matter.

> You charge us with the lack of lofty, noble strivings, of the warm ardor of human love, and the free flight of ideals. We reply to you – you despise us, good. In spite of that we help men more than you, more than all those epochs which you fasten yourself and appeal to; we help them practically, not *with* you because you don't want that, but in spite of you.[43]

The traditional status of the smith as well as the ideology of technological processes were generalized in new ways with the coming of industrial production. The experimental sciences and the notion of progress "takes up and carries forward – in spite of its radical secularization – the millenary dream of the alchemist."[44]

Lewis Mumford brings the mine and the activities of the miner much closer to the context of the war. The perfect symbol for the "paleotechnic" age of industrialization is the mine. Mumford uses the term paleotechnic as a pejorative term to describe the period of the development of heavy industry, a time that stressed quantity, mass, and power out of all proportion to function. The pride of the last half of the nineteenth century lay in its enormous output of steel, coal, and kilowatt hours, and this pride was reflected in public buildings that were designed to give the impression of mass, weight, and solidity. The very materiality of the environment, its artificiality, and its massiveness make the mine a significant reality and symbol.

> The mine to begin with, is the first completely inorganic environment to be created and lived in by man . . . In hacking and digging the contents of the earth, the miner has no eye for the form of things: What he sees is sheer matter, and until he gets to his vein it is only an obstacle which he breaks through stubbornly. . . . If the miner sees shapes on the walls of his cavern, as the candle flickers, they are only monstrous distortions of his own pick and arm: shapes of fear. Day has been abolished and the rhythm of nature broken: Continuous day and night production first came into existence here. The miner must work by artificial light even though the sun be shining outside.[45]

If one might take this as an evocation of a purely technological environment, one can see that the emphasis shifts from the traditional transformative power of the miner and his role as complement to natural processes to an evocation of the transforming power of the environment upon the men who create it. Not surprisingly, Mumford sees a relationship between mining and trench warfare: "Among the hard and brutal occupations of mankind the only one that compares with old-fashioned mining is modern trench warfare."[46] The parallels are explicit enough, for the heavy work in the trenches was done at night. The days were spent in sleeping or watching, and many frontsoldiers complained that their lives were being lived out in darkness. The equipment of war often adapted the equipment of mining. The most frightening – if, objectively, the most humane – weapon of this war, gas, was a hazard miners often dealt with. The gas mask used in war was only a slight modification of the masks first developed by the coal mine industry in Wales and the Ruhr. When Robert Graves went up the line to join the First Welsh battalion, he found himself in the company of miners who had adapted to trench warfare with understandable ease.

The parallels between the symbol of a paleotechnic age and trench warfare intersect in the mining-war under the trenches. The descriptions of this kind of war evoke all of those themes of projection, enclosure, and sensory disorientation called forth by Mumford in his description of the mine. Vignes Rouges, who fought for a year in a French sapper battalion, describes the sensory intensification caused by the environment of the underground.

> The darkness is a huge mass; you seem to be moving through a yielding substance; sight is a superfluous sense. Your whole being is concentrated on the faculty of hearing.[47]

It is easy, Rouges acknowledges, to imagine into the total materiality of the environment "shapes of fear," and these fears are for the most part superstitions and utterly archaic.

> At last, forty yards down, we find ourselves – little moving objects lost in the immensity of inert matter – in the upper section of the Jurassic stratum. A vague superstitious fear seizes the most skeptical minds. What if it be living, this matter upon whose eternal silence we are intruding . . . ? Our presence might, perhaps, enrage mysterious forces here . . . True, the tunnel is boxed in . . . boarded with strong planks, but what a pitiful bulwark against these mighty masses, dense and rugged, that are pulled incessantly toward the center of the globe.[48]

The fear that one is violating a living being, that the earth might be a living breathing body, a mother or a monster, is stimulated by the total foreclosure upon sight and by the realization that one inhabits the "immensity of inert matter." It is an environment that makes it difficult for those working below the surface to prevent themselves from projecting into their material surroundings their worst fears of violation and pollution.

Gaston Bachelard suggests another impression that intrudes upon miners, sappers, divers, and "cellar dreamers": the intensely internal nature of their environment. The tunnel, like the cellar, is a space with no outside, no externality.

> The cellar-dreamer knows that the walls of the cellar are
> buried walls, that they are walls within a single casing, walls
> that have the entire earth behind them, and so the situation
> becomes more dramatic and fear becomes exaggerated . . .
> The cellar then becomes buried madness, walled-in tragedy.[49]

In a mine, as in a cellar, the essential feature of the environment disconnects a key element of perception: the distinction between inside and outside, figure and ground. This feature of the mine makes it a synonym for a total enclosure that directs all questions back upon the questioner. It is precisely the totality and materiality of enclosure that makes mining warfare the perfect setting for interior transformations, a rearrangement of psyche, and, ultimately, the setting for a transformed, perfected warrior.

Ernst Jünger made the most of the formulas of transformation traditionally associated with the mine and technological processes. He, much more intensely than most, was committed to the early expectations that the war would mean an initiation, a "sea change" of personality. With the locking of the front and the denouement of offensive goals, these ideals went underground. The *Frontschwein*, on the surface, would

> . . . never find a solution, for their point of view is already
> problematical, and they search outside for that which is only
> within.
>   Indeed, to them only the surface is of significance . . . If
> they find the guiding thread by which they can grope their
> way out of the labyrinth of war, or desperately cut the Gordian
> knot, they have arrived at the goal of their desire.[50]

Jünger sought a solution for his own war experience, and this solution lay neither on the surface nor in transcendence – in the almost mystic freedom of the flier. It lay in the underground. This underground was a physical place – the abandoned coal mines between the trenches at Lens – and a psychic space – a dimension of depth, of inwardness, in which those few still capable of a solution would find themselves. It is a place where a new man is shaped, the character who becomes the revolutionary type in postwar politics – which is itself the "prosecution of war by other means."

Jünger's myth of the new *Gestalt* fashioned in war is an extremely important fiction. It is important not just for Jünger himself but for many of those young men who had fought the war, or stood waiting impatiently on the sidelines, and who wished to retain some belief that the war had not been *merely* a meaningless orgy of destruction but an event creative of personality, a rebirth and a regeneration of the nation. Jünger's myth of the frontsoldier was accepted and used again and again in the 1920s by those who, for whatever reason, could not accept the fact that in the war they had been used, exploited, maimed, and sacrificed to no personal or national end. Jünger, in the myth of the personality shaped in the underground, fashioned an essential tool in the "saving of appearances" and the rationalization of illusions that function for those who found the postwar world a "formless void," an immobilizing complex of restrictions – as severe and confusing as war had ever been.

In *Sturm* and *Wäldchen 125*, Jünger describes the character shaped by underground war. In effect, the underground intensifies, magnifies, and totalizes those realities characteristic of the surface. Jünger's first and worst war novel, published serially in the *Hannoverscher Kurier* during 1923, tells the story of a pioneer officer commanding, in 1918, a portion of a fiercely contested salient before Lens. Later, in 1925, Jünger expanded this fragment into his best war novel, *Wäldchen 125*. Jünger describes the pioneer officer, later called Vorbeck, as the epitome of the frontsoldier who has grown and flourished in the "gravitational pull of fire" that draws men and matter "incessantly toward the center of the globe." In *Sturm*, the pioneer officer gives his credentials and his story curtly:

> I know what an assault means, and what trench warfare is all about, but that is child's play compared to a fight in the coal

pit. There one has the feeling of being in his tunneled-out grave or already roasting in hell. The weight of enormous masses of earth around you gives you the feeling of complete isolation and makes you think that if you died here no one would ever find you again.[51]

In *Sturm,* Jünger emphasizes the removal of the soldier in the underground from the transcendant eye, the immensity of inert matter, and the nightmare of solitude and death within walls that have a "single casing." But in *Wäldchen 125* the emphasis shifts to the generative power of this totally repressive and isolating environment. He describes, in some detail, the fighting in the "coal pit" and sketches out the strata of confrontation: the air, the surface, and the underground. In telling the pioneer's story of *Minenkrieg,* he draws out the psychic implications of this kind of war.

The pioneer, now Vorbeck, is still the *toll Daraufgänger* of trench warfare, but now he is the model of the assault trooper – the soldier who, by virtue of his exclusive concentration on the tactics of penetration, holds the key to the deadlock of trench warfare. Vorbeck knows the net of trenches from the "Alps to the sea," but with the minute precision of a groundling. He is, explicitly, a man of the depths. In his story of underground warfare, he sounds those plutonic and labyrinthine themes that become such important images in Jünger's validation of the war.

It was at Lens that I first learned to know the war in the mines so well; day and night we were literally standing on a volcano. Under the countryside extended a finely woven network of coal mines many kilometers long which bound both fronts together deep under the topsoil.[52]

For the Germans the mines were a true labyrinth. The French had originally mined this region and were in possession of maps and plans to which the Germans had no access. Lieutenant Vorbeck's unit patiently groped their way through the buried maze of tunnels and galleries, learning its dimensions, and encountering the enemy continually in the process. These deadly, hand-to-hand encounters, ambushes from the dark, continued for weeks until Vorbeck hit upon the idea of planting cannisters of gas in the tunnels and releasing them at the height of enemy activity. "We smoked them out like rats, and had poisoned the entire tunnel system for months."[53] The gas remained in such high concentrations in the tunnels that even with gas masks work was impossible, and the mines were abandoned by both sides.

Vorbeck's story is prosaically told, the terror of this experience casually accepted. But Jünger magnifies this environment, so thoughtlessly poisoned, into the womb of the "new man." The story contains the germs of a number of Jünger's most significant themes: the reappearance of war as a deadly game; the totally confined environment in which decision becomes once again possible; and, most importantly, the refinement of the senses, particularly of hearing, that contributes to the formation of a new type of warrior. In the tunnels, that curtailed and confused vision still possible on the surface is totally extinguished. It is the underground that takes the materiality, the partial blindness, and solitariness characteristic of the surface to its furthest extreme, and it is this extreme that concentrates the forces generative of a new type of man. The story of Vorbeck

> . . . had brought to consciousness the fact that the will to combat was forcing men against one another not only on land, on and under the sea, and high in the air, but that it also led them deep into the abysses of the earth. But are we not in general a plutonic species that – cut off from the joys of existence – is at work upon the future in a subterranean smithy? What we create and for what we are created will first become evident much later than we can expect. Perhaps we ourselves will be most astonished over that.[54]

War in the man-created spaces of the earth leads to a change in which a new man is himself created. But this man is one who has no immediately apparent or even predictable purpose. His distinguishing mark is his hardness, his invulnerability to the terrors of his imagination enflamed by the environment of the underground. The new man forged in the underground stands for the hope that there might exist a future purpose and an intrinsic meaning to the slaughter of war. The underground is not just labyrinth in which a generation goes lost, but a smithy in which a new personality is shaped. The terror and frustration of endless wandering in a totally material world suffused with darkness is now qualified by the creative role that is played out below the surface of the front and below the plane of conscious experience.

The political relevance of this figure was obvious to Jünger. Just as the new man was generated in the pressures of war in the underground, so the revolutionary elite of the 1920s was located below the surface of political life. The dynamite that would explode liberal myths was formulated by Jünger in the mid-1920s; he first discusses this formula in 1927 with members

> . . . of the smallest circle, whom I found ready, and upon whom I happened like a miner who sees the powder-blackened face of a comrade emerging from the breach of his blast hole.[55]

The solution to the contradictions immobilizing the plane of politics lies in the political underground, just as the sword that will slice through the net of tactical difficulties binding the front-soldier would be forged in the smithy of the subterranean labyrinth.

Jünger, as a man committed to the offense, felt these contradictions of war most intensely, for they directly attacked the roots of his own conception of himself. His problematical and aesthetic nationalism receives its intensity from the problem of the war experience, a problem that is initially tactical but that quickly becomes deeply personal – a problem of self-worth, of the function and effect of extreme repression, and of formulating a relationship between solitary man and his alienated means.

His solution to this problem lies in the presumed formation of a special personality and a special elite that operate both on a military and, later, on a political stage.

> It has been proven here that man is capable of enduring more than one could have supposed, that he grows with his means, and that his powers of resistance prevail again and again in this contest. It becomes ever more difficult to approach him; it demands a kind of preparation which borders on magic. One can say that in this arena in which mass national armies and gigantic concentrations of artillery hold the balance, still a second and higher form of warfare begins to unfold: the war of twenty men who alone among the tens of thousands are changed by the gravitational pull of fire and earth, and are still capable of breaking into that elemental, and, in a far deeper sense, decisive stratum where one looks the enemy in the eye.[56]

To those who have the capacity to move in the gravitational field of the front, in both war and peace, the closed, constricted maze of cross-purposes is opened up. The frontsoldier enters the depths of hostile space where confrontation with the enemy and, perhaps, victory is again possible. The conscious exit from the trench labyrinth is granted only to an elite who have regained the power of decision. With this power members of the "twenty" again have hope of assembling an identity, of finding themselves, and of pursuing their direction and purpose with a freedom the mass does not enjoy. For Jünger, the riddle of the trench labyrinth is resolved in depths at once psychic and spatial – in the underground of the mine and in the mind – by men who have mastered the magic of motion in a technological world.

ERNST JÜNGER AND THE MYTH OF THE MACHINE

A great deal of confusion can be caused by the belief that when one talks about the "machine" or the "image of the machine," one is talking about technology. The image of the machine, when it is not purely descriptive, refers not to technology but to human and individual autonomy – how it is gained, lost, constrained, and defined. Actual technologies, the "stuff," provide only the material and the occasion for the examination of ineffable but highly significant matters: to what extent is "man" gaining or losing control over himself, over his fate, his environment? True, the conventional use of technological things – cars, television sets, computers – as the ground for metaphors portraying the degree of individual or collective autonomy, may react back upon our comprehension of concrete things. We may use these things as proofs and demonstrations of the extent to which we have lost control over ourselves or gained control over distance and time. Here the image of the machine begins to enclose those objective, concrete things upon which it is based, using those things to "think with," as ways of arguing about the ultimate fate of humanity within industrial civilization.

It is difficult to see the cultural significance of the image of autonomous technology unless one recognizes its subjective roots.

At bottom this image is, and traditionally has been, a projection and a representation of the drive-regulating structures of the psyche, structures conceived of as "internal" to the individual. In the seventeenth and eighteenth centuries it was popular to regard the human animal as an automaton, and yet here the image carried positive connotations of "self-regulation" and "self-determination." The automaton man, like the machinery of the heavens, was something integral and closed to external sanctions, a system of self-regulating weights and balances that – if free from external interference – would strive toward equilibrium. Significantly, the definition of the machine changed in the nineteenth century to accord with a new conceptualization of "civilized" man. Now the machine was an arrangement of "opposed" parts so arranged as to transform raw energy into work and value. Here the image of the machine is the most objective representation of the bourgeois conception of the psyche as a closed, integral system of psychic parts in balanced conflict, so arranged as to transform "primitive" instincts into civilized values. The coincidence of the image of the machine with modern images of the self is striking enough to suggest that here is something more than just one image among many. The image of the machine has a privileged status as a representation of peculiarly "modern" modes of self-regulation. The image of total self-control, externalized in the figure of the robot, conveys the message that such perfection is inherently "inhuman," destructive of human emotions and potentials. The image of autonomous mechanism is not just a way in which modern men represent "self-control," it is also a way in which they experience and explain their "selves."

The love–hate relationship that natives of industrial societies have maintained with the machine is notorious. Yet it would be a mistake to see this ambivalence purely as a product of the ways technology has destroyed traditional, pre-industrial cultures. I would like to argue that precisely because of its status as an "object," an impersonal, external thing, the image of autonomous mechanism provides a crucial means for the most direct and often bitter expression of the ambivalence that modern men feel toward those structures of inhibition, repression, and self-restraint that are the condition of their social autonomy and individuality. There is a less complex way to say this. The image of the machine is a key element in the code that men in industrial cultures use to speak of their internal regulation *as if* it were a property of the external world. Once this code is learned their self-regulation can be experienced as something imposed upon them by a material environment. It now has the force of "necessity." It is thus that the image of the machine can be spoken of as a true "myth," for it becomes a charter of individual self-regulation, the key ingredient of social regulation. Of course the image of autonomous mechanism is rarely regarded as a myth, but as something that is happening, has happened, or is to be overcome in the future. Perhaps this, more than anything else, suggests the continued vitality of the image. For with it "modernized men" can address to the outer world questions about their inner state. They can see themselves as legitimate products of a human-created but strangely "inhuman" world that tyrannizes over them or "liberates" them, constrains or extends their individual powers.

It is not surprising to find that the image of autonomous mechanism occupies a prominent place in the literature of the First World War. Most often this image is used to represent the forces of repression, those things that victimize the unaccommodated men huddling in the holes and ditches of the trench system. As men experienced the war increasingly as the estrangement of themselves from their "actions," as a loss of control, as a damming up of their potencies, their lost autonomy and repressed energies were invested in an abstraction: "the War," the autonomous mechanism of slaughter. A few participants, Ernst Jünger most prominently, could not resign themselves to the status of common men, passive sufferers of the will of material. They sought to recover their lost potency through an identification with the autonomous mechanism of "the War" that so victimized the "masses." In Jünger's case the identification of himself with autonomous technology became a source of personal power and authorization. Through this identification he could acquire the status of factotum and appendage of a suprapersonal power, a power that lent those who derived their identities from it a renewed, if "amoral" potency. It is in this fashion that one must understand Jünger's assertion that the First World War produced a new *Gestalt,* a "technological man" who was as "hard," "callous," and "unfeeling" as the machinery of war itself.

Through these kinds of identifications the war in general, the image of the war as a "technological," industrial reality in particular, often acquire a deep subjective significance. It is obvious, in Jünger's war books, that the "machine" acquires all the features of other "authorizing" figures that administer suffering while themselves being armored against it – the father imago, the state, the godhead. Jünger's postwar political position, his "radical conservatism," is rooted in an experience of war in which he learned, once more, that the individual gains his potency and autonomy not through rebellion against these figures but through identification with them.

One can begin to see the nature of the personal significance that the image of "autonomous mechanism" began to hold for Jünger when one looks closely at the oft-quoted passage in which he evokes the conventional image of the war as his father and the father of his generation.

> Never before has a generation stepped out into the light from a door so dark and immense as from out of this war. And we cannot lie, however much we wish to do so: the war, father of all things, is also our father. It has hammered, cast and tempered us into what we are. And always, as the whirling wheel of life turns in us, the war will be the axis around which it turns.[57]

The implications of this passage are clear. In so far as the combatant identifies with the mechanisms of war, he is granted autonomy from his parental origins. The war then provides a set of surrogate progenitors, a maternal womb, and a patriarch operating through industrial processes that "hammer, cast, and temper" an entire generation. This transposition of identities from natural parents to "the War" has political implications, as is made clear in a passage written in 1925: "We are the genuine, true and ruthless enemies of the bourgeoisie. . . . We are no bourgeois ourselves but sons of war and civil war."[58]

Jünger was neither the first nor the only combatant to insist upon the creative, initiatory power of war. But he does allow us to see how this age-old convention is personalized, how it ac-

quires a subjective force and an explanatory power. His use of
the image of autonomous technology allows us, too, to see the
ways in which the war experience absorbed, expanded, and articulated pre-existing conflicts. The war experience, in the image of
the machine, absorbs a variety of Oedipal conflicts. Through this
image these conflicts are generalized; they become the tools of
social and political criticism.

For Jünger the war was an experience which liberated sons of
the bourgeoisie from their social origins and turned them against
their bourgeois parents. It is not surprising that Jünger himself
was born, in 1895, into a solid burgher family. Soon after his
birth in Heidelberg, his father, Dr. Ernst Jünger, settled his family in Hannover where he opened a research laboratory in com-
mercial chemicals. In 1901 he established an apothecary shop in
Schwarzenberg, Saxony, which he give up four years later to return to Lower Saxony. After the war, it was the man of science
with whom Ernst identified and not the shopkeeper – the glut-
tonous and bourgeois *Spiessbürger*. The childhood described by
Jünger in the first version of *Abenteuerliche Herz* was occupied
with anatomical specimens and dreams of heroism. His longing
for escape from comfort is little different from the aspirations described by others of his age and station.

> It was the condition well known to many young hearts, of
> homelessness in the middle of a narrow world artificially but-
> tressed with education and bourgeois habit. . . . One found
> oneself not too badly off in the seductive comfort of a liberal
> age. But something must be desired, and desires remaining too
> long without definition, indeed, without conscious awareness,
> break through like a pervasive poison into the blood.[59]

Jünger, unlike most adolescents of his age, acted on his fantasies. In 1913, at the age of seventeen, he ran away from home
and enlisted for a five-year tour of duty with the French Foreign
Legion at Verdun. He was returned from Algiers by official
order, at the request of his parents. August 1914 released him
from the bargain he had made with his father, an agreement to
pass his qualifying examinations before he set out to see the
world.

He missed the early war of movement, arriving at the front in

January of 1915 after a period of training. Only one month was spent in the ranks before he was sent to officer's training school. There he found the comradeship he had initially expected – "for we all came from the same social class."[60] Jünger's war experience is the best-documented portion of his life. But his war diaries, published as *In Stahlgewittern,* do not suggest his success as a soldier. He received the *Pour le Mérite,* Germany's highest decoration, and was wounded fourteen times – five times by bullets, twice by shell fragments, once by shrapnel, four times by hand grenades, and twice by bullet fragments. On four of these occasions he was critically wounded. At the end of the war he could count twenty-one scars on his body. He was one of the few noncareer officers who was allowed to remain in the *Reichswehr,* which was so radically pruned by the Versailles treaty. He left the army in 1922, rejoined it in 1938 – this time as a captain – and, except for a brief tour on the eastern front, spent the Second World War as a deputy provost of Paris.

Jünger's disillusionment in the First World War was little different from that experienced by others. He had brought two things with him into the war, the expectation of adventure and a slender notebook to be filled with daily observations. Jünger acknowledged his early inclination and talent for observation: "I always had a natural inclination toward observation. At an early age I nourished a fondness for telescopes and microscopes with which one sees the large and small."[61]

His brother, Friedrich Georg Jünger, described Ernst as an *Augenmensch:* "He saw with indian eyes . . . from the faintest spoor . . . he drew . . . conclusions that astonished me."[62] The first experience of war was one that confounded both Jünger's expectation of adventure and his talents as an observer. A shell arrived from nowhere and exploded in the midst of his company, producing one corpse and a number of wounded. This was an experience not of adventure but of slaughter administered by an invisible, mechanized enemy.

> What was this? The war had shown its claws and thrown away its comfortable mask. It was so mysterious, so impersonal. One had scarcely given a thought to the enemy, this secret, malignant being, somewhere over there. These events, lying

completely outside one's experience, made such a strong impression that it cost some effort to conceive of the connection. It was a spectral phenomenon in the bright light of midday.[63]

Like others, Jünger experienced the real war as a humiliation, a dreadful resignation. The enemy had disappeared behind a mask of machinery that prevented any confrontation or observation. The next years of war only intensified the contradictions implicit in this first experience. The war was not a test of individual capacities and wills but the suppression of everything that gave value to the individual.

> In war, when the high-velocity shells growled over toward our bodies we felt that no level of intelligence, of virtue, or of courage could distance ourselves from it by even one hair's breadth. As the threat increased, doubt in the value of ourselves weighed down upon us.[64]

Jünger understood with perfect clarity that "combat was a brutal confrontation of the masses, a bloody wrestling match of production and material."[65] He traced those steps taken by Edward Graham and countless others that led from a view of war as an individualizing, ideologically significant project to the view that the world of war could only be the creation of a malevolent, inhuman force, a blind giant, a cosmic power. The very landscape that engraved itself on the pictorial imaginations of the generation as the essence of a technological wasteland asserted that this was a war "empty of men."

> There was nothing to see but the activity of machine work. As far as the eye reached, one shell hole gaped next to another, and man was driven away as from out of the crater landscape of a dead star. And when again and again, even though every square meter had been plowed up and plowed up once more, the steel curtain came down, then these events expressed the features of a cosmic, soulless force before which man almost disappeared.[66]

Now mobility became a fantasy, the offense became a dream, and the war took on its unique internality. Here the hope of resolution acquires a peculiar sexual intensity that is most evident in

Jünger's novels. His first work, *Sturm,* according to Jünger, described those images that naturally evolved at the interface between the individual and his constraining environment. *Sturm* portrayed the contradiction between "the drive for movement [*Bewegungsdrang*] of a singular individual and the limitation of this impulse by the forces which hold him in his surroundings."[67]

But *Fire and Blood,* a novel published in 1925, is preeminently an exploration of movement, of mobility, in which the many levels of significance invested in mobility are outlined. Gerhard Loose, in his examination of this novel, detects five different kinds of movement that make up the structure of the work: quick and explosive movement, the taking up of psychic movement (retrogression), the suspension of movement in philosophical musings, renewal of movement, and exit. But Loose does not mention something that is clear in this work: Both pastoral and mechanized movement are portrayed as an expansion of self from a center to a periphery. There is very little movement in the commonplace sense of the word, in the sense of traversing a space between two fixed points. Movement here means the act of breaking out of the armored, minimal, defensive self into a "free field." Immobility is portrayed as a contraction of self, an anxious drawing inward. Throughout the work, one is reminded insistently of Wilhelm Reich's definition of sexuality as expansion, of anxiety as contraction. "Sexuality and anxiety are one and the same process of excitation, only in opposite directions."[68] With this notion of sexuality, Reich redefined masochism and sadism. The masochist did not seek pain but was willing to tolerate pain in order to release a fund of sexual tension that could find no other outlet. He "wishes to burst and imagines that the torture will bring this about. In this manner alone does he hope to obtain relief."[69] The most consistent fantasy of the masochist is that of being punctured and of obtaining "liberation from the outside, provided by somebody else."[70] Similarly, the fantasy of the sadist is that of puncturing another, of finding gratification in the assertion of his will upon a passive object.

In the picture of motion and mobility offered in *Fire and Blood,* the sadistic element is particularly prominent. The novel opens in a pastoral setting. The protagonist, noting the first signs of spring, goes for a walk in a forest behind the lines. The walk in the woods is motivated by the "desire for solitude that at times overcomes one who has been bound for years in the mass, in the body of the army."[71] The aimless wandering through the woods is the occasion for reassembling pictures of war and drawing parallels between the pastoral and mechanized landscapes. The fruitfulness of the spring makes it clear "that we are like flowers which bloom and like fruits which ripen and fall."[72] Here Jünger draws upon the same store of pastoral imagery catalogued in the British war literature by Paul Fussell. The common equation between flowers and wounds, between the red of flowers and the red of blood, slowly evolves into memories of battles. Jünger is reminded that if spring means the renewal of life, it is also the time of offensives, and this brings him back to an image of the closed, constricted world of the trenches.

> Sometimes we had thought to ourselves during the dull waiting behind fixed breastworks and thick barriers of barbed wire: better a mighty vortex, once more out into the free field, even if the devil himself waits out there; better to show the enemy your teeth than . . . [to remain] . . . here in the twilight, moles creeping about in their dark holes.[73]

The magnitude of the preparations tells Jünger that now it is not a local attack but a major attempt at a breakthrough that is in the offing. This raises the expectation of a "thrust, which we must drive through positions many kilometers in depth."[74] The accumulation of men and material behind the lines, the frustrations of a winter of trench warfare, bring to mind the image of "an actual breakthrough and a concerted movement into free, unbounded space. . . ."[75] The particulars of this breakthrough, what it means and what can be expected of it, Jünger develops in a paragraph. The enemy had become only a concept in trench war, an entity concealed in the trench system and veiled by the power of fire.

> But now we will rip away this veil instead of gingerly lifting its corner. We approach as conquerers, armed with all the means of power. We will force open the closed door and enter by force into the forbidden land. And for us who have, for so

long, been forced to accumulate in desolate fields of shell holes, the idea of this thrust into the depths holds a compelling fascination. We will demolish the dikes and break like a storm-flood into the broad, untouched region. Every day new villages and cities appear to our gaze and rich booty falls into our fist.[76]

The offensive here is the act that resolves all inhibitions. It permits those who have accumulated in trenches and shell holes to behave like freebooters and robbers free of any morality or conscience. The notion of forcibly violating a peaceful landscape in common with others "armed with all the means of power" has a compelling necessity to it, precisely in the inhibiting power of fire, the trench system, and the immobilizing realities of war. Precisely those realities create a fund of men who will burst like a flood into virginal landscapes.

The social core of what seems to be a purely militarized fantasy is revealed in *Sturm*. Here, too, an assaultive personality, bred in war and armed with all the tools of power, is released. But the target of his assault is the burgher. Tronck, a character in one of the many sketches that make up the novel, occupies himself with strolling about the streets of a peaceful city, assaulting its comfortable inhabitants with his penetrating gaze. The eye, the instrument of contemplation, has now become an offensive tool, cutting through the veils of respectability that surround the citizenry and disturbing the equilibrium of the "comfortable."

The burghers were visibly and unpleasantly affected, checking their billfolds and re-establishing the equilibrium of their self-consciousness with the thought of their bank balance or of a duly acquired title.[77]

In Jünger's early work one can see clearly – in the idea of the military and social assault – an overlaying of military and social worlds. Clearly, the experience of war is not, at least not in mind, a discrete experience creative of new psychic strategies. Rather, with the materials of war, Jünger simplifies and intensifies a particularly traditional psychic conflict. On the one side stand all those restrictive and inhibitory realities – technology, the burgher, the image of the father – that serve to protect and defend a fruitful and peaceful landscape. On the other are those creatures of reality and fantasy – the freebooter, the assault soldier, the secret assassins of bourgeois sensibility, youths who are at once "forced back upon themselves" and armed with "all the instruments of power."

Jünger explicitly designed the chracter Tronck as the epitome of a situation obvious in war but also characteristic of social reality.

> We have incorporated ourselves into the movement of a great, necessary event. But often our own movement, that which we call freedom of personality, stands in contradiction to these events. And that for which we strive in this wretched ground – the free unfolding of the personality in the midst of the tightest bonds one could imagine – I wanted to bring to a polished expression in the man Tronck.[78]

This situation is also characteristic of Jünger's experience of pre-war social life. In one of the sketches in *Sturm* the erotic dimension of this fantasy is explicitly developed. The main character of the sketch, Corporal Kiel, is a man of war experience who conducts a search for a prostitute through the streets of the metropolis as a patrol in force. He overlays his sexual quest with images of prior adventures in No Man's Land.

> Just as, previously, these hours of adventure had driven him out over the clicking wire into the wastes of No Man's Land, so, too, now, the inclination for experience drove him out into the whirling surf of the nocturnal metropolis. His sharp gaze, schooled in the essentials, encompassed the passersby, penetrating them, forcing, like a pistol shot coming in answer to a question.[79]

Kiel is self-consciously the professional military man, his professionalism evidenced in the coldness and precision with which he pursues his project. The equipment that constantly accompanies Jünger's description of the character – steel helmets, pistols, and hand-grenades – are the tools with which he puts distance between himself and sentiment. Kiel selects a prostitute, goes to her room, and awakens in the middle of the night to contemplate her "mask-like" face, stamped with the features of her profession. Simultaneously, he remembers his innocence, the days of August 1914, and "a girl he had loved before the war with what was now an inconceivable intensity, although he had, in boyish embarrassment, never exchanged a word with her."[80]

In this overlaying of innocence and experience, one feature doesn't change. With neither the innocent nor the professional object of love is a word exchanged. Both attachments produce no gratification, the first because of "boyish embarrassment," the second because the veteran of war, schooled in violence, has become incapable of that early kind of passion. The encounter with the prostitute is an encounter of masks that permit a sexual exchange without pleasure, guilt, or knowledge of the other. It results not in a sense of gratification, but in a sense of loss, and a suspicion that the object of his campaign had eluded him. But the motive of his "nocturnal patrol" was not contact; rather, it was a search for release.

> He felt the keen desire to pour out the surplus of his energies into some kind of receptacle, to shatter the swollen waves on some kind of woman.[81]

Corporal Kiel is only one of the names Jünger gives to the character formed in the war. At other points this character is given the names of frontsoldier, stormtrooper, worker, *Landsknecht,* and freebooter. Many of the paradoxes of the war can be found imprinted upon this character, for it is a character doubly armored: against suffering and, paradoxically, against gratification. In the sexual arena, Corporal Kiel forms a pair with the prostitute. As a professional, he accomplishes release without pleasure and prosecutes his sexual-military assault without any real resolution of the conflict that forces him to engage in it. In the political arena, the frontsoldier is characterized by a curiously impotent relationship to power. He is defined by his "readiness" (*Bereitschaft*), his hardness, his immersion in the techniques of violence, and by his inability to consummate any political change without the authorization of a leader. In the social arena the man emerging from the "dark door" of war is the bitter enemy of the bourgeoisie. Yet he assaults this bourgeoisie only with his gaze, and penetrates them only with words "like pistol shots." He does not attack them physically or act upon his anger. All of these situations have the same structure of energies enormously compressed to the point where the individual is ready for release, although he never accomplishes a release in actuality – only in the garb provided by fantasy.

In all of these areas, the character of the soldier is marked by a heightened tension that has become habitual. In pathological terms, this character is founded upon a stasis, a tense equilibrium, that continually energizes fantasies of release. If one wished to reconstruct the path marked out in Jünger's work that leads from the experience of war to a thoroughly ambivalent ideology combining authoritarianism with revolution, one would have to begin with the actual situation of trench warfare. This was a situation in which the drives and the mobility of the individuals fighting it were inhibited by technology, resulting in a monstrous physical stasis. But this stasis, in the case of Jünger, resulted in a fixation upon technology, which assumed the status of a parent of a generation. This point marks the boundary of the realities of war and the fantasies engendered by it. These fantasies can be recognized as at once sadistic in structure and incestuous in content. In taking on the garb of the repressive technology and identifying with the "father of all things," select individuals become artists in penetration, free from moral inhibitions, conquerers of a placid, fruitful landscape. In fantasy, at least, gratification is attained in the offensive thrust through "positions many kilometers in depth," and anxiety is reduced in taking on the mask of those powers that, in reality, immobilize the individual. The "passive sufferer" has now become the administrator of the fate of which he was formerly, in reality, the victim.

5. An Exit from the Labyrinth – Neuroses and War

INDUSTRIALIZED WAR AND NEUROSIS

Neurosis in the Great War is more significant when it is viewed as a complex psycho-sociological phenomenon than when it is seen purely as an event in the history of psychology. Other than the quantity, variety, and protractedness of neurotic symptoms, medical authorities found little that was new or surprising in war neuroses. The symptoms of shell-shock were precisely the same as those of the most common hysterical disorders of peacetime, though they often acquired new and more dramatic names in war: "the burial-alive neurosis," "gas neurosis," "soldier's heart," "hysterical sympathy with the enemy." True, what had been predominantly a disease of women before the war became a disease of men in combat.[1] But uniformed physicians immediately recognized the kinship between the symptoms covered by the term shell-shock and those prewar hysterical disorders that followed upon train wrecks and industrial disasters.[2] Even the social distribution of symptoms was the same in war as it had been in peace. Neurasthenia, a generalized anxiety syndrome that had been found primarily in private hospital rooms and exclusive sanitaria, was most common among officers. Hysterical neuroses with gross physical symptoms of paralysis, spasms, mutism, blindness, and the like – the disorders usually found in public wards or outpatient clinics before the war – predominated in the ranks.[3] In war, as in peace, the notion that disease could be without physiological signs, that it could have a purely behavioral expression, seemed to be the exclusive property of the higher social orders.

Neither did the flood of neuro–psychiatric cases that began to flow through clearing stations beginning in the winter of 1915 stimulate the development of new theories of therapies. The war provided an extensive testing ground of already developed theoretical principles and therapeutic regimens. The consensus among medical officers after the war justified Freud's satisfaction that the war had, if nothing else, supplied abundant confirmation of the psychoanalytic view of neurosis.[4] War neurosis, like neurosis in peacetime, was a flight from an intolerable, destructive reality through illness.

But if war neurosis offered little that might surprise professional psychiatrists, it must engage the attention of social and cultural historians at a number of levels. Neurosis was a psychic effect not of war in general but of industrialized war in particular. Prior to the thoroughgoing mechanization of war the most common psychic disability was homesickness, or what the French in the Napoleonic wars called *nostalgie,* a form of intense separation anxiety.[5] The range of hysterical symptoms that the First World War brought forth on an enormous scale was unprecedented in combat. In 1916 M. D. Eder, a British neurophysician, enunciated the consensus: "From the combatant's point of view this has been described as industrial warfare; from the medical point of view it might be described as nerve warfare."[6] Psychiatrists in the rear and troops at the front immediately saw the relationship between the industrial features of war and the incidence of neurosis. The dominance of long-ranged artillery, the machinegun, and barbed wire had immobilized combat, and immobility necessitated a passive stance of the soldier before the forces of mechanized slaughter. The cause of neurosis lay in the dominance of material over the possibilities of human movement. In a real sense the neuroses of war were the direct product of the increasingly alienated relationship of the combatant to the modes of destruction.

The relationship between the industrialization of war and war neuroses had already been noted in the Russo-Japanese war by R. L. Richards, who was astonished at the number of psychiatric casualties sent back through the military hospitals at Harbin. He attributed the rise in combat neurosis to the effects of "long ranged artillery" and the enlarged theatre of war. But it would be a mistake to regard the increase in the incidence of neurosis solely as an effect of purely technological realities. True, prewar technological and industrial development produced a set of tactical realities in which combatants were forced to erect thicker and more complex defenses against their own fear. And yet the increase in the incidence of neurosis is a response not simply to changes in the "infrastructure of war" but also to transformations of the "superstructure," to new techniques of discipline, control and domination. The very acceptance of neurosis as a condition "appropriate" to combat troops constitutes a problem. For many officers resisted the acceptance of the shell-shock victim as a legitimate casualty of war. They believed that such an acceptance would mean a massive change in the assumptions that underlay military discipline, a change in the values and official image embodied in the military personality, a change in the ethics of aggression that underlay this image. The enormous numbers of psychic casualties in this war raises the question of why neurosis was officially acknowledged as a category of behavior appropriate to combatants. In what ways was neurosis functional not simply for the combatant fleeing the war through illness but also for those authorities responsible for keeping the combatant in the war? In part this question can be answered by looking closely at the scene of therapy, for if neurosis was a "legitimate" exit from the war it was in therapy that the legitimacy of the symptom was judged. Here the exit from war was policed and administered. Within the drama of therapy the traditional "offensive" soldierly role was clarified and fitted upon those who desperately wished to repudiate it. At worst, the therapies administered to those made neurotic in war were acts of pure domination; at best, it was the scene of negotiations between the demands of authority and the needs of the victims of war.

THE POLITICS OF NEUROSIS

Many military officers inside and outside the medical corps regarded the acceptance of neurosis as a condition appropriate to soldiers in combat as a political issue. Many insisted that to allow neurosis the privileges of "disease" would open a gaping hole in the structures of discipline that kept soldiers in the war. They insisted that war neurosis was not so much a condition of the individual soldier as a recategorization of behavior that had traditionally been filed under "cowardice," "indiscipline," or neurological wounds with unexplained causes. A number of witnesses testifying before the War Office Committee on Shell-Shock in 1922, noted that the public acceptance of war neurosis was a disaster. To the "public mind" any pathology that stemmed from the trenches and gave rise to the presumption that the individual was no longer in control of his behavior began to be described as "shell-shock."[7] With the popular acceptance of the term "shell-shock," victims of neurosis were accorded the regard and sympathy that should legitimately be reserved for the physically disabled. They complained that, at the front, the term created an area of presumed psychic incompetence and that troops were quick to take advantage of this. They came to believe that a particularly close hit by a heavy shell or a prolonged barrage produced mysterious transformations in the soldier's nervous system, which damaged his self-control. Sudden flight, hysterical weeping, a refusal to go forward, inability to "hear" an order could be, and were, ascribed to the effects of the previous shelling. Between the acceptance of the legitimacy of neurosis at home and at the front, traditional-minded officers who wished to enforce the moral categories of courage, honor, and duty often had no choice but to resign themselves to neurosis as a legitimate disease of war. Lt. Col. G. Scott-Jackson proudly reported to the Committee that he had not a single case of shell-shock in his battalion throughout the entire year of 1915. He would not "permit it." But when the signs and symptoms of shell-shock were thoroughly familiar even to fresh troops, and when the psychic victims of war received support and sympathy when they returned home, he found he could no longer "hold out."[8] Increasing numbers of men reported to the clearing hospitals in the rear – blind, mute, deaf, with halting gaits, spasms of the face, neck, or limbs.

It was immediately obvious that war neurosis was a "functional" disorder for soldiers. It removed them from the war and this was the conscious or unconscious "aim" of the symptom.

> The psychological basis of the war neuroses (like that of neuroses in civil life) is an elaboration with endless variations, of one central theme: escape from an intolerable situation in real life to one made tolerable by neurosis.[9]

But as the war continued it was increasingly obvious that neuroses were as functional for military authorities as they were for individual soldiers. W. M. Maxwell observed that, in spite of the propaganda of drill sergeants, this was a war that offered few outlets to the aggressions and hostilities of the troops. The realities of war built up enormous funds of repressed hostility that, increasingly, found outlet against improper targets: those in authority, the "rear," the "staff," politicians at "home." "The anger which could not expend itself against the enemy . . . was . . . transferred against a staff which seemed at fault."[10] Many, like Phillip Gibbs, a British War correspondent, noted the growing hatred of the men in the trenches for the staff officer. "They desired his death exceedingly . . . This hatred of the staff was stoked high by the fires of passion and despair."[11] In Germany too, the repressions of war produced inevitable hostilities turned back upon authority. Ernst Simmel insisted that this fund of repressed aggression found expression in the neurotic symptom, particularly in the symptom of mutism. Mutism and speech disorders were the most common symptoms of war neurosis, and Simmel argued that this was so because the soldier was required to be silent, to accept the often suicidal edicts of authority and to hold back or severely edit any expression of hostility toward those who kept him in a condition of mortal peril.[12] Rather than cursing, striking, or shooting his superior officer, he distorted his speech or completely denied himself that faculty. Support for this view was given, independently, by Frederick W. Mott, senior neurologist to Maudsley neurological clearing hospital during the war. Mott observed that "whereas mutism is common

among soldiers and noncommissioned officers, it is compara-
tively very rare in officers."[13]

The neurotic symptom, as all recognized, was a compromise.
With the symptom the soldier who was unable to tolerate any
longer the strains of war removed himself from the sphere of
military obedience to the more lenient sphere of medical obedience. To acknowledge the neurotic as a legitimate casualty of
war was to tacitly acknowledge the nature of the compromise
implicit in the symptom. Simmel, like many psychoanalysts,
argued that the neurosis should be ratified as a flight from the
war for the soundest political reasons. It was better to have the
power of command evaded through an individualized symptom
than challenged directly in mutiny. Behind the neurotic symptom lay more dangerous possibilities, a more permanent psychosis, or a direct challenge to the war and those continuing it.

Neurosis was functional for authorities precisely because it
provided a category for behavior that was fundamentally ambiguous in moral and legal terms. Within this category the unconscious wishes of the soldier and the imperatives of duty could be
negotiated with little permanent prejudice to the moral stature of
the patient and – more importantly—without calling into question the legitimacy of the war. George Stertz, like many German
neurologists, was quite aware of the value of this ambiguous category in removing potential sources of dissent from the front
lines. He treated a number of cases of what he called "eccentric
fanatics," patients whose eccentricities tended to assume a political form. A typical case involved K. K., a noncommissioned
officer and a volunteer of 1914, who wrote a letter to his commanding officer expressing sentiments against the war. This
earned him field punishment that was revoked due to "weakness
of the nerves." As Stertz summarized K. K.'s views: "the subor-
dinate is a slave in Germany . . . injustice without end . . . too
tired for hate and revenge."[14] Stertz found him to have strong
"paranoid fanatic traits" and recommended a period of treatment
and discharge from the army upon cure. It would seem here that
Stertz is illegitimately treating "political matters" as mental disease. But it is better to take a broader view. Neurosis was a functional category of behavior for authorities because it included
a very broad range of deviant behavior, the symptoms of which

could be treated. The very breadth of the category and its ambiguities (it sheltered potential revolt and indiscipline as well as psychosomatic disorders) made it an effective means of identifying disciplinary and morale problems, isolating the aberrant, and treating him on an individual basis in a medical rather than a judicial setting.

There was a general recognition on the part of medical officers that in administrating the ambiguities of neurosis and in judging the "legitimacy" of the symptom, they had assumed certain judicial and political functions. They were not just doctors curing disease, but spokesmen and executors of authority and officially sponsored views of the soldierly character. Inevitably this raised problems of conscience. William Bailey, a British psychiatrist, was not the only one in charge of the mental hygiene of the troops who asked whether it was right for a doctor – sworn to the alleviation of suffering – to inflict pain upon a patient to the point where he relinquished his symptom and returned to duty. He answered that, in the special circumstances of a war for civilization, the doctor had such a right. "In many patients persuasive measures are sufficient. But when they fail, disciplinary measures should be made available."[15] Neither was Bailey the only psychiatrist in uniform to qualify this prescription in the face of social realities. Officers, he recognized, were inappropriate subjects of disciplinary or "electrical" treatments because "the treatment of neurosis in officers is generally more difficult."[16]

The moral ambiguities of neurosis necessarily made the therapist's role ambiguous. He was to administer a "cure" that, if unsuccessful, became a "punishment." And yet it was recognized that the cure of neurosis was a very different matter than the cure of a physical wound. The task of the therapist was to induce the patient to resume his official, socially ratified, military role. The therapy subjected the patient to official views of himself and imposed painful sanctions upon him if he refused to accept that view. Often therapies even dispensed with the trappings of the "medical." Lortat-Jacobs reported that he had obtained good results in Paris with shell-shocked soldiers merely by appealing to the "individual's sense of honor and by publicly administering the oath."[17]

But there was a great deal of disagreement about *how* the soldier who had chosen the exit of neurosis was to be reacculturated to a role that common sense and a familiarity with the realities of war had caused him to reject. In the actual treatment of war neurosis one can identify two very different therapeutic scenes, two different techniques of domination, rooted in two different conceptual frameworks and visions of human nature. In "disciplinary" treatments the therapy served to dramatize and clarify the moral issues involved in the conflict between public duty and the private intentions of the patient. Disciplinary therapists operated with a traditionally moral – one might almost say "rhetorical" – scheme of human motives based upon long-established categories of virtues and vices.

The moral view of neurosis that fashioned disciplinary treatments contrasts sharply with the "analytic" view, which is best represented by, but by no means identical with, psychoanalysis. Those who used the analytic perspective saw the therapist's role as that of a "medium" of unconscious conflicts that were represented in the symptom. They operated with a view of the mind as a mechanism of opposed parts that processed – often below the level of consciousness – the needs of the individual and accommodated these needs to the imperatives of reality. Clearly the debates between disciplinary and analytical therapists neither began nor ended with the First World War. But the circumstances of war raised with particular urgency the issue of the adequacy, efficiency, and even the morality of the various techniques by means of which men were socialized to tasks that, by any objective estimate, were self-destructive. In the scene of therapy analysts were forced to reckon individual needs against social costs. In many instances this reckoning lead to an excruciating awareness of the human costs of war.

DISCIPLINARY THERAPY AND THE
MORAL VIEW OF NEUROSIS

Those who administered disciplinary therapies fashioned a therapeutic scene that closely resembled a judicial ordeal. "Moralists" like André Leri were particularly anxious to maintain the distinction between neuroses that had a physical cause in a fall or the explosion of a shell (commotional disorders) and those that had a purely psychic basis (emotional disorders). Only commotional disorders deserved the rights and privileges of disease. Emotional disorders should be dealt with in a disciplinary fashion, for they were rooted in the will of the patient rather than in the soma.

> After a severe emotional shock, accompanied or not by physical commotion or wounds, the brave soldier becomes a coward. He is shorn of his warrior courage. When he hears the guns he is afraid, trembles and can neither conquer nor hide his confusion.[18]

Leri, like many who served in the clearing stations directly behind the front, regarded men made neurotic in war as "moral invalids." By virtue of some inherited taint or familial degeneracy made overt in war, they had become incapable of controlling their fear. The war neurotic "can no longer resist victoriously the agony of the battlefield. He is a moral invalid, one wanting in courage."[19] This same view was expressed before the War Office committee, where E. MacPather testified that he could see no difference between shell-shock and cowardice: "Cowardice I take to mean action under the influence of fear, and the ordinary kind of shell-shock, to my mind, was chronic and persisting fear."[20]

Disciplinary therapists collapsed any distinction between legitimate neurosis and malingering. The legitimacy of the neurosis was tested in the therapy itself. Here the therapist determined the quantum of will that the patient had put at the disposal of his own desire for survival. The task of the therapist was to make the consequences of the symptom painful and to pursuade the patient to relinquish it and resume his official, soldierly, and manly function.

Too, those who took a moral view of war neurosis were inclined to read the symptom back into a biological or familial degeneracy. The neurotic symptom, which the war merely made overt, was rooted in inherited abnormalities. This tendency had two functions: It marked the neurotic soldier with a sign of moral inferiority; it removed the symptom from the context of the war, for now this context was only a severe test that brought out latent abnormalities. This view thus accorded with the prevailing Darwinian ideologies of war that saw war as a test of the "fitness" and survival power of nations as well as individuals. Of course the "latent" degeneracy was always found *after* it had become overt in the neurotic symptom. Laurent noted the frequency of "strange first names" in degenerate families. But he made this correlation only after a private, with the extraordinary name of Agapithe, had gone over the top and surrendered to the Germans, crying out, "Comrades, what difference does it make to me whether I am German or French? My officers are imbeciles that drink the blood of us unlucky ones."[21] When repatriated and institutionalized, the inherited taint that lurked behind his name was isolated and identified.

But even moralists were forced to recognize that combat in industrialized war overrode pre-existing adaptations or maladaptations. Soldiers with a history of previous emotional instability occasionally throve in the climate of war, while those with no previous history of mental illness broke down, and broke down in great numbers. Even when an inherited predisposition could be demonstrated, the conditions of war seemed to be the determining, even overdetermining cause of neurosis. Southard reports the case of a soldier whose family had a history of epilepsy. But it required two years of active service at the front, four wounds, the death of a father and five brothers and, finally, the experience of being buried three times in one day to make his epilepsy overt. In the only study of this question, Douglas Thom found that the incidence of poor inheritance among shell-shock victims was insignificant. "There is not a great deal of difference between those who broke down and those who carried on." He found that five percent of a sample of shell-shock victims had a history of neurosis in their families, while three to five percent of a control sample of "normal" soldiers had an equally "poor inheritance."[22]

The difference between the moral and the analytical perspectives can be seen most clearly in the question of malingering. From the moral point of view, neurosis was nothing but an evasion of duty that appropriated physical symptoms. In essence it was no different from going "sick," or working the system by simulating the symptoms of venereal disease. The sole difference between the outright malingerer and the neurotic was the ability of the latter to maintain his symptom under severe and painful treatment – a difference, in short, in the force of will the "true" neurotic had put into the project of escaping from the war. J. A. Secard distinguished in practice between two kinds of malingerers: the *simulateur de création* who pretended a symptom to escape death and the *simulateur de fixation* who fixed and maintained an initial neurotic symptom long after the condition had actually disappeared. Every genuine victim of shell-shock was a potential *simulateur de fixation* who, if he met with pity, attention, received the rewards of disease, would become incurable.[23] A. F. Hurst noted that strict simulation was very rare among soldiers, while the fixation, exaggeration, and prolongation of symptoms was very common.[24] In the British army it was quickly acknowledged as a mistake to send those suffering from shell-shock home, where the danger of the fixation of symptoms was much greater than if they remained in France.

The line between malingering and neurosis, the degree of malingering within the neurosis, was actually determined in the course of the disciplinary treatment. The methods of disciplinary therapy were many and were essentially the same in all belligerent armies. The *manière forte* and *torpillage* in the French army, the "quick cure" and "queen square" methods among the British, the Kaufmann technique in Austria, and the *Überrumplung* ("hustling") technique in Germany, all used principles and techniques derived from animal training: pain administered usually by an electrical apparatus, shouted commands, isolation, restricted diet with promise of relief upon abandonment of the symptom. Bellin and Vernet report on the disciplinary treatment of a *poilu* afflicted with hysterical deafness and aphonia. After being in several hospitals, the "front-cure" was tried. The patient was taken to a dugout near the front lines that was frequently shelled. He was given a subcutaneous injection of ether. "Such patients had always been cured, and a drug injected under the skin – not dangerous but extremely painful – would cure them." The patient lost his deafness but it recurred the next day. "He was given a half-hour to exercise his voice in and told that he must succeed unless he was a simulator."[25] Whereupon his deafness was cured, although for how long is not reported.

The Kaufmann method, which was played up in the Allied

press as yet another demonstration of German bestiality, was almost identical to "quick cure" methods used by the French and British. It combined powerful electrical shocks with shouted commands to perform certain exercises. Kaufmann kept up the treatment until the patient was cured, even if it took hours of treatment with progressively stronger electrical shocks. As with all disciplinary therapies, a great many cures were effected, although German critics pointed to the frequency of relapse, the number of patients who committed suicide upon cure, and the death of two patients in therapy as invalidating consequences of these kinds of cures.

According to Lewis Yealland, the most outspoken British proponent of disciplinary therapies, "electricity is the great sheet-anchor of treatment in these cases . . ."[26] Yealland was proud of the fact that he could cure cases of hysterical mutism that had lasted for months in a matter of minutes. One of Yealland's typical cases was that of a 24-year-old private who had been totally mute for nine months. The private had taken part in the retreat from Mons, the Battle of the Marne, Aisne, and the First and Second battles of Ypres. He had also fought at Hill 60, Neuve Chapelle, Loos, and Armentières. Sent to Salonica to take part in the Gallipoli expedition, he collapsed from the heat and woke up mute. His condition was particularly stubborn, having resisted many therapies, including the following:

> He had been strapped down in a chair for twenty minutes at a time while strong electricity had been applied to his neck and throat: lighted cigarette ends had been applied to the tip of his tongue and "hot plates" had been placed at the back of his mouth.[27]

Yealland insisted that such techniques had failed because they had not been applied with thoroughness and consistency, nor had they been combined with the properly authoritative attitude on the part of the therapist. He took the private into the darkened electrical room and locked the doors, informing the patient that he would not be permitted to leave until he acted normally. Electricity was applied for one hour, at the end of which the patient could say "ah." After two hours, the patient tried to get out of the room but could not. He signalled that he could tolerate no more electricity whereupon Yealland said: "Suggestions are not wanted from you. When the time comes for more electricity, you will be given it whether you want it or not."[28] He raised the voltage to very strong shocks and continued for a half hour until the spasms of the neck had disappeared and the patient could speak in a whisper with no spasms or stammer. Yealland, after curing the primary symptoms, often had enough time left for loose ends. To one patient he said: "You have not recovered yet; your laugh is most offensive to me; I dislike it very much indeed . . . you must be more rational." He left the room for five minutes and returned to find the patient "sober and rational."[29]

Yealland's administration of the disciplinary therapy was not unusual, nor did he consider it unnecessarily cruel.[30] From the moral perspective the scene of therapy could only be a place of judgment and ordeal. The target of the therapy was not so much the symptom itself as the will that the patient had put behind a presumed repudiation of his public role. The electrical apparatus was merely an instrument that tested the fixity of the symptom and determined whether the patient had irrevocably committed himself to private and selfish ends – his own survival. It determined whether the patient could be persuaded, once more, that the survival of the public self, the nation, was a more pressing obligation than the survival of his individual ego. The basic conflict in therapy was conceived as a moral conflict between private and public selves in which the therapist was responsible for the total, unremitting assertion of the demands of duty.

Disciplinary treatment was based upon a traditional ethic of honor, duty, a view of the human personality as director of a will that could be put at the service of either moral or immoral ends. These assumptions were general to the culture and suffused medical practice. There were many "unmedical" kinds of disciplinary treatment, just as neurophysicians recognized that there was much that was judicial and punitive in their own practice. But here again, the circumstances of war overrode any purely medical ethics. The very success of disciplinary therapies gave many professional neurophysicians pause. As Dr. Emil Redlich noted:

The therapeutic success which we have often attained in such cases gives much food for thought, for they can be explained less by any theoretical sophistication than through the energy, indeed the ruthlessness (the milieu and special circumstances of the time demand it) with which they are carried out.[31]

THE ANALYTIC TREATMENT

The criticism that analysts leveled at disciplinary treatment focused not upon the effectiveness but the humanity of its procedures. The cure effected by the moralists was ultimately destructive of the patient. Ernst Simmel pointed out that doctors who devise tortures to make the patient abandon his symptom unconsciously recognize the validity of Freudian theory. "They make a torture of the treatment in order to make the neurotic 'flee into health.' "[32]

The central proposition of analytical therapy in war, as in peace, removed the symptom from the moral arena. The neurosis was not the result of a conscious decision made by the patient. On the contrary, the neurotic soldier was one who could make no decision, who could repudiate neither his desire for survival nor the ideals and moral imperatives that kept him at the front. According to Simmel, both the "hero" and the "slacker"

> . . . are sound . . . unified personalities generated by war. Between them stands the victim of war neurosis. He has the egocentric valuation of his own existence of the malingerer and the altruistic sense of duty of the hero. Incapable of taking the consequences of drawing to one side or the other he "flees" into his illness.[33]

The neurotic was the man in the middle, the everyman. Where disciplinary therapists assumed the weakness of the neurotic's allegiance to duty, analysts tended to emphasize the strength of this commitment and the intensity of the conflict that it imposed upon those who wished to survive the war. A few studies of psychoneurotic veterans tend to bear out the analytic thesis.

Grace Massonneu, in her study of the social backgrounds of veterans in the psychiatric wards of U.S. Public Health Hospital No. 38, was struck by the fact that they had nothing in common but one thing: The overwhelming majority had been volunteers.[34] She thought it logical that men with a high sense of duty to the nation and often idealistic expectations of war would predominate among the "wounded without wounds."

If the moral view of neurosis collapsed any distinction between malingering and emotional disorders and shaped a fundamentally judicial therapeutic situation, the analytic view removed the proposition that underlay the disciplinary treatment. It made the symptom an expression not of the will of the patient but a sign of conflicts that were unconscious. Bernard Glueck went so far as to deny that malingering itself was a consciously chosen form of conduct. He asserted that "in the great majority of instances . . . [malingering] . . . is wholly determined by unconscious motives, by instinctive, biologic forces over which the individual has little or no control."[35] With the claim that the motives crystallized in the symptom were unconscious, analysts annihilated the factor of choice upon which the juridical concept of therapy had been based.

The treatment of the symptom as an expression of motives and experiences that were out of reach of the patient necessarily required a radically different scene of treatment. The symptom was viewed as the key symbol of an internal drama having a history going back to particularly traumatic events of war. The therapist functioned not as a protagonist asserting the moral imperatives shirked by the patient but as an "operator" of a patient who was his own oracle.

In analytic therapy hypnosis replaced the electrical apparatus. It is clear that hypnosis had certain "demand" characteristics in the hands of psychoanalytic therapists like Ernst Simmel. It was an instrument of behavioral control as authoritative and irresistible as the system of tortures fashioned by moralists.[36] The demand characteristics of hypnosis lay in the assumptions with which it was used: the patient would "regress" under hypnosis to *the* event or set of events that precipitated the symptom. The event would be reenacted in the presence of the therapist with all of the affect of its first occurrence. This reenactment would make available to the patient those motives that had become unavailable to him through the repression of his experience.

This kind of therapy was designed to frame and represent the motives conflicting in the symptom and is best illustrated by two cases treated by Ernst Simmel. One of his cases was a *Landstur-*

mann afflicted with tremors in his right arm and a pronounced tic in the left side of his face. Under hypnosis Simmel "placed him" at the front and asked him if he would like to go home. The *Landsturmann* answered, "No – I am no shirker." Simmel led him into battle and asked him if he still wanted to fight.

> A prompt, "yes!" Then I: "the devil, you can't fight. Your right hand is shaking too much. Why, then?" In a tormented voice he answered me: "I'd still like to save my life." Then I said, "your life is saved, you're home, come home." The shaking tremor and the tic disappeared.[37]

Simmel's treatment of the symptom as the symbol of an event, an event in the past that was unconscious and therefore outside of any moral or immoral intentions, is exemplified in his treatment of a Private B., who was afflicted with tremors of the hands and periodic epileptic rigidity. The two symptoms seemed quite distinct, and Simmel thought that they might be imitations of distinctly different events and motives. Under hypnosis B. was asked to relive the precipitating occasion of the second symptom, the complete rigidity of the entire body. B. enacted a Russian attack in which he was cut off. His lieutenant ran away. He had thought: "Nothing will happen to me if I'm dead. The Russians will let me lie." He then assumed the rigidity of a dead man. When he was instructed to recite the setting of the first symptom, the tremors of the right hand, B. told of seeing a doctor in a hospital and wanting to kill him. Simmel asked, "Why the spasm?" and B. replied, "So that I don't do it."[38]

Analysts understood the symptom as a mimetic fragment, the imitation of an action that had great emotional significance to the actor, but there were various degrees of sophistication used in locating the reality behind the symptom. It was not uncommon to find a simple, one-to-one equation drawn between the symptom and its cause.

> Thus a soldier who bayonets an enemy in the face develops an hysterical tic of his facial muscles; abdominal contractions occur in men who have bayonetted enemies in the abdomen; hysterical blindness follows particularly horrible sights; hysterical deafness appears in men who find the cries of the

wounded unbearable and the men detached to burial parties develop anasmia.[39]

Ferenczi and others objected to this kind of simplified equation between the symptom and the event, with its inherently naturalistic biases. To see the symptom as the crystallization of a particularly traumatic event was to miss the importance of the day-to-day climate of warfare. Ferenczi insisted that rarely can the symptom be traced to a single traumatic instance. It is the representation of motives that are consistently in conflict within the environment inhabited by the neurotic. Thus the dragging foot, a common symptom of war neurosis, could not be interpreted as the representation of a time when the individual was caught in the mud or the like. It was the representation of the fundamental psychic state of the combatant who was impelled forward by a sense of duty, obligation, or fear of the authorities while restrained by barely controllable fear of death.[40] The halting gait was the physical representation of the psychic situation of the nightmare, the feeling of being "rooted to the spot" by opposed and conflictual wishes. According to Freud, anxiety neuroses often appear with the first attempts to move toward the setting in which the individual experiences intense anxiety. These places may be generalized in the form of phobias or they may be avoided by the simple measure of blocking out movement or motor functions of specific kinds. Erben tells of patients who were prevented from going forward by violent attacks of tremors, but who could accomplish the much more demanding task of going backwards with little or no difficulty.

At bottom both analysts and moralists attempted, through therapy, to bring the soldier back to a realization of his responsibilities as a citizen and soldier, even though they used very different methods. Both were involved in giving overt expression to the internalized expectations of the soldier's proper role in war. Therapists, whether of disciplinary or analytical persuasion, used coercion to force the neurotic soldier to understand the proper priorities between private intentions and public imperatives. The only difference – and it was fundamental – between disciplinarians and analysts was that the latter used an approach to deviance in which the moral imperative was lacking. Thus, the moral issue ceased to be one that was dramatized in the scene of therapy itself and became an issue appropriate to the context of the war in general. In analytical therapy both patient and therapist were brought to consider the moral and psychic implications of the continuing slaughter. Analysts were much more aware of the human costs of war and tended to raise, implicitly, the issue of who should bear these costs, the society or the individual.

Behind the treatment of the psychic victim of war lay the question of the tolerability of the war itself. Was this industrialized war and its scale of technologically administered violence beyond mere human endurance? If the answer was "yes," then neurosis was an inevitable, even normal consequence of the enormous, invisible threats focused upon those huddled in the trench system. Or was this a war like any other, on a much grander scale, and the shell-shocked soldier merely an individual who had failed the ordeal that his comrades and soldiers in previous wars had survived? The nature of the war became one of the key elements in the evaluation of the legitimacy of neurosis as an exit from the labyrinth of the trenches.

IMMOBILITY, NEUROSIS, AND REGRESSION

Many, both therapists and frontsoldiers, took the position that modern war pushed men beyond the boundaries of their endurance. It was thus difficult to hold the patient responsible for his own illness. Neurosis was, in short, the logical and necessary outcome of the realities of modern combat. The level and scale of mechanized, impersonal violence were uniquely destructive of the psychic defenses of combatants. Equally destructive was the consciousness that war was not a "natural" but a "man-made" disaster, that there was a human agency behind the "implacable mechanisms" that held the frontsoldier immobile and passive, vulnerable to the impacts of shells. War was a matrix of interpersonal motives, whatever the appearance of things; and the death of the soldier, his mutilation, or dismemberment was the outcome of these motives, not of the will of God or nature. Always the randomness of death at the front, the impersonality of violence, was qualified by the recognition that it was men who were operating these machines, men who made and continued the war, men who sought the death of the immobilized men in the trenches. This combination of the impersonality, randomness, and human agency behind the mechanized violence of war was uniquely destructive of the psychic defenses of combatants. Robert Graves insisted that every man who spent more than three months under fire could legitimately be considered neurasthenic. Professional medical men often agreed. One Doctor Hurst, a medical officer during the Gallipoli campaign, claimed that "every man coming out of the Peninsula was neurasthenic, whether he was supposed to be fit or not . . . all were in a condition of profound neurasthenia."[41] One witness before the War Office committee flatly stated, "Under conditions such as existed in France it is inevitable for the man to break down at some time or another."[42]

The most significant variable in the incidence of neurosis was not the character of the soldier but the character of the war. When the war again became a war of movement with the German offences of 1918, even though the fighting was intense and exhausting, the incidence of war neurosis dropped dramatically. It was generally recognized that neurosis was germane to trench warfare and the peculiar emotional states that were generated by stable, seige war. It was precisely the immobilization of combat that seemed to be the most basic underlying reality of the neurotic symptom.

> Experience has shown that a high degree of nervous tension is commonest among men who have . . . to remain inactive while being shelled. For the man with ordinary self-control this soon becomes a matter of listening with strained attention for each approaching shell, and speculating how near it will explode; and behind this thought looms another, namely, how many seconds before he will be blown to pieces. An hour or two of this strain is more than most men can stand.[43]

Psychic defenses were erected against the specific realities of industrialized war just as neurosis, when examined in detail, seemed to be the result of the immobilization of combat. The immobility of war seemed to cause not only overt pathologies but a covert psychic regression that could be seen even in "normal" soldiers. The connections between an immobilized war that represented the "triumph of modern industrialization," neurosis, and regression are best illustrated by a study of W. H. R. Rivers. In his examination of the incidence of neurosis in the air corps, Rivers found that the quantity of neurotic symptoms correlated not with the intensity of battle, the length of an individual's service, or his emotional predisposition, but with the degree of his immobility. In the air corps, as in the trenches, neurosis was a function of the fixity and not the intensity of battle. Rivers learned that pilots, men with some active control over their fate, had the fewest cases of mental breakdown. Observers were much more vulnerable to neurosis. In the balloon service, where men were tethered above the front to offer excellent stationary targets to enemy fliers and artillery, psychic casualties outnumbered physical wounds. This was the only branch of service in which this was so.[44]

Rivers argued that a man's most rational response to anxiety is some kind of manipulative activity. It is through this activity that he acquires a sense of himself as an autonomous actor in a world of instrumentalities. This sense of the manipulability of things, the "technological spirit," and the "health" of the individual who regards himself as the author of his own acts are closely linked. If his ability to manipulate the world is impaired, his sense of autonomy is radically diminished and "you have a prominent condition for the occurrence of neurosis in some form or another."[45] It is ironic that "technological warfare" created the conditions in which men were deprived of their most rational and manipulative defenses against fear. This loss necessarily entailed a regression toward magic, animism, and neurosis. Even more significantly, in this war, this regression must be regarded as a "normal" process experienced by many combatants who did not appear in the psychiatric wards with an incapacitating neurosis.

Immobility created the conditions in which men were forced to process and deal with their fears. The repression of fear was, as most analysts recognized, the root of the neurotic symptom. But neurosis was not the outcome of simple "natural" fear, the kind of "cowardice" treated in disciplinary therapies, but an "educated" fear schooled and modified by the realities of war. Perhaps the best description, by a layman, of the stages through which the anxieties of combatants evolved is that of J. F. C. Fuller. Testifying before the War Office committee, he noted that the fear of combatants went through at least three permutations.

> I have noticed that the normal healthy man arriving from England showed definite signs of physical fear when first coming under fire. This fear very shortly wore off and was replaced by a type of callousness which sometimes increased until a man took very little trouble to protect himself. I noticed in several cases that when this condition was well advanced a man became liable to breakdown mentally or to show a nervousness which may be defined rather as mental terror rather than physical fear. What I noticed was that first of all the man was healthily afraid of what was happening, then he became callous, and after that he sometimes became obsessed with fear.[46]

But what precipitated this process was not "sudden" traumatic danger but "prolonged danger in a static position, where the man cannot get away from it."[47] The same process was identified, in quite different terms, by Sandor Ferenczi while he was working with psycho-neurotic soldiers in the Maria-Valeria Barracks hospital in Budapest during 1915. He suggested that the combatant's encounter with the superior technological forces of war precipitated a disastrous decline in the soldier's self-esteem. The most normal response to the unquestionable superiority of the forces of steel and chemicals, forces that deprived the men in the trenches of any active defense of themselves, was regression and psychic retreat. "Libido withdraws from the object into the ego, enhancing self-love and reducing object love to the point of indifference."[48] The indifference toward his own safety that Fuller noted in the veteran of trench warfare, the "callousness" that many saw in veterans, Ferenczi saw evidenced in the sexual impotence or strongly retarded sexual desires of his patients. Almost all the patients in the neurological section of his hospital complained at some time or another "about their entirely dammed up, or very strongly retarded, sexual libido and potency."[49] In another quarter, on the western front, Lissman noted the same phenomenon. The war with its combination of terror and abstinence, its industrial discipline unrelieved by leisure or regular sexual activity, produced widespread impotence even in normal soldiers. "In the field not a few officers and men of previously sound nerves complained that at the beginning of their leave an erection was either completely lacking or very often extremely defective."[50] Ferenczi regarded this impotence that, in a few cases, lasted long into peacetime, as the most obvious sign of the ways in which war forced the withdrawal of libido from the objective world, the "internalization" of self, an increase in "narcissistic libido."

The callousness of the veteran, his "indifference," seemed to many to be evidence of the pathologies acquired in war, pathologies noted by combatants themselves. It is described by Ernst Simmel as a "narrowing and supression of consciousness" that was the first stage of war neurosis. He regarded the suppression of conscious functions, the elimination of libidinal ties to the world, as an inevitable response to the environment of war. But the effect of this repression is to make the environment of war "unreal" and magical, peopled by forces that cannot be manipulated but only propitiated by the "spells and formulae" used by Carrington. The loss of the sense of what is rightly to be feared, the loss of what Plato defined as "courage," served to magnify and generalize fears to the entire landscape of the front. It is a mistake to regard the fabled "callousness" of the veteran as invulnerability to fear. It is best understood as Fuller and Ferenczi describe it, as a stage in a process that translates "rational" fear into ceaseless, total dread, objectifiable only as a malevolent "giant who pounds the earth with blind hammers." The linking of callousness or indifference to the world with an expanded area of self-love or narcissism is epitomized in Gorch Jachs's description of himself as a combination of "steel-hard nerves" and the "weakest, most pitying heart in the world." William Maxwell summarized his conclusions on the psychic effects of war in terms that closely resemble those used by Ferenczi and Fuller.

> Negative self-feeling was . . . a common emotional state in
> circumstances which made one conscious of one's own per
> sonal impotence and individual unimportance. Given a man in
> whom such a feeling was aroused in reference to some "power

not himself" the sentiment in which it would become organized would not be religion . . . but a fatalism which tended
toward complete indifference.[51]

The increased narcissism, the expanded self-love, which
Ferenczi noted in the psychic victims of war and saw as the result
of the retreat from the threatening world of mechanism, provided one of the strongest and most "positive" bonds that survived the war, the bond of the individual to the men of his unit.
Too, this regression produced a body of men with an enormous
need for care and reassurance, a need combined with anger and
hostility toward the society that had placed them in the position
of victims. This combination of motives explained to many observers the most surprising fact of the war neuroses: their longevity. From 1916 to 1920 four percent of the 1,043,653 British
casualties were psychiatric cases.[52] Little more than a decade after
the war, in 1932, a full thirty-six percent of the veterans receiving
disability pensions from the British government were listed as
psychiatric casualties of the war.[53] Paradoxically enough, "war"
neurosis was a condition more prevalent in "peace" than in war.
A similar phenomenon was noted in other formerly belligerent
countries. In 1942, twenty-four years after the conclusion of the
Great War, Douglas Thom noted that fifty-eight percent of all the
patients being cared for in veterans' hospitals in the United States
(68,000 men) were neuropsychiatric casualties of World War
One.[54] Unkind critics thought that once war neurosis had succeeded in its primary aim, removal of the soldier from war, the
symptom appropriated another aim that made it "functional" in
peacetime – the pursuit of compensation and care. More objective critics recognized that the "maladaptations" of industrial
war could very easily become the "maladaptations" of individuals in industrial society.
    The neuroses of war contained a number of lessons for psychi-
atrists. Psychoanalytically oriented therapists were forced to
abandon, temporarily, many of their most cherished tenets and
to recognize that the uniqueness of combat could override the
predispositions of childhood, that the repression of fear could
constitute a more powerful engine of neurosis than the repression
of sexuality. But perhaps the most significant lesson of the war

neurosis was that it was not unique to war, nor was it an "expression" of individual drives and impulses. On the contrary, the most lasting pathologies of war represented the consequences that result when the individual loses his sense of himself as an autonomous actor in a manipulable world.

WAR NEUROSIS IN POSTWAR SOCIETY

During the war therapists agreed that war neurosis was a functional neurosis with a "limited" aim – the removal of the soldier from an intolerable reality. Analytic therapists occasionally diagnosed a patient as suffering from "only the war" and assumed that with the end to hostilities the symptom would disappear, for its explicit aim would no longer be functional. Kurt Singer, a director of the neuropsychiatric ward of a Berlin hospital, saw his wards emptied in November 1918. When, in 1920, he was asked by Berlin health officials why successful cures of war neurosis had diminished so radically, he answered that cures "are not as good and less frequent because there are no more neurotics."[55] He was exaggerating to show a point. With the beginning of the revolution, twenty patients abandoned the ward without leave, six asked for immediate release, and the remaining ten stayed, Singer suspected, only because they were waiting for warmer weather. The revolution had apparently set aside those conditions in which nervous disorders were functional.

> The Revolution itself terminated the need for the neurotic complex as a protest of the inferior, the suppressed, the subordinated, precisely for that class of men who made up the main contingent of neurotics – the uniformed working proletariat. Those compensations for the feelings of inferiority, defenses against medical opinions, flight into illness . . . were, suddenly, no longer necessary once the existing power relations were so radically transformed.[56]

The absorption of the war into revolution had done two things. It deprived the doctor of his extraordinary powers, the authority he had used to make the illness more painful and immediate than the threat of death in the trenches. "Active therapy was indeed a disguised form of orders and the execution of orders."[57] The end of the war also removed the conditions in which the compromise of neurosis was necessary and functional. In revolution the neurotic could take up arms against those who had ruled him in war. It was not the soldier who was vulnerable now but the apparatus of command that had precipitated the conflict between the survival of the soldier and the fulfillment of his moral obligations. In 1921 Freud repeated the established opinion: "Most of the neurotic diseases which had been brought about by the war disappeared with the cessation of the war conditions."[58]

But within eight years medical authorities learned that they had been too hasty in celebrating the end to war neurosis. The psychoneurotic diseases of war proved to be more enduring, and more expensive to treat, than physical ailments. The pathologies generated by war continued to fill the wards of veterans' hospitals. But just as often these pathologies did not appear in the medical statistics, for they were worked out in offices, households, taverns, and the political arena. Phillip Gibbs, who had hoped that the returning frontsoldiery would lead a movement for national revitalization in England, was forced to recognize that the characteristic readiness for violence of the veteran was inherently apolitical, something that originated in a very deep psychic injury.

> Something was wrong. They put on civilian clothes again and looked to their mothers and wives very much like the young men who had gone to business in the peaceful days before August 1914. But they had not come back the same men. Something had altered in them. They were subject to queer moods and queer tempers, fits of profound depression alternating with a restless desire for pleasure. Many were easily moved to passion where they lost control of themselves, many were bitter in their speech, violent in opinion, frightening.[59]

Robert Graves was much more blunt. What smothered the threat of revolution that the "fighting forces constituted" in 1919 was neither governmental repression nor political co-option, but the "nervous instability" shared by everyone who had spent more than six months under fire. "In most cases the blood was not running pure again for four or five years: and in numerous cases men who had managed to avoid a nervous breakdown during the war collapsed badly in 1921 or 22."[60] While the anger, bitterness, sense of victimization, and familiarity with weapons made the ex-soldier seem a figure with an apparently portentious political destiny, his characteristic neurosis made him – Graves feels – a very bad revolutionary. It was clear that the aberrancies of war would work themselves out in peacetime, often invisibly, outside of the public sphere. Howland believed that aggressions bottled up in the war would inevitably find other targets. "I do not think it will be necessary to remind the returned soldier that 'to spare the rod is to spoil the child,' it is more likely he will spoil the rod."[61] Indeed, through the rod, war neurosis could be transmitted from father to son, as Lidz found out when he learned that one of his patients in the South Seas in 1943, a soldier afflicted with acute panic and severe nightmares, had a father who had been shell-shocked in the First World War. His patient's father had returned home a "useless and cruel man," who kept his home in constant turmoil and was, at times, "out of his mind."[62]

It had been expected that neurotic symptoms originating in the trenches would be "conserved" in peacetime. But what was not expected was that a number of soldiers who had not been hospitalized during the war broke down after the conclusion of hostilities. An American, Roy Grinker, wrote of psychoneurotic veterans of the First World War:

> To our astonishment the majority of the neuroses that are hospitalized today in the convalescent hospitals are people who have developed either the first signs of their neurosis on return to this country or have become worse after landing on these shores.[63]

The war neurosis that appeared in peacetime was something more than a transference of aims from a search for an exit from war to a search for compensation and security. The initial encounter with the home was often disillusioning for men who had served in the war, and this disillusionment could precipitate severe nervous disorders. In combat the soldier had often idealized the home, and this ideal home was an important defense against the dissonances and humiliations of war. As Franz Schauwecker noted, the sentimentalization of the home was an inevitable process in the trenches. "Front and Home – between them arched the rainbow of yearning, bridging everything and tolerating only thoughts, no words."[64] The idealization of the "men and things of the past," those scenes and people that came to seem ever more distant in the trenches, preserved some sense of a possible continuity and sameness, some hope for a unified identity. These idealizations often shattered under the impact of demobilization, unemployment, poverty, and the sheer strangeness of what was once familiar. This last disillusionment often released anxieties that had been kept under control during the war itself, tapping funds of repressed anger and bitterness accumulated during the long years in the trench system. With the collapse of the idealized home went not just an entertaining vision, but an image of a secure self and a solid identity. If the home provided a residence for fantasies of security and esteem, a defense against the realities of war and the sense of inferiority, degradation, and impotence imposed by these realities, then the collapse of the image of the home was the removal of the last defense against a painful consciousness of what, exactly, the soldier had been in war. Disillusionment with the home could produce the "1916 fixation" noted in himself by Charles Carrington. The encounter with the home, paradoxically enough, could lead to a counter-idealization of the war that had just been fought, to an idealization of "comradeship," military life, and the simplicities of war.

A quite different issue was raised by the fact that among veterans psychoses actually increased in absolute terms throughout the 1920s. More pensions for psychotic illnesses were granted by the British government in 1929 than had been granted in the four years immediately after the war.[65] Except for organic heart disease, this was the only category of war-caused illness that rose steeply throughout the decade. During the war Simmel recognized that neurosis not only provided an exit from the trenches but that it protected the soldier from a more permanent psychosis. The neurosis was a way-station on the road to a more fundamental break with reality. While the war was going on it appeared that the large numbers of neuroses had a great deal to do with the surprisingly few psychoses of combat. In peacetime this ratio was reversed.

The encounter with the home might collapse the last, saving

reality. There are numerous examples of men coming home either "normal" or with a slight hysteria to end up, four years later, as schizophrenics. Walter Riese, for example, treated a former corporal in the German army who fought through the entire war and returned in 1918 with a slight, generalized nervous condition. In the next three years the condition of Corporal L. worsened. He was institutionalized and became a terror to doctors and patients in his hospital. His physical symptoms ranged from a partial paralysis of the left arm to verbal and conceptual difficulty, lack of spontaneity and initiative, stiff posture, a spasmodic baring of the teeth, and sudden outbreaks of aggression – all the signs of schizophrenia. Riese could find no evidence of nervous instability in L. before his war experience and concluded that the war was responsible for his illness even though he had experienced nothing abnormally traumatic at the front.[66] P. Reichardt, too, believed that the war was the most significant factor in the rise, immediately after the armistice, in the number of cases of schizophrenia. His belief, like that of Riese, was based upon his clinical practice.

But a final break with reality was not the normal response of men who had seen their own sense of their value shattered in war. Much more common was the search for compensation, or the blank repudiation and repression of the experience of war. Those who repressed their war experience followed the advice most commonly given to frontsoldiers, that they should "forget." This was the reaction of Pierre Van Paassen:

> I had the feeling . . . that I had been the victim of an enormous nonsense . . . I was going to forget the nightmare, burn my uniform as soon as I would be finally discharged, throw away my badges and tokens into Lake Ontario, and efface every trace of my shame and humiliation.[67]

This reaction was also that of Siegfried Sassoon and many others whose "minds were still out of breath and [whose] inmost thoughts [were] in disorderly retreat from the bellowing darkness and men dying out in shell-holes."[68] W. H. R. Rivers believed that the most distressing and protracted symptoms of war neurosis were not necessarily the result of massive trauma, but of attempts to "banish from the mind" distressing memories of war. In effect the repression of the war experience prolonged the memories of war, maintained the affect of those memories, and ensured that veterans, long after the silencing of the guns, would be constantly occupied with *not* "hearing" them.[69] The fear of remembering fixed the minds of veterans upon the war and ensured that the war experience would retain a subjective reality long after the trenches were, once again, farmlands. Siegfried Sassoon was well aware that the repression of war experience could lead to an obsession with that experience.

> It's bad to think of war
> When thoughts you've gagged all day come back to scare you;
> And it's been proved that soldiers don't go mad
> Unless they lose control of ugly thoughts
> That drive them out to jabber among the trees.[70]

But Sassoon also realized that soon enough the war experience would be processed, ideologically integrated, and masked by soothing commonplaces:

> They'll soon forget their haunted nights; their
> Cowed
> Subjection to the ghosts of friends who died, –
> Their dreams that drip with murder; and they'll be
> Proud
> Of glorious war that shattered all their pride . . .[71]

The signs of the repression of the war experience can even be found in the literary fate of the war. Very few war books were published in the 1920s. This period William Karl Pfeiler considered a "latency period" in which an experience that was too destructive of individual and collective selfhood was "forgotten" to be resurrected later in more "acceptable" form. "The war had been driven from the surface of the consciousness in German Society during the first ten years of the Republic, and the Versailles Treaty had taken its place."[72] The trickle of war literature that was published in the decade after the war became, in 1929, a flood that continued through the 1930s. During the decade of the Depression memoires, novels, collections of letters, diaries dealing with the war experience became an extremely popular genre. Charles Carrington thought he understood why the repression of the war experience and the "silence" of the veteran was ended. The Depression had closed the gap between civilian and ex-soldier that had seemed unbridgeable throughout the 1920s. Now, the population as a whole was victimized, reduced to a level of abjectness and dependence with which the former front-soldier could immediately identify. In presenting the details of his "shame and humiliation" to a civilian audience he was, on the other hand, sketching the outlines of an industrial world that had reduced men to microcosmic proportions, to a level that could not be attained in civilian life, even in the conditions of economic collapse.[73] The image of an industrial holocaust was both a comfort and a caution to civilians who had experienced their own disillusionment with an apparently secure industrial world.

6. The Veteran Between Front and Home

COMRADESHIP AND VIOLENCE

Throughout this study I have been concerned with the experience of the First World War as a modernizing experience, an experience in which men who knew that they were living in an "industrial age" learned what that meant in military terms. If the war was a modernizing experience it was so because it fundamentally altered traditional sources of identity, age-old images of war and men of war. The Great War was a nodal point in the history of industrial civilization because it brought together material realities and "traditional" mentalities in an unexpectedly disillusioning way. On the one hand the war deserves the title of the first truly modern war for in it and through it the nature and scale of modern industry was asserted in the most unmistakable and belligerent terms. On the other hand it was a war that mobilized a logic that was deeply rooted in European culture, a logic that asserted the social and existential "otherness" of war as an alternative and a curative to life in civil society. The assumption of the polarity of peace and war was, in 1914, the main ingredient in the widespread affirmation of war as a means of transcending social and economic contradictions. But the disillusioning realization of the inherent similitude of industrial societies and the wars they wage – something that is a commonplace to us – eviscerated, drained, and confounded the logic upon which the moral significance of war and the figure of the warrior had been based. "Total war" was nothing but the assertion that there was no such thing as two realities, two sets of rules, two levels upon which life might be lived and experienced. In war combatants learned that there is *only* an industrial world, the reality of which defined them in war much more than it had in peace. In the trenches men learned that mechanized destruction and industrial production were mirror images of each other.

This clash between traditional images of war and the realities of war continued in the character and behavior of veterans of the First World War. The veteran is a traditional figure, a role at least as old as written literature. Conventionally he is an initiated man who carries within him an experienced knowledge of the fragility of his own substance and humanity. The figure of the veteran is a subcategory of what might be called the "liminal type." He derives all of his features from the fact that he has crossed the boundaries of disjunctive social worlds, from peace to war, and back. He has been reshaped by his voyage along the margins of civilization, a voyage in which he has been presented with wonders, curiosities, and monsters – things that can only be guessed at by those who remained at home.

All of these features can be found in Ernst von Salomon's description of the returning German soldiery, a description that – with all its gothic features – could stand as a portrayal of any soldiery returning, defeated, from the land of battles.

> The eyes lay deep under the shadow of the helmet rim, embedded in dark-grey, sharply edged hollows; these eyes glanced neither right nor left. Ever straight ahead as if fixed upon a terrible goal, as if peering over a torn-up ground from out of clay holes and trenches – before them free space. They spoke no word. . . .
>
> The emaciated, unmoving faces beneath the steel helmets, the bony limbs, the decayed, dusty uniforms! Stride on stride they marched past, and around them was an infinite void. Yes, it was as if they drew around themselves a magic circle in

which – invisible to the eyes of the uninitiated – dangerous powers, secret beings worked.[1]

Salomon, as a young naval cadet, had just missed getting into the fighting. He suffered no disillusionment and was able to draw upon all the sources of mystification that surround the figure of the veteran, the initiate of death, the man of dangerous powers. The veteran is a man defined and refined by war, stripped of every social superfluity, stripped to his essence.

These qualities are not unique to the figure of the veteran. The features that have traditionally defined the veteran character are also those that have been ascribed, in folk-tales throughout the world, to all professional travelers: the itinerant actor, the wandering blacksmith, the conjurer and mountebank, the peripatetic merchant, preacher, and mendicant. These are the figures who are at home between the boundaries of settled societies, the figures that practice transformations upon themselves, roles, metals, values, spiritual and physical states. Those at home both fear the power generated in these transformations and desire to attach this power for domestic use. The "liminal type" has always provided the ground upon which those at home project their ambivalence toward the social order they inhabit: their fear of disorder and their fear of petrifaction. The veteran, like those other liminal figures formed on the boundaries of domestic life, embodies the anxieties, acts out the guilts, and attenuates the boredom native to domesticity.

In essence the traditional figure of the veteran is derived from everything that is presumed to lie "outside" the boundaries of domestic existence. What is thought to lie outside is usually a function of how people experience the social structure in which they live. Different views of the veteran and his political intentions after 1919 reflect not different views of the war but different conceptualizations of the social order. Those, both socialists and conservatives, who conceived of modern society in terms of estrangement, privatization, self-interest, and class conflict saw the veteran as a "comrade," a man of community. He had been formed amidst the "natural" solidarities that underlay the artificial divisions of class and status. He thus constituted the best hope for a resolution to those tensions that defined capitalist society. Those, on the other hand, who conceived of society in terms of "civilization," as a structure of morally necessary restraints, inhibitions, and controls upon "primitive" asocial instincts, saw war as an arena of instinctual liberation. The figure educated in this arena was necessarily someone who had been primitivized, barbarized, and infantilized, demoted on the scales that measure and define civilized adulthood. The veteran, with his dangerous powers and his penchant for violence, was a threat to the society of his origins. He was someone who had to be reintegrated, reacculturated, reeducated.

Ex-soldiers returning from the front found their way into society by using these traditional definitions of the veteran character. But they used these definitions of their selves not as an assertion of a newly acquired, positive dignity, but as a way of compensating themselves for their exploitation, their victimization, their demotion from "heroes" to eminently superfluous men used up by an industrialized war.

Both images – that of the comrade, the communal man, and the man of violence – were functional. Ex-soldiers could use the image of the man of community to assert their superiority to civilian politicians who acted as if the machinery of communal life was simply a means for the prosecution of class interests. The veteran could claim to best represent the whole of the nation for he had "sacrificed himself" for the survival of the community. As a man who had lived for years in No-Man's-Land, he knew the nation and its pathologies from an exterior perspective. The ex-soldier could also act within the image of the man of violence, the individual intolerant of all civilized restraints. He could, and did, use this image to extort the care, esteem, and support normally due those who had sacrificed their self-interest, their private egos in defense of the whole. Normally these alternatives were asserted by civilians and veterans as "effects" that the war had upon combatants, ways in which the experience of war changed the character of the soldier. But it is better to view these traditional images of the liminal type as a means of communication and negotiation between civilians and men who had been socially, psychologically, and physically abused and, in the process, had become strange to themselves as well as others. In

Ernst H. Posse's description of those ex-soldiers who joined the political *Kampfbunde* in Germany, one can see both of these images of the veteran character at work.

> As a man released from his social past, a man from a particular class or estate who had become a comrade, the frontsoldier offered a unique sociological phenomenon. His ideology inclined him toward the notion of class harmony rather than toward class affiliation . . . But he had behind him a life of activity and struggle which inclined him to deeds and the gratification of his desires . . . A portion of the frontsoldiery was inclined to join any movement that permitted him to continue the adventurousness of his former life, either because of subjective reasons or because he could no longer attach himself to any vocational activity.[2]

Posse, like others who were interested in the political role of the returning frontsoldiery, had difficulty in unravelling their political motives. They were "comrades," men of community, and thus inclined toward "class peace." Thus, they might be expected to play a conservative part in the reconstruction of Germany. On the other hand they were accustomed to violence and to "the gratification of their desires," and thus potential enlistees in any kind of political adventure, whether revolutionary or reactionary. Another version of the veteran as "comrade" lay in the assertion that the frontsoldiery constituted a "new proletariat" of "instinctive" socialists. Phillip Gibbs saw them in this light. The frontsoldiery had been divorced from civil society by the war while demobilization had placed them back in civil society. They were a group whose grievances were universal because their sufferings had been unimaginable. They were men who no longer enjoyed a secure civil status and were completely opposed to the assumptions of the statesmen who had fed them into the maw of war. The war constituted, for the soldiery, a fundamental break with the past.

> More died [at the front] than the flower of our youth and German manhood. The old order of the world died there, because many men who came alive out of that conflict were changed and vowed not to tolerate a system of thought which had led

to such a monstrous massacre of human beings who prayed to the same God, loved the same joys of life, and had no hatred of one another except as it had been lighted and inflamed by their governors.[3]

Unlike a traditional proletariat the returning frontsoldiery were "highly organized, disciplined . . . trained to fight."[4] At least in Germany, they were also armed. Moritz Liepmann, in his study of the relationship between the war and postwar criminal statistics, noted with alarm that 1,895,052 rifles, 8,452 machine guns, and 4,000 trench mortars had been "lost" by the army on retreat.[5]

It was common to find the assertion that the propertiless soldier, wedded to his comrades and estranged from bourgeois society, was an "instinctive" socialist. The frontsoldiery were socialists, according to Hans Zehrer, "not because they understood Marx, but because they . . . felt social injustice deeply and could thus understand the justification for the social resentment that lived within the working class."[6] The soldiery had learned their socialism not from books but from the dramatic structures of war. The experienced nature of their social knowledge gave their stance toward established political orders a different moral weight than the criticism of intellectuals. Emilio Lussu, an Italian socialist and veteran of the war, makes this claim for the Italian frontsoldiery: "The veterans were philosocialists, not because they were familiar with the classics of socialism, but because of their profound internationalism and their hunger for land."[7] Otto Braun, a student volunteer, then junior officer who died at the front in 1918, also believed that the men in the trenches had become socialists. But he – correctly, I think – stressed the negative, "reactionary" nature of this socialism.

> Any leaning the soldier may have toward socialism is, after all, mainly negative. He is furious with the whole rotten bourgeois society, furious with the stay-at-homes, in fact furious with everything at home. I see no signs of constructive political ideas . . . [When the soldiers return] . . . there will be a great amount of knowledge and a consciousness of power in back of them. In order to guide these masses into the paths of productive activity, one will have to know and be able to direct their gigantic mass of uncontrolled energy.[8]

Braun introduces a number of important qualifications into the characterization of the frontsoldiery as a new proletariat of instinctive socialists. True, the war had radically severed the soldier from his society and generated in him a profound sense of anger. This anger, fury, and violence came from a sense of being the victim of a profound injustice. But the experience of war did not provide its participants with a new vision of community, the realization of which would transform existing political and social arrangements. The "experience of comradeship" was identical in many ways with the anti-bourgeois attitudes of the proletariat. But the war, a "silent teacher," had not provided combatants with an ideology that would provide a common ground and basis of appeal to diverse social groups. The frontsoldier had been stripped of ideologies and this made him "silent," a man of deeds rather than words. If, as Braun insists, the war had provided the soldier with a consciousness of power, it must be recognized that this consciousness had little in common with political power. On the contrary, it was a consciousness appropriate to functionaries, to instruments of command, to men who had survived as passive sufferers of the "will of war." In 1926, Ernst Jünger was one of those who called for veterans to become political activists. And yet, when it comes time to describe this activism, it appears to be little more than a translation of the soldier's place in the war. In peace, as in war, he was to become an instrument of some mysterious, unspecified fate.

> The concept of power can only be realized in the idea of a leader. But the great leader has not yet appeared. His appearance is equivalent to an act of nature. It cannot be taken for granted or influenced by any expedients. To prepare the way, however, that is the task of the frontsoldiery. It consists of removing our inner dissensions, in the clarification of our thought . . . and in the consolidation of ourselves into a disciplined instrument of power with which one can work.[9]

Here the political activism of the soldiery is a kind of political incantation consisting in a process of "self-definition" that is necessary before the coming of a redeemer. The frontsoldier is an initiate in a field of force who has, apparently, no demands except to be allowed to be used as a tool of some future destiny. Here "power" is an attribute of identity, not an ability to manipulate others in the political arena for the realization of a specific plan. This, insisted Leopold Schwarzschild, editor of the Social Democratic journal *Das Tagebuch,* was not politics in the usual sense of the word.

It is clear that the Marxian conceptions both of the proletariat and of socialism had to be stretched out of shape to accommodate the range of attitudes found in the frontsoldiery. Those who hoped that frontsoldiers would be in the vanguard of a postwar revolutionary movement quickly became aware that the soldier's life on the margins of society had given him a contradictory set of political motives. The conventionally "socialist" features of the war experience – the equality of the ranks, the comradeship, the propertilessness of the soldier, the unformity of conditions – these were a product of defenselessness before authority and technology. The comradeship of the front was inextricable from the formula coined by T. E. Lawrence: "Except under compulsion there is no equality in the world."

The soldier was a man who had lived for a seemingly endless period of time beyond civilian social categories, beyond any but purely formal and mechanical status distinctions. The experience of living outside of class, but in ranks, as socially declassified or not yet classified individuals, was productive of an undeniable sense of comradeship among those who shared this situation. But it was also productive of an inability to link up the social experience of war with the social problems and political issues of postwar society. It is not surprising that those who wished to make the war experience the basis for an attack upon a bourgeois, liberal order had recourse to the most contradictory self-definitions: "revolutionary nationalism," "radical conservatism," "national socialism." These self-identifications might not have seemed so contradictory to men whose identities were shaped by an experience that, while giving new relevance to archaic, formalistic concepts of authority, could also be experienced as a kind of militarized proletarianization in which men were reduced to the status of anonymous functionaries of impersonal mechanisms of destruction.

But frontsoldiers, immediately after the war, were much more visible and recognizable in the role of the "man of violence" than in that of the "comrade" and man of community. As Gibbs observed, many former soldiers were "bitter in their speech, violent in opinion, frightening." Willard Waller talked with returned soldiers on the streetcorners of Chicago in 1919. He was astonished at the "intensity of their fury. They were angry about something; it was not clear just what . . . But there was never any mistaking their temper. They hated somebody for something."[10] Theodore Bartram, who tried to organize returning soldiers into a political party, learned that the thing they had most in common was not a political ideology but a consuming hatred for civilians, a hatred he shared. "One finds wounded comrades begging on the *Kurfurstendamm,* and you must force your fury back into your throat so that you don't smash your fist into the face of the next playboy you see."[11]

Many saw the anger, fury, and violence of veterans as "irrational." It was evidence that the war had forced a regression from the standards of mature civilized behavior. A few veterans agreed with this characterization of the fury of returned soldiers, and acknowledged that in war they and their comrades had been decivilized and disacculturated. Henry de Man wrote:

> The plain truth is that if I were to obey my native animal instincts – and there was little hope for anything else while I was in the trenches – I should enlist again in any future war, or take part in any sort of fighting, merely to experience again that voluptuous thrill of the human brute who realizes his power to take away life from other human beings who try to do the same thing to him. What was first accepted as a moral duty became a habit, and the habit . . . had become a need.[12]

There was no question that the frontsoldiery were violent when they returned home. This is not a matter of impressions, conjecture, or self-analysis, but a matter of record. From January 6 to January 10, 1919, there were demonstrations, disturbances, and incidents of mass insubordination involving 10,000 troops at Fokestone Camp, Surrey; 2,000 men were involved in similar incidents at Dover, and 8–9,000 at Bromley. There were similar, though less serious disturbances at Osterly and the Ilford airdrome. Also in January, 2,000 soldiers – details of the elite guards regiments – mutinied at Shoreham camp. At the same time Lord Byng was sent by the War Office to deal with a "soviet" established by the ordnance corps and 2,000 striking infantry from other units in Calais. From March 7 to March 10, Canadian troops rioted against their officers at Kinmel Camp at Ryl. Five men were killed, twenty-three wounded, and a good part of the installation burned. An officer sent by the War Office to report on the situation felt it necessary to remind troops just back from Flanders of an essential distinction, that it "was murder for Canadians to kill Canadians."[13] The London *Times* called the riots the "worst that had happened in England" and implied that such behavior was to be expected from Canadians who generally had a reputation for rowdiness during the war.[14] During the mustering out of Canadian troops in Montreal, the fury of the troops turned against civilians. Pierre Van Paassen describes the events.

> Dismissed from parade . . . thousands of men marched into the city, tearing down street signs in the French language on the way. Streetcars were commandeered; local citizens found driving in their sleighs were stopped, pushed out and forced to surrender their conveyances to the veterans. The walking sticks, donated by the patriotic citizens of Quebec, were used to batter in their own shop windows.[15]

In June, 1919, the "Khaki riots" reached their height in England. During this month, 1,500 soldiers of Allenby's corps mutinied in Plymouth; Canadian soldiers again fought their officers in Kinmel Camp; four to five hundred Canadian soldiers burned the police station at Epsom, killing one policeman. In Surrey, at Sutton Camp, three regiments mutinied and two battalions of guards and one machine-gun company were sent to restore order. In this last incident, 400 mutineers were arrested and 1,800 others were dispersed to various depots. Most of these riots and mutinies were caused by the impatience of troops for release from uniform, an impatience that was frustrated by the British plan of releasing first only those soldiers who had firm offers of employment.[16] In the winter of 1919 this plan was abandoned. But in the spring and summer the violence of veterans turned increasingly toward civilian targets. Carrington describes the civilian-soldier battles that were an unscheduled feature of Victory Day (July 19) parades in Glasgow, Coventry, Epsom, and

Lutton. The Lutton riots were "one of the most dangerous outbreaks in modern English history, although it seems generally
forgotten."[17] At Lutton ex-servicemen set the town hall afire
and from nine o'clock until dawn fought off police and firemen
attempting to extinguish the blaze. The Victory Day events at
Lutton cost 100 casualties. At the trial of the ringleaders, the public prosecutor could excise four years of war from his summation
and ascribe the riots to "Bolshevism, anarchy, drunkenness and
animality."[18] The United States, the nation least damaged by the
war, was not immune from veteran violence. Veterans broke up
socialist meetings in New York and were prominent in the race
riots in East St. Louis during 1919. On April 6, 1919, an
ex-serviceman's soviet affiliated with the I. W. W., fought police
on the streets of Tacoma, Washington, and, a few days later,
similar incidents occurred in Seattle. Beginning on May 28 veterans conducted "patrols in force" on the Yale campus, injuring
one hundred students and damaging nearly all the buildings. The
disturbances, begun when students insulted veterans parading
past their dormitories, were ended when the 102nd Infantry and
the state militia were called in.

Commonly the violence of the veteran was seen as an "expression" of his estrangement from social norms, and his habituation
to the arts of violence. It was, clearly, an after-effect of living in
an environment that educated only man's "native animal instincts." Or this penchant for violence could be seen in Faustian
terms and the veteran regarded as a man of "deeds" rather than
words. Schauwecker insisted that "whoever comes home from
the front is silent. He steps from a region ruled by the deed into a
region where the word is everything."[19] In this context the violence of the veteran could be seen as a repudiation of effeminate
bourgeois politics and the "hall of winds" in which politics were
normally conducted. Indeed, the general tendency is to see the
violence of veterans as an "expression" of themselves or an "acting out" of repressed aggressions. But it is better to regard the
actions of veterans in the terms most often used by them. Many
veterans felt that as a group they had been the victims of injustice, and that they were "retaliating" against civilian society for
the injustice done them. Governments and civilians had trans-
gressed against the "unwritten rules" that established the status

of the soldier in war and maintained his social place. The violence
of veterans must be understood in the context of that mutuality
of sacrifice that defines relations between front and home. It was
the collapse of this mutuality that, more than anything else, gave
veterans a consciousness of themselves as an exploited and
abused group.

THE ECONOMY OF SACRIFICE AND ITS
  COLLAPSE

The citizen-soldier has always been a central figure in what
might be called an "economy of social guilt" and public sacrifice.
He is the holder of a blood-debt upon the society he has defended
and can demand restitution for his "sacrifice of himself" as well
as for that of his comrades who have died. War may be objectively seen as Gaston Bouthouls sees it – a way of solving demo-
graphic embarrassments such as a surplus of young men – and
yet this, clearly, is not a reason why young men go to war.
Commonly the exchange of roles demanded of the citizen-soldier
is also understood within the language of sacrifice. Here sacrifice
is essentially an exchange, perhaps the very paradigm of
exchange. Within the national ideologies that reigned in 1914,
the civilian exchanged his private self and his individual self-
interest for a public and communal identity represented in the
uniform. For this temporary loss of a private self, the soldier can
demand restitution in the form of honor, prestige, or financial
rewards. Anyone can see how the language that imposes the
burden of "self-sacrifice" upon sons in the name of the preservation of the home accords with the normal outcome of the Oedipal situation, in which the child is forced to resign himself to the
failure of his sexual ambitions in order to maintain the family
structure.

But it is not the economy of sacrifice but its disruption that
created the anger, sense of injustice, and status ambiguity that
characterized veterans of the First World War. This disruption
was experienced as the fragmentation of the moral nexus between front and home, the nexus that made the suffering and
death at the front meaningful in terms of the preservation of the
larger entity, the "nation," the home. The "estrangement" of

front and home was the most significant factor in intensifying psychic identification's with the "front" on the part of the soldier, in making the "comradeship" of the front into the "mental internment" camp from which men like Charles Carrington could not escape until the 1930s.

In 1914 the ideology of the nation provided the formula that made the exchange of public for private roles meaningful as a "release" and a "liberation" from social contradiction. It was commonly felt that, in August, "society" – a cluster of competing interests – had become a "community" that unified diverse private interests into a common destiny. The volunteer was someone who embodied this transformation, for he was the individual who voluntarily submerged his private ego into a national persona. In the language of the day the volunteer was motivated by his *Opferbereitschaft,* his readiness to sacrifice himself in the realization of the suddenly palpable national destiny. This was more than just a way of speaking. Many experienced the beginning of the war as a dismantling of private egos, the transcendence of privacy, the tearing down of barriers that had preserved discrete social selves.

In August the civil death of the soldier, his "estrangement" from society, was accompanied by the sense that society, that market place of status, had been replaced by community. But the soldier's attitude toward the nation and toward his own public status changed markedly once he entered the labyrinth of trenches. Here, the liberation from bourgeois society came to seem like a death, abandonment, a severance from life. Gotthold von Rhoden, a young German volunteer, felt that he and his comrades were somehow estranged from the "men and things of the past" and that this estrangement created a situation in which "death can no longer sever our ties too painfully." What was, initially, a liberation from domesticity began to be experienced as a loss of the home.

But the most significant factor in the anger and bitterness of veterans was the perception that in the four years of war the "nation" of 1914 reverted to a marketplace of status. The home, which conducted "business as usual," was no longer a community. With this perception – given to many soldiers on leave or convalescing from a wound – the experience of war could only be understood in the classic terms of social injustice. Those at home were abstaining from "not a single pleasure," and were justifying their continued comfort and security in terms of their social or economic indispensability. This could only mean that those "heroes at the front" were eminently dispensable and superfluous to the home. This diminished status was repetitively confirmed by the realities of war – the countless, futile attacks, the constant waiting for a random, meaningless death.

But it was most often the encounter with the "profiteer" that permanently severed the moral relationship between front and home and collapsed the economy of sacrifice that was to define the relationship of combatant to noncombatant. The profiteer was a symbol of those who engrossed the medium of exchange – blood — for their private profit. But more significantly, he was also someone who had risen in status during wartime. His rise made it impossible for the frontsoldier to ignore the possibility that his "self-sacrifice" was an actual, and perhaps irrecoverable, social and economic loss. Franz Schauwecker encountered his profiteer in a restaurant during his final leave home in 1918. He describes the profiteer as a man with a "coarse, vacant face without any sign of mental activity, with plump, giant fists" and dressed in expensive fabrics and jewelry. Once he has identified the type, Schauwecker locates many of the "war rich" pushing their attentions on "young, refined women." In uncharacteristically laconic tones, Schauwecker concludes: "One appears alien in one's own country. It is best to go out there again. Out there, meaning, to the front."[20] Siegfried Sassoon also encounters the profiteer in a restaurant, in Liverpool rather than Berlin, yet his impressions are almost identical to Schauwecker's. "In the dining room I began to observe that some noncombatants were doing themselves pretty well out of the war. They were people whose faces lacked nobility, as they ordered lobsters and colossal cigars."[21]

For both Sassoon and Schauwecker, the one a member of the English gentry, the other the son of a man high in the German Imperial civil service, the encounter with the profiteer places their war experience in a new moral and ideological framework. Not only is the front exploited by the home, not only has the frontsoldier suffered a precipitous diminution of status from the "armed representative of the nation" to a "day laborer of death," but it may be that there is no longer a place to which the front-soldier might return when the war is over. The profiteer signals unmistakably the conversion of the economy of sacrifice to a market place where social status is being negotiated along with bills of exchange. This encounter precipitates Sassoon's protest against the war, a protest that is actually against the home.

> On behalf of those who are suffering now I make this protest against the deception which is being practiced on them; also, I believe that I may help to destroy the callous complacence with which the majority at home regard the continuance of those agonies which they do not share, and which they have not sufficient imagination to realize.[22]

It became abundantly clear in the four years of war that, in going to war, the soldier had not escaped the contradictions of capitalist society. At the front, and even at home, many realized that the war epitomized the contradiction of an "individualistic, profit-directed economy" subsisting in the midst of the "unconditional solidarity of the people." Capitalist society had not ceased being capitalist society by virtue of the war, in spite of the initial, overpowering sense of community. This was the greatest disillusionment of many who believed that the war would bring with it a spiritual, communal transformation. In the trenches, and in numerous encounters with the home, it was shown that the economy of sacrifice and blood had been absorbed in the market of goods, capital, and labor.

The voyage of the soldier beyond the boundaries of his home was a voyage to the place where the contradictions of industrial, capitalist society were most densely impacted. It was a voyage to the place where inequalities of wealth and status became inequalities of sacrifice and suffering. The difference between the front and the home became, in the long years of war, a difference between those who continued to live and live well and those who were daily faced with the reality of dying a mean, passive, and purposeless death. The actual sufferings of civilians, particularly in Germany during the "turnip winter," could not efface the image of the profiteer, the playboy, those who sacrificed nothing.

It is not surprising that, after the war, veteran's groups were organized around the demand for restitution, and that the violence of veterans was one of the most convincing arguments that society should compensate the soldier for his loss. The first leaflet of the *Bulletin* of the National Federation of Discharged and Demobilized Sailors and Soldiers, translated the social injuries of war into the classic terms of exploitation. The returned serviceman looks at Britain, the country he had "saved,"

> . . . and sees much in it that was not worth saving . . . Wealth still remains uncontrolled . . . He says, if my life was conscripted to save this wealth, why shouldn't it be conscripted to save my life and the lives of the dependents of the men who have fallen to save it? Now this is, of course revolutionary. It is very awkward to those who have lost least in this war. And so they attempted to fob it off with a bribe – in this case £1,000,000 spent on clubs, buns and billiards.[23]

Postwar veterans organizations tried to fit the veteran's sense of his own victimization with political and economic demands. The demand for compensation was the coin in which ex-soldiers and civilians negotiated their differences. And yet one cannot miss the depth and subjectivity of the injury that many incurred in war. Even the most innocent demands of veterans reveal this injury. Thus Ralph Perry, an American veteran, justified the demand for the bonus in the most subjective terms. This demand was just not because veterans had "earned" it. The bonus was first of all "revenge" against the home, and then a "test" of the love and affection of the home for those whom war had stripped of their pride.

> It is important to remember that in the veteran's eyes the bonus is a retaliation for injustice. The veteran regards the bonus as a moral issue, a test case to determine the attitude of the nation toward the men who abandoned their private concerns to meet a national emergency.[24]

The bonus issue was a plea for the society to resolve the psychic and social ambiguities that defined the place of the veteran in the postwar world. This sense of status ambiguity can also be found in what was perceived to be the dominant characteristic of veterans of the First World War: silence. Walter Benjamin ob-

served: "Was it not noticeable at the end of the war that men returned from the battlefield grown silent – not richer but poorer
in communicable experience? What, ten years later, was poured
out in floods of war books was anything but experience that goes
from mouth to mouth."[25] Benjamin attributed the silence of veterans to the contradictoriness of their experience, for "never has
experience been contradicted more thoroughly than strategic experience by positional warfare . . . physical experience by technological warfare."[26] Hemingway recognized that the experience of war had collapsed all those words that had once fixed the
elevated status of the soldier. Perhaps the most painful word was
now "sacrifice."

> Now, for a long time . . . I had seen nothing sacred and the
> things that were glorious had no glory and the sacrifices were
> like the stockyards at Chicago if nothing were done with the
> meat except to bury it. There were many words which you
> could not stand to hear and finally only the names of places had
> dignity.[27]

Particularly in the mouths of civilians words like "honor," "sacrifice," "duty" became intolerable assertions of the lie that nothing had changed. These words illuminated too starkly the victimization of those at the front. A bitter silence was the only
recourse for men who wished neither to ratify their own mor-
tification nor liberate the home from its putative guilt.

The traditional character of the warrior as a man who has
inhabited the margins of society as an extra-social being, half
man, half beast, means one thing in traditional societies where
status is fixed by law, custom, and ceremony. But the "temporary" marginalization of millions of men means quite another
thing in industrial societies where status is not fixed, where it is a
matter of success in the competition for wealth. When society
conducts "business as usual" those who exist outside the market
of status experience an absolute loss of their place. It may become
impossible for the soldier to reintegrate himself into society
without daily experiencing the reality of his loss.

I have argued throughout this study that there is a particular
structure to the ways in which Europeans had understood the
relationship of peace to war. This structure, which appears in the

ideologies of national war, also has a subjective status in the sense that it provides combatants with a particular conception of themselves and a specific sense of the value of their own suffering and death. We can see this structure most clearly in its collapse on the western front, its subjective reality in the psychic consequences of this collapse.

THE INTERNALIZATION OF WAR

The "otherness" of war was extinguished in the battles of material, and with it the poles that defined the meaning of the soldier's sacrifice of himself. Now war could only be experienced as a proletarianization, the only positive value of which was "comradeship." But in most cases this comradeship was a sense of sharing, in common, the status and powerlessness of victims. The psychic effects of the collapse of the economy of sacrifice can be found in the attempts of soldiers to evolve an identity from out of the war and to find a "home" at the front.

This was the response of Franz Schauwecker. It was better to go "out there" to the isolated, abandoned, cut-off world of the front. After issuing his protest against the home, undergoing a period of therapy in the Craiglockhart Hospital for shell-shock victims, and returning to his unit, Sassoon began, increasingly, to seek all emotional sustenance from his unit. When abandoned by the "callous complacence" of the majority of Britons, the battalion was the only place that retained any moral validity.

And yet this turning to the front and to one's comrades as a replacement for the lost home could have disastrous psychological consequences. The unit was an unstable entity, continually decimated by shellfire; old, familiar faces were being continually replaced by new, strange ones. To identify with the battalion at war and with the narrow circle of one's comrades was to open a large, vertiginous emotional drain, and to begin a seemingly endless process of mourning. Sassoon's last year of war was spent in a losing battle to maintain the constantly unravelling ties to friends and comrades.

> I had lost my faith in . . . [the war], and there was nothing left to believe in but the "battalion spirit." The battalion spirit

meant living oneself into comfortable companionship with the officers and N.C.O.'s around one . . . But while exploring my way into the war I had discovered the impermanence of its humanities. One evening we could all be together in a cosy room in Corbie . . . a single machinegun or a few shells might wipe out the whole picture within a week . . . And now there was a steel curtain down between April and May, on the other side of the curtain, if I was lucky, I should meet the survivors, and we should begin to build up our little humanities all over again.[28]

In war the psychic dangers of identification with the men of one's unit are obvious, and yet this was the reaction that was often necessary given the emotional severence from the home. This identification ensured that the death of every comrade would be a loss of self. No longer could the death of a friend be justified with the comfort that this was a loss that preserved the life of the whole. Each departure could be compensated for only by an intensification of the bonds to those who remained, and this guaranteed that the next, inevitable loss would mean an even more severe, even less tolerable extinction of self. At the end of this process one's own demise could be welcomed as a resolution to an insupportable, continuous mourning. As Freud pointed out in the analysis of bereavement he wrote during the war: "Mourning is regularly the reaction to the loss of a loved person, or to the loss of some abstraction which has taken the place of a loved one, such as country, liberty, an ideal and so on."[29] The loss of the home was the loss of such a "substitute" for a loved one, and this loss precipitated a search for a replacement amidst the "impermanent humanities" of the front. As Schauwecker insisted, the "front is now home." In 1918 this was true in a double sense. The front was the only available refuge for men who were continually confronted with the reality of their loss of status. This psychic home, the abandoned nation of victims, now confronted a Germany that, with the revolution, had compounded its moral betrayal of the frontsoldiery.

The internalization of war begins with the loss of the abstraction that had "taken the place" of a loved one. The substitute for this abstraction, the "home," the "nation," was found at the front, among one's comrades. But this narcissistic reaction to the loss of the home, a reaction that consisted in drawing into the ego the narrow circle of one's comrades, necessarily precipitated a "fixation" upon the dead and the living, a set of identifications that lasted long into peacetime. The mourning of soldiers for the dead, the "cowed subjection" of survivors to the ghosts of "friends who died," was reinforced in the pageants, memorials, rituals, and songs of veteran's groups. Not the least important function of these groups was that of mortuarial associations that organized the process of mourning for the dead and the revenge against the home. The casualties of war became the central figures in a cult of suffering and self-sacrifice. The dead became an obligating symbol for survivors, a symbol that represented most perfectly the soldier's once totally insecure and vulnerable state.[30]

This organized mourning, like the blank repression of the war experience, was the most acceptable way in which the war continued to define the identities of combatants. Much more dangerous was the reaction of those who found their way into the rightist combat leagues in Germany, Italy, and France. It was possible for the veteran to acknowledge the social and psychic injury he had received, to accept this as a distinction, to affirm his social dislocation as a permanent state, and to manipulate his status ambiguity in a game of social and political extortion. This was the reaction that most frightened Erich Weniger, who despaired over those who "still remain, even in their youth, only as a veteran on the other side of daily life."[31] Many ex-soldiers ritualized their liminal status, their position between the front and the home. Nels Anderson found a large number of veterans among the "homeless men" of Chicago. These men "worked" their war experience to maintain themselves on the peripheries of society. Friedrich Sieburg – one of the many junior officers who mustered out of the army to join the irregulars fighting in the Baltic – admitted that he embraced his status as a marginalized man and gloried in the liberties that this status permitted him.

> I never again want to go home; I would like to live my life walking along this road, searching the sky, measuring the world by co-ordinate squares and division combat sectors,

evaluating the daylight hours by the strength of the artillery fire . . . My Germany begins where the flares go up and ends where the train for Cologne departs. I can't go home again and live the old life.[32]

The First World War was the first holocaust. It was destined to be repeated again in the twentieth century, again on a mass scale, again with no apparent purpose or meaning. Those who had internalized the war, its peculiar relationship between victims and victimizers, the liminality that it imposed upon combatants, were destined to play a significant part in this repetition. For many could not resolve the ambiguities that defined their identities in war and resume their place in civilian society without acknowledging their status as victims. Friedrich Wilhelm Heinz, a veteran to become a *Gruppenfuhrer* of the S.A., insisted that the war did not end in 1918.

Those people told us the war was over. That was a laugh. We ourselves are the war: Its flame burns strongly in us. It envelops our whole being and fascinates us with the enticing urge to destroy. We obeyed . . . and marched onto the battlefields of the post-war world just as we had gone into battle on the western front.[33]

The community of the front was formed of those uprooted from their social matrix to serve as instruments in the defense of the established order. In this defense many learned the indefensibility of this order. In the experience of war the "home" became more alien than any enemy, and the hypocrisy of those who used the soldier was repetitively demonstrated in his performance of duty. No "rites of reaggregation" could efface the memory of utter defenselessness before authority and technology. No ceremonial conclusion to the war could restore the continuities it had ended, or recreate those "fictions" that had been left behind in the labyrinth of trenches.

Notes

1. THE STRUCTURE OF THE WAR EXPERIENCE

1 Phillip Witkop, ed., *Kriegsbriefe gefallener Studenten* (Munich: 1936), p. 3.
2 *Ibid.*, p. 88.
3 Quoted in Paul Fussell, *The Great War and Modern Memory* (London, Oxford, and New York: 1975), p. 64.
4 This I have taken from Jerome Kagan, who has challenged the dominance of "continuity" in cognitive psychology. See his "Emergent Themes in Human Development," *American Scientist, 64,* 2 (March–April 1976), pp. 186–96.
5 Erik Erikson, *Childhood and Society* (London: 1967), p. 37.
6 Quoted in Ludwig Scholz, *Seelenleben des Soldaten an der Front. Hinterlassene Aufzeichnungen des im Kriege gefallenen Nervenartzes* (Tübingen: 1920), p. 184.
7 A full description, and a comparison of these models, can be found in Richard Sipes, "War, Sports and Aggression: An Empirical Test of Rival Theories," *American Anthropologist, 75,* 1 (February 1973), pp. 64–86.
8 See, for example, Peter Loewenberg's "Arno Mayer's 'Internal Causes and Purposes of War in Europe,' an Inadequate Model of Human Behavior, National Conflict and Historical Change," *Journal of Modern History, 42* (1970), 628–36. Also, Franco Fornari, *The Psychoanalysis of War* (Garden City, New York: 1974).

9 Arno Mayer, "Internal Causes and Purposes of War in Europe, 1870–1955: A Research Assignment," *Journal of Modern History, 44,* 3 (September 1969), p. 291. Also, Michael Gordon, "Domestic Conflict and the Origin of the First World War: The British and German Cases," *Journal of Modern History, 46,* 2 (June 1974), 191.

10 Ludwig Lewinsohn, *Die Revolution an der Westfront* (Charlottens-burgh: 1919), p. 63.

11 Laurence Housman, *War Letters of Fallen Englishmen* (London 1930), p. 60.

12 For a development of this point of view, see Robert Jay Lifton's *Home from the War. Vietnam Veterans: Neither Victims nor Executioners* (New York: 1972). The shortcomings of the work lie precisely in an insufficient appreciation of the frustration of aggression native to war, and to partisan war in particular.

13 Carrol Lija Nichols, "War and Civil Neuroses – a Comparison," *Long Island Medical Journal, 13* (August 1919), p. 259.

14 W. M. Maxwell, *A Psychological Retrospect of the Great War* (London: 1923), p. 85.

15 S. L. A. Marshall, *Men Against Fire* (New York: 1966), p. 78.

16 See Chapter 3 under "The Defensive Personality."

17 Ernst Jünger, *Feuer und Blut* (Magdeburg: 1925), p. 18.

18 Roger Abrahams, "Rituals in Culture," unpublished paper, p. 19. U. of Texas-Austin.

19 Charles Edmund Carrington, "Some Soldiers," *Promise of Great-ness. The War of 1914–1918,* ed. George A. Panichas (New York: 1968), p. 157.

20 Charles Edmunds (pseudonym for Charles Edmunds Carrington), *Soldiers from the Wars Returning* (London: 1965), p. 250.

21 Mircea Eliade, *Rites and Symbols of Initiation:* Ch. V, "Heroic and Shamanic Initiations" (New York, Evanston, San Francisco, and London: 1958).

22 Harry Halbert Turney-High, *Primitive War: Its Practice and Concepts* (Columbia, S.C.: 1949).

23 Georges Dumezil, *The Destiny of the Warrior* (Chicago and London: 1969), p. 40.

24 Arnold Van Gennep, *The Rites of Passage* (Chicago: 1972), p. 39.

25 Edmunds (Carrington), *Soldiers from the Wars Returning,* p. 87.

26 Victor Turner, "From Liminal to Liminoid in Play, Flow and Rit-ual: An Essay in Comparative Symbology," *The Anthropological Study of Human Play,* Rice University Studies, *60,* 31 (Summer 1974), p. 57.

27 Gertrude Bäumer, *Lebensweg durch eine Zeitwende* (Tubingen: 1933), p. 280.

28 Carl Zuckmayer, *Als wär ein Stück von Mir* (Vienna: 1936), p. 221.

29 Victor Turner, "Betwixt and Between: The Liminal Period in *Rites de Passage*," Warner Modular Publication, Reprint 772; also Ch. IV of Turner's *Forest of Symbols* (Ithaca and London: 1973), p. 99.

30 *Ibid.*, p. 7.

31 Mary Douglas, *Purity and Danger. An Analysis of Concepts of Pollution and Taboo* (New York and Washington: 1963), p. 36.

32 F. C. Bartlett, *Psychology and the Soldier* (Cambridge: 1927), p. 176.

33 W. H. R. Rivers, "The Repression of War Experience," *Lancet*, I (*1918–1;* p. 173).

34 Robert Michaels, *Briefe eine Hauptmanns an seinen Sohn* (Berlin: 1916), p. 69.

35 Marshall, *Men Against Fire*, p. 45.

36 Henri Massis, in Panichas, *Promise of Greatness. The War of 1914–1918*, p. 282.

37 *Ibid.*

38 Housman, *War Letters of Fallen Englishmen*, p. 60.

39 Emilio Lussu, *Sardinian Brigade* (New York: 1939), p. 167.

40 Sigmund Freud, "The 'Uncanny'," *The Complete Works, XVII*, pp. 219–52.

41 Witkop, *Kriegsbriefe gefallener Studenten*, p. 210.

42 Siegfried Sassoon, *Memoirs of George Sherston* (containing *Memoirs of a Fox-Hunting Man, Memoirs of an Infantry Officer*, and *Sherston's Progress*), (New York: 1937), p. 373.

43 Zuckmayer, *Als wär ein Stück von Mir*, p. 213.

44 Ernst Simmel, *Kriegsneurosen u. Psychisches Trauma* (Munich: 1918), p. 10.

45 Dr. P. Grasset, "The Psychoneuroses of War," *Medical Press and Circular, 150* (1915), p. 562.

46 E. E. Southard, *Shell-Shock and Other Neuro-Psychiatric Problems Presented in Five Hundred and Eighty-nine Case Histories* (Boston: 1919), p. 250.

47 Turner, "From Liminal to Liminoid in Play, Flow and Ritual," p. 57.

48 Simone de Beauvoir, *Memoirs of a Dutiful Daughter* (New York: 1974), p. 180.

49 John Keegan, *The Face of Battle* (New York: 1976), p. 221.

50 Turner, "Betwixt and Between," p. 9.

51 John Masters, *The Ravi Lancers* (New York: 1973).

52 T. E. Lawrence, *The Mint* (New York: 1963), p. 32.
53 Quoted in Irene Willis, *England's Holy War* (New York: 1928), p. 145.
54 *Ibid.,* p. 148.
55 Quoted in Keegan, *The Face of Battle,* p. 276.
56 *Ibid.,* p. 221.
57 Carl Zuckmayer, *Pro Domo* (Stockholm: 1938), p. 42.
58 David Jones, *In Parenthesis* (New York: 1961), p. x.
59 Turner, "From Liminal to Liminoid in Play, Flow and Ritual," p. 73.
60 Turner, "Betwixt and Between," p. 17.
61 Witkop, *Kriegsbriefe gefallener Studenten,* p. 100.
62 Quoted in Hannah Hafkesbrink, *Unknown Germany. An Inner Chronicle of the First World War Based on Letters and Diaries* (New Haven: 1948), pp. 65–6.
63 In Jean Norton Cru, *Temoins. Essai D'Analyse et de Critique des Souvenirs de Combattants Edités en Français de 1915 à 1928* (Paris: 1928), p. 140.
64 David Jones, *In Parenthesis,* p. x.
65 Friedrich Dessauer, *Streit um der Technik* (Frankfurt A/M: 1956), p. 26.
66 Turner, "Betwixt and Between," p. 5.
67 Henry de Man, *The Remaking of a Mind. A Soldier's Thoughts on War and Reconstruction* (London: 1919), p. 178.
68 *Ibid.*
69 Rudolf Binding, *A Fatalist at War* (Boston and New York: 1929), p. 61.
70 Karl Marx, *Capital, I* (Chicago: 1908), p. 424.
71 *Ibid.,* p. 402.
72 Paul Ricoeur, "The Model of the Text: Meaningful Action Considered as a Text," *New Literary History, V,* 1 (Autumn 1973), p. 98.
73 Sandor Ferenczi, "Uber zwei Typen der Kriegsneurosen," *Int. Zeitschrift f. ärtztliche Psychoanalyse, IV* (1916–1917), pp. 131–45.
74 Werner Beumelberg, *Sperrfeuer über Deutschland* (Oldenberg: 1929), p. 171.

2. THE COMMUNITY OF AUGUST AND THE ESCAPE FROM MODERNITY

1 Zuckmayer, *Pro Domo,* p. 35.
2 Gertrude Bäumer, *Lebensweg durch eine Zeitwende* (Tubingen: 1933), p. 264.

3 Magnus Hirschfeld and Andrea Gaspar, *Sittengeschichte des Ersten Weltkriegs* (Hanau am Main: 1929), p. 50.

4 *Ibid.*

5 Maxwell, *A Psychological Retrospect of the Great War*, p. 57.

6 Bäumer, *Lebensweg durch eine Zeitwende,* p. 265.

7 Roger Caillois, *Man and the Sacred* (Glencoe, New York: 1950), p. 177.

8 For an anthology of studies on the relationship of primitive war to political and social values in a variety of premodern societies, see Paul Bohannon, ed., *Law and Warfare. Studies in the Anthropology of Conflict* (Garden City, New York: 1969). In spite of its theoretical deficiencies, Turney-High's *Primitive War* is still the standard monograph in English.

9 See Marcel Mauss, *The Gift: Forms and Functions of Exchange in Archaic Societies* (London: 1954) for an intriguing discussion of the interface between conventions of war and exchange.

10 Walter Scheller, *Als die Seele Starb, 1914–1918* (Berlin: 1930), p. 2.

11 Stefan Zweig, *The World of Yesterday. An Autobiography* (New York: 1945), p. 224.

12 Quoted in Hafkesbrink, *Unknown Germany,* p. 37.

13 Rudolf Binding, *Erlebtes Leben* (Frankfurt A/M: 1928) p. 237.

14 Quoted in Victor Turner, *Ritual Process* (Chicago: 1969), p. 126.

15 *Ibid.,* p. 131.

16 In E. Loehrke, ed., *Armageddon: The World War in Literature* (New York: 1930), pp. 44–5.

17 Quoted in Hirschfeld and Gaspar, *Sittengeschichte des Ersten Weltkriegs,* p. 57.

18 See Hirschfeld. Although Hirschfeld's clinical data are unreliable – he's been known to have manufactured data — his book is a mine of information on the popular press during the war. See also the "dream of love – service in wartime" reported by Freud in his *Introductory Lectures, The Complete Psychological Works, XV* (London: 1968), p. 137.

19 Caillois, *Man and the Sacred,* p. 166.

20 McKim Marriott, "The Feasts of Love," in *Krishna: Myths, Rites and Attitudes,* Milton Singer, ed. (Honolulu, 1966), p. 212.

21 Zuckmayer, *Pro Domo,* p. 130.

22 For an examination of this theme in European literature and festivals, see Natalie Zeman Davis, "Women on Top," *Society and Culture in Early Modern France* (Stanford, Calif.: 1975), pp. 124–51.

23 Hirschfeld and Gaspar, *Sittengeschichte des Ersten Weltkriegs,* p. 53.

24 Maxwell, *A Psychological Retrospect of the Great War,* p. 57.

25 Rainer Maria Rilke, *Wartime Letters, 1914–1921* (New York: 1940), p. 22.
26 Richard and Clara Winston, eds., *The Letters of Thomas Mann, 1889–1955* (New York: 1975), p. 67.
27 Friedrich Meinecke, *The German Catastrophe* (Boston: 1963), p. 25.
28 Bäumer, *Lebensweg durch eine Zeitwende,* p. 280.
29 Zuckmayer, *Pro Domo,* pp. 34–5.
30 Ernst Gläser, *Class of 1902* (New York: 1929), p. 94.
31 Quoted in Carl Schorske, *German Social Democracy, 1905–1917* (Cambridge, Mass.: 1955), p. 390.
32 *Ibid.*
33 Jules Romains, *Men of Good Will,* Vol. 7: *Death of a World* (New York: 1938), p. 533.
34 *Ibid.*
35 Zweig, *The World of Yesterday,* p. 224.
36 Binding, *Erlebtes Leben,* p. 237.
37 Rilke, *Wartime Letters, 1914–1921,* p. 21.
38 Mikhalyi Csikszentmihalyi, *Beyond Boredom and Anxiety. The Experience of Play, in Work and Games* (San Francisco, Washington, and London: 1975), p. 36.
39 *Ibid.,* p. 47.
40 Johan Huizinga, *Homo Ludens: A Study of the Play Element in Culture* (Boston: 1970; first published 1944), p. 13.
41 Morton Marks, "Ritual Structure in Afro-American Music," in *Religious Movements in Contemporary America,* Irving I. Zaretsky and Mark P. Leone, eds. (Princeton, N. J.: 1974), pp. 60–134. Also, see Karl Bücher, *Arbeit und Rhythmus* (Leipzig: 1902), p. 397.
42 Franz Schauwecker, *The Fiery Way* (London and Toronto: 1921), p. 29.
43 Graves, *Goodbye to All That* (London: 1929), p. 239.
44 Turner, *Ritual Process,* p. 194.
45 Alfred Vagts, *The History of Militarism* (New York: 1959), p. 13.
46 Zuckmayer, *Pro Domo,* p. 37.
47 *Ibid.*
48 See Fussell on Wilfred Owen, "Soldier Boys," Ch. VIII of *The Great War and Modern Memory* (London, Oxford, and New York: 1975).
49 Hafkesbrink, *Unknown Germany,* p. 43.
50 Bäumer, *Lebensweg durch eine Zeitwende,* p. 280.
51 Binding, *Erlebtes Leben,* p. 263.
52 Zuckmayer, *Als wär ein Stück von Mir,* p. 221.
53 *Ibid.,* p. 199.

54 Zuckmayer, *Pro Domo*, p. 34.

55 Thomas Mann, "In My Defense," *Atlantic Monthly, 174,* 4 (October 1949), p. 101.

56 Winston, *The Letters of Thomas Mann*, p. 67.

57 Christian Graf von Krockow, *Die Entscheidung. Eine Untersuchung über Ernst Jünger, Carl Schmitt, Martin Heidegger* (Stuttgart: 1958), p. 42.

58 Hafkesbrink, *Unknown Germany*, p. 43.

59 In Loehrke, *Armageddon*, p. 56.

60 Bäumer, *Lebensweg durch eine Zeitwende*, p. 281.

61 E. M. Forster, "The Machine Stops," in Arthur O. Lewis, Jr., *Of Men and Machines* (New York: 1963), p. 274.

62 Fritz Kreisler, *Four Weeks in the Trenches* (Boston and New York: 1915), p. 63.

63 See P. Fussell, *The Great War and Modern Memory*, Ch. VII: "Arcadian Recourses" (London, Oxford, and New York: 1975).

64 For the literature detailing the impact of industrialization upon interior decoration, literature and style, see: Lily Litvak, *A Dream of Arcadia. Anti-industrialism in Spanish Literature, 1895–1905* (Austin, Texas, and London: 1975); and Herbert Sussman, *Victorians and the Machine* (Cambridge, Mass.: 1968). Still most valuable are the works of Giedion (*Mechanization Takes Command*) and Lewis Mumford (*Technics and Civilization*).

65 Thorstein Veblen, *Imperial Germany and the Industrial Revolution* (New York: 1946; first published 1915), p. 85. The standard works on the impact of industrialization on Wilhelmine Germany by and large fall short of 1914 chronologically or pass over it. See: Kenneth Barkin, *The Controversy over German Industrialization, 1890–1902;* Ralf Dahrendorf, *Society and Democracy in Germany* (New York: 1967); and Fritz Stern, *The Politics of Cultural Despair. A Study in the Rise of the German Ideology* (Berkeley: 1961). The work of Alexander Gerschenkron is invaluable. See his *Bread and Democracy in Germany* (New York: 1966), and particularly his *Backwardness in Historical Perspective* (Cambridge, Mass.: 1962).

66 Veblen, *Imperial Germany and the Industrial Revolution*, p. 236.

67 Ernst Jünger, "Krieg als äusseres Erlebnis," *Standarte* (Supplement to *Der Stahlhelm*), I, 1 (September 27, 1925).

68 Carl von Clausewitz, *On War* (London: 1968), p. 117.

69 Zuckmayer, *Als wär ein Stück von Mir*, p. 199.

70 Ernst Gombrich, *Art and Illusion* (Princeton, N. J.: 1969), p. 110.

71 Bäumer, *Lebensweg durch eine Zeitwende*, p. 281.

72 Ernst Jünger, *Der Kampf als inneres Erlebnis* (Berlin: 1922), pp. 25–6.

3. WAR IN THE LABYRINTH: THE REALITIES OF WAR

1 Rudolf Binding, *Fatalist at War*, p. 60.
2 Ernst Jünger, "Unsere Politiker," *Standarte*, 1 (September 6, 1925).
3 Charles Edmunds (Carrington), *Subaltern's War* (London: 1929), 217–218.
4 Franz Schauwecker, *So war der Krieg* (Berlin: 1927), p. 17.
5 Henri Massis in Panichas, *Promise of Greatness*, p. 277.
6 Henri Barbusse, *I Saw it Myself* (New York: 1928), pp. 19–20.
7 Zweig, *The World of Yesterday*, p. 224.
8 Zuckmayer, *Als wär ein Stück von Mir*, p. 21.
9 Zuckmayer, *Pro Domo*, p. 33.
10 Zuckmayer, *Als wär ein Stück von Mir*, p. 195.
11 *Ibid.*, p. 207.
12 *Ibid.*, p. 221.
13 Karl Jannack, *Wir mit der roten Nelke* (Boutzen: 1959), p. 57.
14 Zuckmayer, *Als wär ein Stück von Mir*, p. 208.
15 Franz Schauwecker, *The Fiery Way*, p. 217.
16 Franz Schauwecker, *Im Todesrachen. Die Deutsche Seele im Weltkrieg* (Halle: 1921), p. 22.
17 *Ibid.*, p. 4.
18 *Ibid.*, p. 39.
19 *Ibid.*, p. 264.
20 This formula was fashioned by Fr. Wilhelm Heinz. See his *Die Nation greift an. Geschichte und Kritik des soldatischen Nationalismus* (Berlin: 1933), p. 16.
21 Schauwecker, *The Fiery Way*, p. 152.
22 Franz Schauwecker, *Aufbruch der Nation* (Berlin: 1930), p. 395.
23 Zuckmayer, *Als wär ein Stück von Mir*, p. 217.
24 Ernst Jünger, *Werke, V,* (Stuttgart: 1965), p. 38.
25 Jünger, "Der Krieg als äusseres Erlebnis," *Der Stahlhelm, Beilage, "Standarte," I*, 4 (September 27, 1925).
26 Witkop, *Kriegsbriefe gefallener Studenten*, p. 3.
27 *Ibid.*, p. 12.
28 This point is made by Jannack, *Wir mit der roten Nelke*, p. 59.
29 Henry de Man, *The Remaking of a Mind. A Soldier's Thoughts on War and Peace* (London: 1919), p. 161.
30 *Ibid.*, p. 162.
31 Jünger, "Der Krieg als Inneres Erlebnis," *Standarte, I*, 6 (October 12, 1925).
32 Quoted in Hafkesbrink, *Unknown Germany*, p. 66.

33 J. F. C. Fuller, *The Conduct of War, 1789–1961* (New Brunswick, N. J.: 1961), p. 140.
34 *Ibid.*, p. 137.
35 R. L. Richards, "Mental and Nervous Diseases During the Russo-Japanese War", *Military Surgeon, 26* (1910), pp. 178–9.
36 Quoted in Fuller, *The Conduct of War, 1789–1961*, p. 130.
37 David Lloyd George, *War Memoirs* (London: 1933), p. 365.
38 Fuller, *The Conduct of War, 1789–1961*, p. 161.
39 Panichas, *Promise of Greatness*, p. 150.
40 F. Winteringham, *The Story of Weapons* (Boston: 1943), p. 164.
41 Cru, *Temoins*, p. 439.
42 Clausewitz, *On War*, p. 164.
43 *Ibid.*, p. 165.
44 Jünger, *Werke, I*, p. 252.
45 Jünger, *Das Wäldchen 125. Eine Chronik aus den Graben Kampf 1918* (Berlin: 1925), p. 21.
46 *Ibid.*, p. 21.
47 *Ibid.*, p. 21.
48 Beumelberg, *Sperrfever über Deutschland*, p. 136.
49 Jacques Mayer, "Verdun, 1916," in Panichas, *Promise of Greatness*, p. 58.
50 Panichas, *Promise of Greatness*, p. xxi.
51 Schauwecker, *Im Todesrachen*, p. 275.
52 *Ibid.*, p. 275.
53 A. E. Ashworth, "The Sociology of Trench Warfare," *British Journal of Sociology, XIX*, 4 (December 1968), p. 417.
54 Chaim F. Shatan, M.D., "Through the Membrane of Reality: 'Impacted Grief' and Perceptual Dissonance in Vietnam Combat Veterans," *Psychiatric Opinion, 11*, 6 (October 1974), p. 10.
55 Cru, *Temoins*, p. 92.
56 Irene Willis, *England's Holy War* (New York: 1928), p. 153.
57 *Ibid.*, p. 153.
58 Southard, *Shellshock*, p. 211.
59 *Ibid.*, p. 319.
60 *Ibid.*, p. 224.
61 Basil Liddell-Hart, *Memoirs, I* (London: 1962), p. 13.
62 Witkop, *Kriegsbriefe gefallener Studenten*, p. 144.
63 Fritz Kreisler, *Four Weeks in the Trenches: The War Story of A Violinist* (Boston and New York: 1915), p. 69.
64 *Ibid.*, p. 69.
65 Robert Graves, *Goodbye to All That*, p. 107.
66 *Ibid.*, p. 119.

67 A. E. Ashworth, "The Sociology of Trench Warfare," *British Journal of Sociology, XIX,* 4 (December 1968), p. 418.
68 Graves, *Goodbye to All That,* p. 228.
69 Wilhelm von Schramm, in *Krieg und Krieger,* E. Jünger, ed. (Berlin: 1930), p. 41.
70 Massis, in Panichas, *Promise of Greatness,* p. 283.
71 *Ibid.,* p. 277.
72 Edmunds (Carrington), *Soldiers from the Wars Returning,* p. 252.
73 Ernst Jünger, *Feuer und Blut. Ein Kleiner Ausschnitt aus einer grossen Schlacht* (Magdeburg: 1925), pp. 46–7.

4. MYTH AND MODERN WAR

1 Fussell, *The Great War and Modern Memory,* p. 115.
2 Cru, *Temoins,* p. 4.
3 Fussell, *The Great War and Modern Memory,* p. 131.
4 Ruth Benedict, "Myth," *Encyclopedia of the Social Sciences,* E. R. A. Seligman, ed., *11* (New York: 1933), pp. 178–81.
5 Roland Barthes, *Mythologies* (New York: 1975), p. 129.
6 *Ibid.,* p. 144.
7 Claude Lévi-Strauss, "The Story of Asdival," in *The Structural Study of Myth and Totemism,* Edmund Leach, ed. (Edinburgh: 1967), p. 30.
8 Claude Lévi-Strauss, *The Raw and the Cooked. Introduction to a Science of Mythology, I* (New York and Evanston: 1969), p. 3.
9 See: Leo Marx, *The Machine in the Garden* (New York: 1964); and Henry Nash Smith, *Virgin Land: The American West as Symbol and Myth* (New York: 1950).
10 Quoted in Fussell, *The Great War and Modern Memory,* p. 51.
11 Kreisler, *Four Weeks in the Trenches,* p. 2.
12 *Ibid.,* p. 12.
13 Ernst Jünger, *Werke, V,* pp. 80–1.
14 Jünger, *Werke, I,* p. 302.
15 Witkop, *Kriegsbriefe gefallener Studenten,* p. 34.
16 "The Great Years of Their Lives," *Listener, 86,* 2207 (July 15, 1971), p. 74.
17 J. C. Carothers, "Culture, Psychiatry and the Written Word," *Psychiatry* (November 1964), p. 313.
18 Graves, *Goodbye to All That,* p. 160.
19 Edmunds (Carrington), *Subaltern's War* (London: 1929), p. 67.
20 Ulric Neisser, *Cognitive Psychology* (New York: 1967), p. 297.
21 *Ibid.*

22 *Ibid.*, p. 298.
23 Rodney Needham, "Percussion and Transition," *Man, 2,* 4 (December 1967), p. 606.
24 Quoted in Needham, p. 608.
25 Marks, "Ritual Structure in Afro-American Music," p. 64.
26 Witkop, *Kriegsbriefe gefallener Studenten,* p. 82.
27 *Ibid.*, p. 83.
28 Edward F. Graham, in *War Letters of Rochester's Veterans, II* (Rochester, New York: 1929), p. 241.
29 *Ibid.*, p. 243.
30 *Ibid.*, p. 245.
31 Schauwecker, *Im Todesrachen,* p. 148.
32 E. von Ludendorff, *Der Totale Krieg* (Munich: 1936), p. 52.
33 Antoine St. Exupéry, *Night Flight* (New York: 1932), p. 43.
34 Jünger, *Werke, I,* p. 368.
35 Quoted in Fussell, p. 54.
36 *Ibid.*, p. 55.
37 Jünger, *Werke, I,* p. 361.
38 A. Marwick, *The Deluge* (London: 1961), p. 84.
39 A. F. Wedd, *German Student's War Letters* (London: 1965), p. 201.
40 H. D. Trounce, *Fighting the Boche Underground* (New York: 1918), p. 2.
41 Mircea Eliade, *The Forge and the Crucible* (London: 1962), p. 169.
42 Marcel Mauss, *A General Theory of Magic* (London and Boston: 1972), Ch. 3.
43 Dessauer, *Streit um der Technik,* p. 23. Also see Hannah Arendt, *The Human Condition* (Chicago, 1970).
44 Eliade, *The Forge and the Crucible,* p. 172.
45 Lewis Mumford, *Technics and Civilization* (New York: 1934), pp. 69–70.
46 *Ibid.*, p. 71.
47 Vignes Rouges, "Bourru," in Loehrke, *Armageddon,* p. 399.
48 *Ibid.*, p. 398.
49 Gaston Bachelard, *The Poetics of Space* (New York: 1964), p. 20.
50 Jünger, *Werke, V,* pp. 85–6.
51 Jünger, "Sturm," *Hannoverscher Kurier,* Installment 9.
52 Jünger, *Wäldchen 125,* p. 58.
53 *Ibid.*, p. 60.
54 Jünger, *Werke, I,* pp. 381–2.
55 Jünger, "Schlusswort zu einem Aufsatz," *Widerstand, V* (1930) 1, p. 10.
56 Jünger, *Werke, I,* p. 352.

57 Jünger," "Kampf als inneres Erlebnis," *Werke, V,* p. 13.
58 Jünger, "Wesen des Frontsoldatentums," *Standarte, I,* 1 (September 6, 1925).
59 Jünger, *Werke, VII,* p. 51.
60 Jünger, *Storm of Steel* (New York: 1929), p. 28.
61 Armin Mohler, ed., *Die Schleife: Dokumente zum Weg von Ernst Jüngers* (Zurich: 1955), p. 55.
62 Friedrich Georg Jünger, *Spiegel der Jahre. Erinnerungen* (Munich: 1958), p. 11.
63 Junger, *Werke, I,* p. 13.
64 Jünger, "Sturm," *Hannoverscher Kurier,* Installment 2.
65 *Ibid.*
66 Jünger, "Materialschlacht," *Standarte, I,* 5 (October 4, 1925).
67 Jünger, "Sturm," *Hannoverscher Kurier,* Installment 2.
68 Wilhelm Reich, *Selected Writings* (New York: 1961), p. 116.
69 *Ibid.,* pp. 117–18.
70 *Ibid.,* p. 105.
71 Jünger, *Feuer und Blut,* p. 11.
72 *Ibid.,* p. 33.
73 *Ibid.,* p. 18.
74 Jünger, *Werke, I,* p. 470.
75 *Ibid.*
76 Jünger, *Feuer und Blut,* pp. 46–7.
77 Jünger, "Sturm," *Hannoverscher Kurier,* Installment 5.
78 *Ibid.,* Installment 6.
79 *Ibid.,* Installment 10.
80 *Ibid.,* Installment 11.
81 *Ibid.*

5. AN EXIT FROM THE LABYRINTH– NEUROSES AND WAR

1 Carrol Lija Nichols, "War and Civil Neurosis – A Comparison," *Long Island Medical Journal, 13,* 8 (August 1919), pp. 257–68.
2 Francis X. Dercum, "So-Called 'Shell-Shock': The Remedy," *Archives of Neurology and Psychiatry, 1* (1919), p. 66.
3 *Ibid.,* p. 68, and Nichols, "War and Civil Neurosis," p. 259.
4 Sigmund Freud (Karl Abraham, Ernest Jones, Sandor Ferenczi, *et al.*), *Psychoanalysis and the War Neuroses:* Introduction (London, Vienna, and New York: 1921), p. 2.
5 George Rosen, "Nostalgia, a Forgotten Psychological Disorder," *Psychological Medicine, 5,* 4 (1974), pp. 340–54.

6 M. D. Eder, "Psychopathology of the War Neurosis," *Lancet* (August 12, 1916), p. 2.

7 Great Britain. Army. *Report of the War Office Committee of Enquiry into "Shell-shock"* (London: 1922), p. 6. (Henceforth *War Office*.) This and Karl Birnbaum's on-going summary of the medical literature published in Germany (in *Zeitschrift für die gesammte Neurologie und Psychiatrie, Referate und Ergebnisse,* 1914–1919) during the war are the two most essential sources on war neurosis.

8 *Ibid.,* p. 38.

9 Thomas W. Salmon, M.D., *The Care and Treatment of Mental Diseases and War Neuroses ("Shell-Shock") in the British Army* (New York: 1917), p. 30. For the same point see Sidney Schwab, "The Mechanism of the War Neuroses," *Journal of Abnormal Psychology, XIV* (April–June 1919), p. 1.

10 W. M. Maxwell, *A Psychological Retrospect of the Great War* (London: 1923), p. 85.

11 Phillip Gibbs, *Now it Can Be Told* (New York: 1920), p. 4.

12 Ernst Simmel, in *Psychoanalysis and the War Neuroses* (London, Vienna, and New York: 1921), p. 95.

13 Frederick W. Mott, *War Neurosis and Shell-shock* (London: 1919), p. 95.

14 George Stertz, "Verschrobene Fanatiker," *Berliner Klinische Wochenschrift, 56* (1919), p. 586.

15 W. Bailey, "War Neurosis, Shell-Shock and Nervousness in Soldiers," *Journal of the American Medical Association, 71* (1918), p. 215.

16 *Ibid.*

17 Dercum, "So-Called 'Shell-Shock,' " p. 75.

18 André Leri, *Shell-Shock, Commotional and Emotional Aspects* (London: 1919), p. 118.

19 *Ibid.*

20 War Office, p. 28.

21 E. E. Southard, ed., *Shell-Shock and Other Neuro-Psychiatric Problems Presented in Five Hundred and Eighty-Nine Case Histories* (Boston: 1919), p. 60.

22 Douglas Thom, "War Neurosis. Experiences of 1914–1918," *Journal of Laboratory and Clinical Medicine, 28* (1943), p. 499.

23 War Office, p. 24.

24 *Ibid.,* p. 26.

25 Southard, *Shell-Shock and Other Neuro-Psychiatric Problems,* p. 781.

26 Lewis Yealland, *Hysterical Disorders of Warfare* (London: 1918), p. 12.

27 *Ibid.,* pp. 8–9.

28 *Ibid.*, p. 23.

29 *Ibid.*, p. 22.

30 See Southard for many identical therapies.

31 Emil Redlich, "Einzige allgemeine Bemerkungen über den Krieg und unser Nervensystem," *Medizinische Klinik, 11,* 17 (April 25, 1915), p. 472.

32 Simmel, *Psychoanalysis and the War Neuroses,* p. 43.

33 Ernst Simmel, *Kriegsneurosen und psychisches Trauma* (Munich, 1918), p. 33.

34 Grace Massonneau, "A Social Analysis of a Group of Psychoneurotic Ex-servicemen," *Mental Hygiene, 6* (1922), pp. 575–91.

35 Bernard Glueck, "The Malingerer: A Clinical Study," *International Clinics, III,* 25th Series (1915), p. 201.

36 See Julian Jaynes's remarks on the history of hypnosis in *The Origins of Consciousness and the Breakdown of the Bicameral Mind* (Boston: 1977), p. 399. A number of doctors used hypnosis with the same assumptions as Simmel. Most notable and successful in Britain was William Brown who, in "Hypnosis, Suggestion and Dissociation," *British Medical Journal, I* (June 14, 1919), pp. 734–36, reports the cure of one hundred and twenty-eight cases of mutism in sixteen months. All these patients "spoke when forced to live again through their experiences."

37 Simmel, *Kriegsneurosen und psychisches Trauma,* p. 30.

38 *Ibid.*, p. 35.

39 Salmon, *The Care and Treatment of Mental Diseases and War Neuroses,* p. 30.

40 Ferenczi, "Über zwei Typen der Kriegsneurosen," p. 135.

41 War Office, p. 25.

42 *Ibid.*, p. 5.

43 Maxwell, *A Psychological Retrospect of the Great War,* p. 66.

44 War Office, p. 57.

45 *Ibid.*, p. 58.

46 *Ibid.*, p. 29.

47 *Ibid.*

48 Ferenczi, "Über zwei Typen der Kriegsneurosen," p. 140.

49 *Ibid.*, p. 137.

50 Quoted in Hirschfeld and Gaspar, *Sittengeschichte des Ersten Weltkriegs,* p. 168. See also, Iwan Block, "Über Traumatische Impotenz," *Zeitschrift für Sexualwissenschaft, 5* (1918–1919), pp. 135–41; Friedel Pick, "Über Sexualstörungen im Kriege," *Weiner Klinische Wochenschrift, 30* (1917) 45, pp. 1418–25; and H. Fehlinger, "Krieg und Geschlechtsleben," *Zeitschrift für Sexualwissenschaft, 3–4* (1916–1918), pp. 124–27.

51 Maxwell, *A Psychological Retrospect of the Great War*, p. 100.
52 Maj. T. J. Mitchell, *Official History of the War. Medical Services. Casualties and Medical Statistics* (London: 1931), p. 255.
53 Emanuel Miller, ed., *The Neurosis in War* (New York: 1942), p. 212.
54 D. A. Thom, "War Neuroses, Experiences of 1914–1918," p. 497.
55 Kurt Singer, "Was ist's mit dem Neurotiker vom Jahre 1920?" *Medizinische Klinik, 16,* 2 (September 12, 1920), p. 951.
56 Kurt Singer, "Das Kriegsende und die Neurosenfrage," *Neurologisches Zentralblatt, 38* (1919), p. 331.
57 Singer, "Was ist's mit dem Neurotiker vom Jahre 1920?" p. 951.
58 Freud, *Psychoanalysis and the War Neuroses*, p. 1.
59 Gibbs, *Now It Can be Told*, pp. 547–48.
60 Graves, *Lost Weekend*, p. 27.
61 Goldwin W. Howland, "Neuroses of Returned Soldiers," *American Medicine*, New Series, 12A (May 1917), p. 315.
62 Theodore Lidz, "Nightmares and the Combat Neuroses," *Psychiatry, 9* (1946), p. 44.
63 Roy Grinker, "The Medical, Psychiatric and Social Problems of War Neuroses," *Cincinnati Journal of Medicine, 26* (1945), p. 245.
64 Schauwecker, *Im Todesrachen.*
65 Mitchell, *Official History;* see Chart opposite his p. 328.
66 Walter Riese, "Krieg und Schizophrenie," *Allgemeine Ärtzliche Zeitschrift f. Psychotherapie und Psychologische Hygiene, 2* (1929), pp. 741–52.
67 Pierre Van Paassen, *Days of Our Years* (New York: 1934), p. 91.
68 S. Sassoon, *Memoirs of George Sherston*, p. 233.
69 W. H. R. Rivers, "The Repression of War Experience," *Lancet, (1918–*1; p. 173).
70 S. Sassoon, "Repression of War Experience," *Counter-attack and Other Poems* (New York: 1919), p. 51.
71 S. Sassoon, "Survivors," *Counter-attack and Other Poems* (New York: 1919), p. 55.
72 William Karl Pfeiler, *War and the German Mind* (New York: 1941), p. 16.
73 Edmunds (Carrington), *Soldiers from the Wars Returning*, p. 252.

6. THE VETERAN BETWEEN FRONT AND HOME

1 Ernst von Salomon, "Heimkehr," in *Die Front kehrt Heim. Das Reich im Werden*, V (Frankfurt A/M: 1933), p. 34.
2 Ernst H. Posse, *Die politische Kampfbünde Deutschlands*, series,

Fachschriften zur Politik und Staatsbürgerlichen Erziehung, Ernst v. Hippel, ed., (Berlin: 1931), p. 5.

3 Gibbs, *Now It Can Be Told*, p. 44.

4 *Ibid.*, p. 515.

5 Moritz Liepmann, *Krieg und Kriminalität in Deutschland*, No. 5, Wirtschafts und Sozialgeschichte des Weltkrieges. Deutsche Serie. Carnegie Foundation for World Peace, J. Shottwell, ed. (Stuttgart: 1930), p. 38.

6 Quoted in Hans-Peter Schwarz, *Der Konservative Anarchist* (Frieburg-im-Breisgau: 1962), p. 77.

7 Quoted in M. A. Ledeen, "Italy: War as a Style of Life," in *The War Generation*, Stephen Ward, ed. (Port Washington, New York, and London: 1975), p. 108.

8 Otto Braun, in *Diary*, Julie Braun (Vogelstein), ed. (London: 1924), p. 171.

9 Jünger, "Wesen des Frontsoldatentums," *Standarte*.

10 Willard Waller, *The Veteran Comes Back* (New York: 1944), p. 95.

11 Theodore Bartram, *Der Frontsoldat. Ein Deutsches Kultur und Lebensideal* (Berlin-Tempelhof: 1934), pp. 5–6. A reprint of speeches delivered in 1919.

12 Henry de Man, "European Unrest and the Returned Soldier," *Scribner's Magazine*, 66 (1919), p. 437.

13 London *Times* (March 8, 1919), p. 11b.

14 *Ibid.*

15 Pierre Van Paassen, *Days of Our Years*, p. 98.

16 See Ministry of Reconstruction. Committee on the Demobilization of the Army, *1st and 2nd Interim Report* (London: 1917).

17 Edmunds (Carrington), *Soldiers from the Wars Returning*, p. 276.

18 London *Times* (July 31, 1919), p. 11b.

19 Schauwecker, *Im Todesrachen*, p. 52.

20 *Ibid.*, p. 123.

21 Sassoon, *Memoirs of George Sherston*, p. 150.

22 Quoted in Graves, *Goodbye to All That*, p. 260.

23 National Federation of Discharged and Demobilized Sailors and Soldiers, Leaflet Series, #1.

24 Ralph R. Perry, "The Bonus. A Veteran's Opinion," *Outlook, 128* (1921), pp. 512–13.

25 Walter Benjamin, *Illuminationen* (Frankfurt A/M: 1961), p. 410.

26 *Ibid.*

27 Ernest Hemingway, *A Farewell to Arms* (New York: 1929), p. 196.

28 Sassoon, *Memoirs of George Sherston*, pp. 195–6.

29 S. Freud, "Mourning and Melancholia," *Complete Works, XIV*, p. 234.

30 For an excellent analysis of memorials and ceremonies in France, see Antoine Prost, *Les Anciens Combattants et La Société Française 1914–1939, III.* Mentalites et Ideologies (Paris: 1977), Chs. 1 and 2.

31 Erich Weniger, "Das Bild des Krieges. Erlebnis, Erinnerungen, Uberlieferung," *Die Erziehung. Monatschrift für den Zusammenhang von Kultur u. Erziehung,* Vol. 5, No. 1 (Oct., 1929), p. 5.

32 Quoted in Hagen Schulze, *Freikorps und Republik* (Boppard-am-Rhein: 1969), p. 56.

33 Quoted in R. D. L. Waite, *Vanguard of Nazism* (Cambridge, Mass.: 1952), p. 41.

Bibliography

Abraham, Karl, Ernest Jones, Sandor Ferenczi, *et. al. Psychoanalysis and the War Neurosis*. London, Vienna, and New York, 1921.

Abrahams, Roger. "Rituals in Culture," Unpublished paper.

Appell, John, M. C. Gilbert *et al.* "Comparative Incidence of Neuropsychiatric Casualties in World War I and World War II," *American Journal of Psychiatry, 103* (1946–1947). Pp. 196–9.

Armeson, Robert B. *Total Warfare and Compulsory Labor. A Study of the Military-Industrial Complex in Germany During WW I.* The Hague: 1964.

Ashworth, A. E. "The Sociology of Trench Warfare." *British Journal of Sociology, XIX,* 4 (December 1968). Pp. 407–20.

Bailey, W. "War Neurosis," *Journal of the American Medical Association, 71* (1918). Pp. 2148–53.

Barbusse, H. *The Inferno.* New York, 1918.

Ein Mitkämpfer Spricht. Aufsatz und Reden aus den Jahren 1917–1921. Basel, 1922.

Thus and Thus. London, 1927.

I Saw it Myself. New York, 1929.

Under Fire. New York, 1965.

Bardy, E. "Konservierte Kriegswaffen und andere ideele Kampfsmittel in ihren ("Richtigen") verhältnis zur Socialordnung." *Kölner Zeitschrift für Soziologie, V* (1952–1953). Pp. 502–12.

Barkin, K. D. *The Controversy over German Industrialization 1890–1902.* Chicago and London, 1970.

Barth, H. *Masse und Mythos: Die ideologische Krise an der Wende zum 20 Jahrhundert und die Theorie der Gewalt: Georges Sorel.* Hamburg, 1959.

Barthes, R. *Mythologies.* New York, 1975.

Bartlett, F. C. *Psychology and the Soldier.* Cambridge, 1927.

Bartram, T. *Der Frontsoldat, ein deutsches Kultur- und Lebensideal.* Berlin/Tempelhof, 1934.

Bäumer, G. *Lebensweg durch eine Zeitwende.* Tübingen, 1933.

Beauvoir, S. de. *Memoirs of a Dutiful Daughter.* New York, 1974.

Benedict, R. "Myth," *Encyclopedia of the Social Sciences, 11,* ed. E. R. A. Seligman. New York, 1933. Pp. 178–81.

Berger, P. L. *et al. The Homeless Mind: An Approach to Modern Consciousness.* New York, 1973.

    ed. "Some General Observations on the Problem of Work," in *The Human Shape of Work.* New York, 1964.

Beumelberg, W. *Sperrfeuer über Deutschland.* Oldenberg, 1929.

Bidwell, S. *Gunners at War.* London, 1970.

Biedenkopf, K. *Kriegserlebnis eines im Felde Erblindeten.* Hamburg, 1916.

Binding, R. *Erlebtes Leben.* Frankfurt A/M, 1928.

    A Fatalist at War. Boston and New York, 1929.

Binswanger, O. *Die Seelischen Wirkung des Krieges. 12,* series Der Deutsche Krieg. Stuttgart and Berlin, 1914.

Birnbaum, K. "Kriegsneurosen und -Psychosen auf Grund der gegenwartigen Kriegs-Beobachtungen," *Zeitschrift für die gesamte Neurologie und Psychiatrie, 11–19* (1915–1919).

Block, I. "Über Traumatishe Impotenz," *Zeitschrift für Sexualwissenschaft, 5* (1918–1919), 135–41.

Bohannon, P. *Law and Warfare. Studies in the Anthropology of Conflict.* Garden City, N.Y., 1969.

Braun, O. *Diary.* ed. Julie Braun (Vogelstein). London, 1924.

Brown, W. "Hypnosis, Suggestion and Dissociation," *British Medical Journal, I* (June 14, 1919), 734–6.

Bruchmüller, G. *Die Deutsche Artillerie in dem Durchbruchschlachten des Weltkrieges.* Berlin, 1922.

Buchner, M. *Der Marxismus im Weltkrieg und sein Einfluss auf des deutsche Heer.* Munich, 1925.

Caillois, R. *Man and the Sacred.* Glencoe, N.Y., 1950.

    Man, Play and Games. Glencoe, N.Y., 1961.

Campbell, J., and Alex Jamieson. "Ex-servicemen at Grips." Pamphlet. Glasgow, 1920.

Carothers, J. C. "Culture, Psychiatry and the Written Word," *Psychiatry* (November 1964). Pp. 16–36.

Carrington, C. E. *Soldiers from the Wars Returning*. London, 1965.
  A Subaltern's War. London, 1929.
von Clausewitz, K. *On War*. New York, 1911.
Cousins, A. "The Sociology of the War Novel," *Indiana Journal of Social Research, 2*, 2 (July 1961). Pp. 83–90.
Cru, J. N. *Temoins. Essai D'Analyse et de Critique des Souvenirs de Combattants Edités en Français de 1915 à 1928*. Paris, 1928.
Csikszentmihalyi, M. *Beyond Boredom and Anxiety. The Experience of Play, Work and Games*. San Francisco, Washington, and London, 1975.
Cysarz, H. *Zur Geistesgeschichte des Weltkriegs. Die Dichterischen Wandlungen des deutschen Kriegsbild 1910–1930*. Halle/Salle, 1931.
Dahrendorf, R. *Society and Democracy in Germany*. Garden City, N.Y., 1967.
Davis, N. Z. *Society and Culture in Early Modern France*. Stanford, Calif., 1975.
Dercum, F. X. "So-called 'Shell-Shock': The Remedy," *Archives of Neurology and Psychiatry, 1* (1919). Pp. 65–70.
Douglas, J. *Veterans on the March*. New York, 1934.
Douglas, M. *Purity and Danger. An Analysis of Concepts of Pollution and Taboo*. New York and Washington, 1963.
Drexel, J. "Im Westen nichts neues," *Widerstand, 4* (April 1929). P. 97.
Dumas, G., and Henri Aime. *Neuroses et Psychoses de Guerre chez les Austro-Allemands*. Paris, 1918.
Dumezil, G. *The Destiny of the Warrior*. Chicago and London, 1969.
Earle, E. M., ed. *Makers of Modern Strategy. Military Thought from Machiavelli to Hitler*. Princeton, N.J., 1944.
Eaton, R. M. "The Social Unrest of the Soldier," *International Journal of Ethics, 31* (April 1920), 279–88.
Eder, M. D. "Psychopathology of the War Neurosis," *Lancet* (August 12, 1916), 264–8.
Ehrmann, J. "Homo Ludens Revisited," *Yale French Studies,* No. 41 (1968). Pp. 31–58.
Eliade, M. *The Forge and the Crucible*. London, 1962.
  Rites and Symbols of Initiation. New York, Evanston, San Francisco, and London, 1958.
Ellul, J. *The Technological Society*. New York, 1965.
Erikson, E. H. *Childhood and Society*. London, 1965.
Everth, E. *Von der Seele des Soldaten im Felde. Bemerkungen eines Kriegsteilnehmers*. Jena, 1915.
Fagerberg, E. P. *The "Anciens Combattants" and French Foreign Policy*. Ambilly-Annemosse, 1966.

Fehlinger, H. "Krieg und Geschlechtsleben," *Zeitschrift für Sexualwissenschaft, 3–4* (1916–1918). Pp. 124–7.

Feldman, G. P. *Army, Industry and Labor in Germany 1914–1918.* Princeton, N.J., 1966.

Ferenczi, S. "Über zwei Typen der Kriegsneurosen," *Int. Zeitschrift für Ärztliche Psychoanalyse, IV* (1916–1917). Pp. 131–145.

Fischer, F. *Germany's Aims in the First World War.* New York, 1967.

Fischer, H. "Der Deutsche Infanterist von 1917," *Widerstand, 9* (January 1934). Pp. 6–11.

Flex, W. *Der Wanderer zwischen beiden Welten. Ein Kriegserlebnis.* Munich, 1918.

Ford, F. M. *No More Parades.* New York, 1925.

Fornari, F. *The Psychoanalysis of War.* Garden City, N.Y., 1974.

Forster, E. M. "The Machine Stops," in *Of Men and Machines,* Arthur O. Lewis, ed. New York, 1963. Pp. 266–79.

Forsyth, D. "Functional Nerve Disease and the Shock of Battle," *Lancet,* 1915, 2 (December 1915). Pp. 1395–1401.

Foucault, P. "Experiences Sur la Fatigue Mentale," *Revue Philosophie, 79* (1915). Pp. 505–26.

Frank, L. *Der Mensch ist Gut.* Potsdam, 1917.

Freud, S. *The Complete Psychological Works.* London, 1968.

Fuller, Maj.-Gen. J. F. C. *The Conduct of War, 1789–1961.* New York, 1961.

A Study of the Impact of the French, Industrial and Russian Revolutions on War and its Conduct. New Brunswick, 1961.

Fussell, P. *The Great War and Modern Memory.* London, Oxford and New York, 1975.

Gaupp, R. "Hysterie und Kriegsdienst," *Münchener Medizinische Wochenschrift, 62,* 1 (March 16, 1915). Pp. 361–3.

van Gennep, A. *The Rites of Passage.* Chicago, 1972.

Ginsburg, I. "National Symbolism," in *Modern Germany: a Study of Conflicting Loyalties,* P. Rosak, ed. Chicago, 1933. Pp. 2902–325.

Gläser, E. *Class of 1902.* New York, 1929.

Glueck, B. "The Malingerer: A Clinical Study," *International Clinics, III,* 25th Series (1915). Pp. 200–51.

Gombrich, E. *Art and Illusion.* Princeton, N.J., 1969.

Graham, S. "The Ex-Service Mind of Europe," *Contemporary Review, 123* (1923). Pp. 290–300.

Grasset, Dr. F. "The Psychoneuroses of War," *Medical Press and Circular, 150* (1915). Pp. 586–7.

Graves, R. *Goodbye to All That.* London, 1929.

Graves, R., and Alan Hodge. *The Long Weekend: A Social History of Great Britain 1919–1939.* New York, 1963.

Great Britain. Army. *Report of the War Office Committee of Enquiry Into "Shell-shock."* London, 1922.

Grinker, R. "The Medical, Psychiatric and Social Problems of War Neuroses," *Cincinnati Journal of Medicine, 26* (1945). Pp. 241–59.

Hafkesbrink, H. *Unknown Germany. An Inner Chronicle of the First World War Based on Letters and Diaries.* New Haven, 1948.

Halevy, E. *The World Crisis of 1914–1918.* Oxford, 1930.

Haller, H. "Naturgeschichte einer Generation?" *Widerstand, 4* (1930). P. 205.

Hartung, W. *Grosskampf, Männer und Grenaten.* Berlin, 1930.

Heinz, F. W. *Die Nation Greift an. Geschichte und Kritik des Soldatischen Nationalismus.* Berlin, 1933.

Hirschfeld, M., and Andrea Gaspar. *Sittengeschichte des Ersten Weltkriegs,* 2 vols. Hanau am Main, 1929.

Hoelz, M. *Vom "Weissen Kreuz" zur Roten Fahne. Jungend- Kampf- und Zuchthauserlebnisse.* Berlin, 1929.

Hoffman, R., ed. *Der Deutsche Soldat: Briefe aus dem Weltkrieg.* Munich, 1937.

Housman, L., ed. *War Letters of Fallen Englishmen.* London, 1930.

Howland, G. W. "Neuroses of Returned Soldiers," *American Medicine,* New Series *12A* (May 1917). Pp. 312–19.

Hübner, H. H. "Die Strafrechtliche Begulachtung von Soldaten," *Proceedings, Psychiatrischer Verein der Rheinprovinz. Allgemeine Zeitschrift für Psychiatrie, 72* (1915–1916). Pp. 518–21.

Huizinga, J. *Homo Ludens. A Study of the Play Element in Culture.* Boston, 1970.

Hulpert, H. J. "Gas Neurosis Syndrome," *American Journal of Insanity,* 77 (1920–1921). Pp. 213–16.

Jannack, K. *Wir mit der Roten Nelke.* Boutzen, 1959.

Jaynes, J. *The Origins of Consciousness and the Breakdown of the Bicameral Mind.* Boston, 1977.

Jirgal, E. *Die Wiederkehr des Weltkriegs in der Literatur.* Vienna/Liepzig, 1931.

Johnson, A. S. "The Socialism of Modern War," *Unpopular Review,* (1915). Pp. 139–53.

Jolly, P. "Kriegshysterie und Beruf," *Archiv für Psychiatrie, 59* (1918). Pp. 873–82.

Jones, D. *In Parenthesis.* New York, 1961.

Jung, E. *Der Herrschaft der Minderwertigkeit.* Berlin, 1930.

Jünger, E. "Die andere Seite," *Widerstand, IV,* 3 (1929). Pp. 76–81.

ed. *Das Antlitz des Weltkrieges. Fronterlebnis deutscher Soldaten.* Berlin, 1930.

"Ausbildungsvorschrift für die Infanterie," *Militär-Wochenblatt,* (1922).

Feuer und Blut. ein Kleiner Ausschnitt aus einer grossen Schlacht. Magdeburg, 1925.

"Der Frontsoldat und die wilhelminische Zeit," *Der Stahlhelm, Beilage, "Standarte,"* I, 3 (September 20, 1925).

"Die Geburt des Nationalismus aus dem Kriege," *Deutsches Volkstum,* No. 8 (1929). Pp. 777–81.

"Grosstadt und Land," *Deutsches Volkstum,* No. 8 (1926). Pp. 577–81.

"Der Krieg als äusseres Erlebnis," *Der Stahlhelm, Beilage, "Standarte,"* I, 4 (September 27, 1925).

"Der Krieg als inneres Erlebnis," *Der Stahlhelm, Beilage, "Standarte,"* I, 6 (October 11, 1925).

ed. *Krieg und Krieger.* Berlin, 1930.

Der Kampf als Inneres Erlebnis. Berlin, 1922.

ed. *Der Kampf um das Reich.* Essen, 1929.

"Die Mobilmachung des Deutschen," *Widerstand, V,* 4 (1930). Pp. 109–12.

"Die Materialschlacht," *Der Stahlhelm, Beilage, "Standarte,"* I, 5 (October 4, 1925).

" 'Nationalismus' und Nationalismus," *Das Tagebuch,* X, 38 (September 21, 1929). Pp. 1552–8.

"Reinheit der Mittel," *Widerstand, IV,* 10 (1929). Pp. 295–7.

"Revolution um Karl Marx," *Widerstand, VI,* 5 (1929). Pp. 144–6.

"Skizze moderner Gefechtsführung," *Militär-Wochenblatt* (1920). Pp. 433–5.

In Stahlgewittern. Berlin, 1922.

"Sturm," in *Hannoverscher Kurier* (April 11–27, 1923).

"Technik in der Zukunftsschlacht," *Militär-Wochenblatt* (1921). Pp. 288–289.

"Unsere Politiker," *Der Stahlhelm, Beilage, "Standarte,"* I, 1 (September 6, 1925).

"Untergang oder neue Ordnung," *Deutsches Volkstum,* XV, 10 (May 1, 1933). Pp. 413–19.

Das Wäldchen 125. Eine Chronik aus den Grabenkampf 1918. Berlin, 1925.

Werke, 10 vols. Stuttgart, 1965.

"Wesen des Frontsoldatentums," *Der Stahlhelm, Beilage, "Standarte,"* I, 1 (September 6, 1925).

Jünger, F. G. *Aufmarsch des Nationalismus.* Berlin, 1926.

Machine und Eigentum. Frankfurt A/M, 1949.

Die Perfektion der Technik. Frankfurt A/M, 1946.

Spiegel der Jahre. Erinnerungen. Munich, 1958.

Junior, R., ed. *Hier Spricht der Feind.* Berlin, 1931.

Jurr, W. *Um die proletarische Wehrorganisation.* Berlin, 1930.

Kagan, J. "Emergent Theories in Human Development," *American Scientist, 64,* 2 (March–April, 1976). Pp. 186–96.

Kaiser, H. *Mythos, Rausch und Reaction: Der Weg Gottfried Benns und Ernst Jüngers.* Berlin, 1962.

Kankleit, O. "Heldentum und Verbrechen," *Monatschrift für Kriminalische Psychologie, 16* (1925). Pp. 193–201.

Karpe, Richard, and Isidore Schnap. "Nostopathy – A Study of Pathogenic Homecoming," *American Journal of Psychiatry, 109* (1952–3). Pp. 46–51.

Keegan, J. *The Face of Battle.* New York, 1976.

Keeling, F. H. *The Keeling Letters.* London, 1918.

Kreisler, F. *Four Weeks in the Trenches. The War Story of a Violinist.* Boston and New York, 1915.

Kriegsbriefe gefallener deutscher Juden. Stuttgart-Degerloch, 1961.

von Krockow, C. Graf. *Die Entscheidung.* Stuttgart, 1958.

Landes, D. *The Unbound Prometheus. Technological Change and Industrial Development in Western Europe.* Cambridge, Mass., 1969.

Laquer, W. *Young Germany. A History of the German Youth Movement.* New York, 1962.

Lawrence, T. E. *The Mint.* New York, 1963.

Leach, E. ed. *The Structural Study of Myth and Folklore.* Edinburgh, 1967.

Leri, A. *Shell-Shock, Commotional and Emotional Aspects.* London, 1919.

Lévi-Strauss, C. *The Raw and the Cooked. Introduction to a Science of Mythology, I.* New York and Evanston, 1969.

Lewinsohn, L. *Die Revolution an der Westfront.* Charlottenburg, 1919.

Liddel-Hart, B. *Memoirs.* London, 1962.

Lidz, T. "Nightmares and the Combat Neuroses," *Psychiatry, 9* (1946). Pp. 37–49.

Lifton, R. J. *Home From the War. Vietnam Veterans: Neither Veterans nor Executioners.* New York, 1970.

Lloyd-George, D. *War Memoirs.* London, 1933.

Loehrke, E., ed. *Armageddon: the World War in Literature.* New York, 1930.

Loewenberg, P. "Arno Mayer's 'Internal Causes and Purposes of War in Europe,' an Inadequate Model of Human Behavior, National Conflict and Historical Change," *Journal of Modern History, 42,* 3 (September 1970). Pp. 628–36.

Loose, G. *Ernst Jünger, Gestalt und Werk.* Frankfurt A/M, 1957.

Löwy, M. "Zur Behandlung des Psychotraumatiker des Krieges im Krieg und nach Friedensschluss," *Monatschrift für Psychiatrie und Neurologie, XLIII,* 1 (October 1917). Pp. 59–65.

von Ludendorff, E. *Der Totale Krieg.* Munich, 1936.

Lussu, E. *Sardinian Brigade.* New York, 1939.

Lutz, R. H. *The German Revolution 1918–1919.* Stanford University Publications, *1,* No. 1.

MacCurdy, J. T. *The Psychology of War.* London, 1917.

de Man, H. "European Unrest and the Returned Soldier," *Scribner's Magazine, 66* (1919). Pp. 432–8.

The Remaking of a Mind: A Soldier's Thoughts on War and Reconstruction. London, 1919.

Mann, T. "In My Defense," *Atlantic Monthly, 174,* 4 (October 1949). Pp. 100–104.

Manwaring, G. B. *If We Return; Letters of a Soldier of Kitchner's Army.* London, 1918.

Marc, F. *Briefe, Aufzeichnungen und Aphorismen.* Berlin, 1920.

Marks, M. "Ritual Structure in Afro-American Music," in *Religious Movements in Contemporary America,* ed. Irving I Zaretsky and Mark P. Leone. Princeton, N.J., 1947.

Marriott, M. "The Feasts of Love," in *Krishna: Myths, Rites and Attitudes,* ed. Milton Singer. Honolulu, 1966.

Marshall, S. L. A. *Men Against Fire.* New York, 1966.

von Martin, A. *Der Heroische Nihilismus und seine Uberwindung.* Krefeld, 1948.

Marwick, A. *The Deluge.* London, 1961.

Marx, K. *Capital, I.* Chicago, 1908.

Marx, L. *The Machine in the Garden.* New York, 1964.

Massonneau, G. "A Social Analysis of a Group of Psychoneurotic Ex-Servicemen," *Mental Hygiene, 6* (1922). Pp. 575–91.

Masters, J. *The Ravi Lancers.* New York, 1973.

Mauss, M. *A General Theory of Magic.* London and Boston, 1972.

The Gift: Forms and Functions of Exchange in Archaic Societies. London, 1954.

Maxwell, W. M. *A Psychological Retrospect of the Great War.* London, 1923.

Mayer, A. J. *Dynamics of Counterrevolution in Europe, 1870–1956. An*

Analytic Framework. New York, Evanston, San Francisco, and London: 1971.

"Internal Causes and Purposes of War In Europe," *Journal of Modern History, 44,* 3 (1969). Pp. 291–303.

Meinecke, F. *The German Catastrophe.* Boston, 1963.

Mendelssohn-Bartholdy, A. *The War and German Society. The Testament of a Liberal.* New Haven, 1937.

Michels, R. *Briefe eines Hauptmanns an seinen Sohn.* Berlin, 1916.

Miller, E., ed. *The Neurosis in War.* New York, 1942.

Mitchell, Maj. T. V. *Official History of the Great War. Medical Services. Casualties and Medical Statistics.* London, 1931.

Mohler, A. *Die Konservative Revolution in Deutschland. Grundriss ihrer Weltanschauungen.* Stuttgart, 1950.

Die Schleife. Dokumente zum Weg von Ernst Jüngers. Zurich, 1955.

Mosse, G. L. *The Crisis of German Ideology: Intellectual Origins of the Third Reich.* New York, 1964.

Mott, F. W. *War Neuroses and Shell Shock.* London, 1919.

Mumford, L. *Technics and Civilization.* New York, 1934.

Münster, I., and F. von Ham. "Kriegswaffen und Sozialordnung. (Grundlinie einer Soziologische-systematischen Studie über ihre gegenseitige Abhängigkeit)," *Kölner Zeitschrift für Soziologie, V* (1952–3). Pp. 118–86.

Myers, C. S. "A Contribution to the Study of Shell-shock," *Lancet,* 1915, 1 (February 13, 1915). Pp. 316–20. The first report on shell-shock.

Needham, R. "Percussion and Transition," *Man, 2,* 4 (December 1967). Pp. 606–10.

Neisser, U. *Cognitive Psychology.* New York, 1967.

Neumann, S. *Permanent Revolution. The Total State in a World at War.* New York and London, 1942.

Neymann, C. "Some Experiences in the German Red Cross," *Mental Hygiene, 1* (1917). Pp. 392–6.

Nichols, C. L. "War and Civil Neuroses – a Comparison," *Long Island Medical Journal, 13* (August 1919). Pp. 259–268.

Obermann, E. *Soldaten, Bürger, Militaristen, Militär und Demokratie in Deutschland.* Stuttgart, 1958.

Oberdorf, C. P. "On Retaining the Sense of Reality in States of Depersonalization," *International Journal of Psychoanalysis, 20* (April 1939). Pp. 137–47.

van Paassen, P. *Days of Our Years.* New York, 1934.

Panichas, G. A., ed. *Promise of Greatness. The War of 1914–1918.* New York, 1968.

Pfeiler, W. K. *War and the German Mind: The Testimony of Men of Fiction Who Fought at the Front*. New York, 1941.

Pfemfert, F., ed. *Das Aktionsbuch*. Berlin-Wilmersdorf, 1917.

Pick, F. "Über Sexualstörungen im Kriege," *Wiener Klinische Wochenschrift, 30,* 45 (1917). Pp. 1418–25.

Prost, A. *Les Anciens Combattants et la Société Française 1914–1939*, 3 vols. Paris, 1977.

Redlich, E. "Einzige allgemeine Bemerkungen über den Krieg und unser Nervensystem," *Medizinische Klinik, 11,* 17 (April 25, 1915). Pp. 467–73.

Remand, R. "Les Anciens Combattants et la Politique," *Revue Français de Science Politique, V,* 2 (April–June 1955). Pp. 267–69.

✗Remarque, E. M. *All Quiet on the Western Front*. Boston, 1929.

Rene-Hocke, G. *Die Welt als Labyrinth. Manier und Manie in der Europäischen Kunst*. Hamburg, 1963.

Renn, L. *Krieg*. Frankfurt A/M, 1929.

Nachkrieg. Berlin, 1930.

Richards, R. L. "Mental and Nervous Diseases During the Russo-Japanese War," *Military Surgeon, 26* (1910). Pp. 177–93.

Ricoeur, P. "The Model of the Text: Meaningful Action Considered as a Text," *New Literary History, V,* 1 (Autumn 1973). Pp. 91–117.

Riese, W. "Krieg und Schizophrenie," *Allgemeine Artzliche Zeitschrift für Psychotherapie und Psychologische Hygiene, 2* (1929). Pp. 741–52.

Rilke, R. M. *Later Poems*. Trans. J. B. Leishman. London, 1938.

Wartime Letters 1914–1921. Trans. D. Herter Norton. New York, 1940.

Rivers, W. H. R. "The Repression of War Experience," *Lancet, 1918–1*. Pp. 171–8.

Romains, J. *Men of Good Will*, Vol. 7: *Death of a World*. New York, 1938.

Ropp, T. *War in the Modern World*. Durham, N.C., 1959.

Rosen, G. "Nostalgia, a Forgotten Nervous Disorder," *Psychological Medicine, 5,* 4 (1974). Pp. 340–54.

Rosenstock, E. *Die Hochzeit des Kriegs und der Revolution*. Berlin, 1920.

Rosenstock-Huessy, E. *Out of Revolution. Autobiography of Western Man*. New York, 1938.

Rosinski, H. *The German Army*. New York, 1940.

Rubiner, L. *Der Mensch in der Mitte*. Berlin-Wilmersdorf, 1917.

✗St. Exupéry, A. *Night Flight*. New York, copy. 1932.

Salmon, T. W. *The Care and Treatment of Mental Disease and War Neuroses ("Shell-Shock") in the British Army*. New York, 1917.

von Salomon, E. *Fragebogen.* Hamburg, 1967.

Sassoon, S. *Counter-Attack and other Poems.* New York, 1919.

Memoirs of George Sherston (Containing: *Memoirs of a Fox-Hunting Man, Memoirs of an Infantry Officer,* and *Sherston's Progress*). New York, 1937.

Schauwecker, F. *Aufbruch der Nation.* Berlin, 1930.

The Fiery Way. London and Toronto, 1921.

So ist der Friede: Die Revolution der Zeit in 300 Bilder. Berlin, 1928.

So War der Krieg. Berlin, 1927.

Im Todersrachen. Die Deutsche Seele im Weltkrieg. Halle (Salle), 1921.

Scheler, M. *Der Genius des Krieges und der Deutsche Krieg.* Leipzig, 1915.

Scheller, W. *Als die Seele Starb 1914–1918. Das Kriegserlebnis eines Unkriegerischen.* Berlin, 1931.

Schmitt, C. *Ex Captivite Salus. Erfahrungen der Zeit 1945–1947.* Köln, 1950.

Gesprach über die Macht und dem Zergang zur Machthaber. Metzingen, 1954.

Die Kernfrage des Völkerbunds. Munich, 1926.

Politische Romantik. Munich and Leipzig, 1919.

Politische Theologie. Munich, 1943.

Theorie des Partisanen. Zwischen-Bemerkung zum Begriff des Politischen. Berlin, 1963.

Schoenberger, S. "Disorders of the Ego in Wartime," *British Journal of Medical Psychology, 21* (1947–8). Pp. 248–53.

Scholz, L. *Seelenleben des Soldaten an der Front. Hinterlassene Aufzeichnungen des im Kriege gefallenen Nervenartzes.* Tübingen, 1920.

Schorske, C. *German Social Democracy 1905–1917.* Cambridge, Mass., 1955.

Schüddekopf, O. E. *Das Heer und die Republik. Quellen zur Politik der Reichswehrführung 1918–1933.* Hannover and Frankfurt A/M, 1955.

Linke Leute von Rechts. Die nationalrevolutionären Minderheiten. Stuttgart, 1960.

Schulze, H. *Freikorps und Republik.* Boppard am Rhein, 1969.

Schwab, S. "The Mechanism of the War Neuroses," *Journal of Abnormal Psychology, XIV* (April–June, 1919). Pp. 1–8.

Schwarz, H. P. *Der Konservative Anarchist. Politik und Zeitkritik Ernst Jüngers.* Freiburg im Breisgau, 1962.

Shklovsky, V. *A Sentimental Journey. Memoirs 1917–1922.* Ithaca, N.Y., and London, 1970.

Simmel, E. *Kriegsneurosen und psychisches Trauma.* Munich, 1918.

Singer, K. "Das Kriegsende und die Neurosenfrage," *Neurologisches Zentralblatt, 38* (1919). Pp. 327–36.

"Was ist's mit dem Neurotiker vom Jahre 1920?" *Medizinische Klinik,* *16,* 2 (September 12, 1920). Pp. 947–55.

Sipes, R. "War, Sports and Aggression. An Empirical Test of Rival Theories," *American Anthropologist, 75,* 1 (February 1973). Pp. 64–86.

Smith, H. N. *Virgin Land: The American West as Symbol and Myth.* New York, 1950.

Sokel, W. *The Writer in Extremis: Expressionism in 20th Century German Literature.* Palo Alto, Calif., 1959.

Solberg, P. A. "Attitudes of Canadian Veterans to Political and Economic Issues," *Journal of Social Psychology, 38* (1953). Pp. 73–86.

Sontheimer, K. *Antidemokratisches Denken in der Weimarer Republik: Die Politischen Ideen des Deutschen Nationalismus zwischen 1918 und 1933.* Munich, 1962.

Soucy, R. "Romanticism and Realism in the Fascism of Drieu La Rochelle," *Journal of the History of Ideas, XXXI* (January–March 1970). Pp. 69–89.

Southard, E. E. *Shell-Shock and Other Neuro-Psychiatric Problems Presented in Five Hundred and Eighty-Nine Case Histories.* Boston, 1919.

Stadtler, E. *Als Politische Soldat, 1914–1918.* Düsseldorf, 1936.

Stekel, W. *Unser Seelenleben im Kriege. Psychologische Betrachtungen eines Nervenarztes.* Berlin, 1916.

Stertz, G. "Verschrobene Fanatiker," *Berliner Klinische Wochenschrift, 56* (1919). Pp. 583–90.

Stewart, J. P. "The Treatment of War Neuroses," *Archives of Neurology and Psychiatry, 1* (1919). Pp. 14–24.

Die Stimme der Toten. Series. Deutsches Schriften. Frankfurt A/M, 1933.

Stumpf, R. *War, Mutiny and Revolution in the German Navy. The World War I Diary of Richard Stumpf,* ed. Daniel Horn. New Brunswick, N.J., 1967.

Swan, J. M. "An Analysis of Ninety Cases of Functional Disease in Soldiers," *Archives of Internal Medicine, 28* (1921). Pp. 586–602.

Terraine, J. *The Western Front 1914–1918.* London, 1964.

Thom, D. "War Neurosis. Experiences of 1914–1918," *Journal of Laboratory and Clinical Medicine, 28* (1943). Pp. 498–505.

Toller, E. *I Was a German.* London, 1943.

Trotsky, L. *My Life. An Attempt at an Autobiography.* New York, 1930.

Trounce, H. D. *Fighting the Boche Underground.* New York, 1967.

Turner, V. W. *Forest of Symbols.* Ithaca and London, 1967.

"From Liminal to Liminoid in Play, Flow and Ritual: An Essay in

Comparative Symbology," *The Anthropological Study of Human Play, Rice University Studies, 60,* 31 (Summer 1974). Pp. 53–90.

The Ritual Process. Chicago, 1974.

Vagts, A. *A History of Militarism.* New York, 1959.

Veblen, T. *Imperial Germany and the Industrial Revolution.* New York, 1946, copyright 1915.

Viets, H. "Shell-Shock. A Digest of the English Literature," *Journal of American Medicine, 69,* 1779–86.

Volkmann, E. O., and B. Schwertfeger, eds. *Das Soldatentum des Weltkriegs,* Vol. I: *Die Deutsche Soldatenkunde.* Leipzig, 1937.

Waller, W. *The Veteran Comes Back.* New York, 1944.

War in the Twentieth Century. New York, 1940.

War Letters of Rochester's Veterans, 3 vols. Rochester, N.Y., 1929.

Ward, S. R. *British Veteran's Organizations of the First World War.* Cincinnati, 1969. Unpublished dissertation.

ed. *The War Generation.* Port Washington, New York, and London, 1975.

Wedd, A. F., ed. *German Student's War Letters.* New York, 1930.

Weniger, E. "Das Bild des Krieges. Erlebnis, Erinnerungen, Überlieferung," *Die Erziehung. Monatschrift für den Zusammenhang von Kultur und Erziehung, 5,* 1 (October 1929). Pp. 1–22.

Wheeler-Bennet, J. W. *The Nemesis of Power: the German Army in Politics 1918–1945.* London, 1953.

Williamson, H. *A Soldier's Diary of the Great War.* London, 1929.

Willis, I. *England's Holy War.* New York, 1928.

Winston, R. and Clara, eds. *The Letters of Thomas Mann 1889–1955.* New York, 1975.

Winteringham, F. *The Story of Weapons.* Boston, 1943.

Witkop, P., ed. *Kriegsbriefe gefallener Studenten.* Munich, 1936.

Wooton, G. *The Official History of the British Legion.* London, 1956.

Wright, H. "Postbellum Neuroses: A Clinical Review and Discussion of their Mechanism," *Archives for Neurology and Psychiatry, 3* (1920). Pp. 429–434.

Yealland, L. *Hysterical Disorders of Warfare.* London, 1918.

Zuckmayer, C. *Als wär ein Stück von Mir.* Vienna, 1966.

Pro Domo. Stockholm, 1938.

Zweig, S. *The World of Yesterday. An Autobiography.* New York, 1945.

Index